Communications
in Computer and Information S

T0238131

Tai-hoon Kim   Laurence T. Yang
Jong Hyuk Park   Alan Chin-Chen Chang
Thanos Vasilakos   Sang-Soo Yeo (Eds.)

Advances in Communication and Networking

Second International Conference on Future Generation
Communication and Networking, FGCN 2008
Sanya, Hainan Island, China, December 13-15, 2008
Revised Selected Papers

 Springer

Volume Editors

Tai-hoon Kim
Hannam University, Daejeon, Korea
E-mail: taihoonn@empal.com

Laurence T. Yang
St. Francis Xavier University, Antigonish, NS, Canada
E-mail: ltyang@stfx.ca

Jong Hyuk Park
Kyungnam University, Kyungnam, South Korea
E-mail: jhpark1@kyungnam.ac.kr

Alan Chin-Chen Chang
National Chung Cheng University, Chiayi County, Taiwan
E-mail: ccc@cs.ccu.edu.tw

Thanos Vasilakos
University of Western Macedonia, West Macedonia, Greece
E-mail: vasilako@ath.forthnet.gr

Sang-Soo Yeo
Mokwon University, Daejeon, South Korea
E-mail: ssyeo@msn.com

Library of Congress Control Number: Applied for

CR Subject Classification (1998): C.2, D.2, H.3, C.3, D.3

ISSN   1865-0929
ISBN-10   3-642-10235-2 Springer Berlin Heidelberg New York
ISBN-13   978-3-642-10235-6 Springer Berlin Heidelberg New York

springer.com

© Springer-Verlag Berlin Heidelberg 2009
Printed in Germany

Typesetting: Camera-ready by author, data conversion by Scientific Publishing Services, Chennai, India
Printed on acid-free paper   SPIN: 12791514   06/3180   5 4 3 2 1 0

Preface

As computational science and engineering (CSE) become specialized and fragmented, it is easy to lose sight that many topics in CSE have common threads and because of this, advances in one sub-discipline may transmit to another. The presentation of results between different sub-disciplines of CSE encourages this interchange for the advancement of CSE as a whole. Of particular interest is the hybrid approach of combining ideas from one discipline with those of another to achieve a result that is more significant than the sum of the individual parts. Through this hybrid philosophy, a new or common principle can be discovered which has the propensity to propagate throughout this multifaceted discipline.

This volume comprises the selection of extended versions of papers that were presented in their shortened form at the 2008 International Conference on Future Generation Communication and Networking (http://www.sersc.org/FGCN2008/) and 2009 Advanced Science and Technology (http://www.sersc.org/AST2009/).

We would like to acknowledge the great effort of all in the FGCN2008 and AST 2009 International Advisory Board and members of the International Program Committee, as well as all the organizations and individuals who supported the idea of publishing these advances in communication and networking, including SERSC (http://www.sersc.org/) and Springer.

We would like to give special thanks to Rosslin John Robles, Maricel O. Balitanas, Farkhod Alisherov Alisherovish, Feruza Sattarova Yusfovna. These graduate school students of Hannam University attended to the editing process of this volume with great passion.

We strongly believe in the need for continuing this undertaking in the future, in the form of a conference, journal, or book series. In this respect we welcome any feedback.

April 2009

Tai-hoon Kim
Laurence T. Yang
Jong Hyuk Park
Alan Chin-Chen Chang
Thanos Vasilakos
Sang-Soo Yeo

Organization

Steering Co-chairs

Tai-hoon Kim   Hannam University, Korea
Laurence T. Yang   St. Francis Xavier University, Canada

General Co-chairs

Jong Hyuk Park   Kyungnam University, Korea
Alan Chin-Chen Chang   National Chung Cheng University, Taiwan
Thanos Vasilakos   University of Western Macedonia, Greece

Program Co-chairs

Yang Xiao   University of Alabama, USA
Charalampos Z. Patrikakis   National Technical University of Athens, Greece
Sang-Soo Yeo   Hannam University, Korea

Symposium Co-chairs

Yan Zhang   Simula Research Laboratory, Norway
Damien Sauveron   University of Limoges, France

Workshop Co-chairs

Xingang Wang   University of Plymouth, UK
Young-Sik Jeong   Wonkwang University, Korea

International Journals Coordinating Co-chairs

Yan Zhang   Simula Research Laboratory, Norway
Qun Jin   Waseda University, Japan
Irfan Awan   University of Bradford, UK

International Advisory Board

Wai Chi Fang   NASA JPL, USA
Hsiao-Hwa Chen   National Sun Yat-Sen University, Taiwan
Han-Chieh Chao   National Ilan University, Taiwan
Hamid R. Arabnia   The University of Georgia, USA
Gongzhu Hu   Central Michigan University, USA
Byeong-Ho KANG   University of Tasmania, Australia

Publicity Co-chairs

Ching-Hsien Hsu   Chung Hua University, Taiwan
Hangbae Chang   Daejin University, Korea
Houcine Hassan   Polytechnic University of Valencia, Spain

Publication Chair

Sajid Hussain   Acadia University, Canada

Program Committee

A Min Tjoa   Vienna University of Technology, Austria
Ai-Chun Pang   National Taiwan University
AL FALOU Ayman   ISEN-Brest, France
Alex Sprintson   Texas A&M University, USA
Amar Balla   Institut National dInformatique, Algeria
Andres Iglesias Prieto   University of Cantabria, Spain
Andrzej Jajszczyk   AGH University of Science and Technology, Poland
Athanasios (Thanos) Vasilakos   University of Western Macedonia, Greece
Avinash Srinivasan   Florida Atlantic University, USA
Bin Luo   Anhui University, China
Biplab K. Sarker   Innovatia Inc., Canada
Byungsoo Koh   DigiCaps, Korea
Chao-Tung Yang   Tunghai University, Taiwan
Chia-Chen Lin   Providence University, Taiwan
Chin-Feng Lee   Chaoyang University of Technology, Taiwan
Cho-Li Wang   The University of Hong Kong, Hong Kong
Christophe Fouqueré   LIPN, Paris-Nord University and CNRS, France
Christos Douligeris   University of Piraeus, Greece
Chu-Hsing Lin   Tunghai University, Taiwan
Clement Leung   Victoria University, Australia
Cliff Shaffer   Virginia Tech, USA
Damien Sauveron   University of Limoges, France
Der-Chyuan Lou   National Defense University, Taiwan
Dimitrios D. Vergados   University of Piraeus, Greece
Don-Lin Yang   Feng Chia University, Taiwan
Driss Mammass   Ibn Zohr University, Morocco
Fang-Rong Hsu   Feng Chia University, Taiwan
Fevzi Belli   University of Paderborn, Germany
Gang Pan   Zhejiang University, China
Gianluigi Ferrari   University of Parma, Italy
Gongzhu Hu   Central Michigan University, USA
Hao Zhu   Florida International University, USA
Hongyi Wu   University of Louisiana at Lafayette, USA
Hsiao-Hwa Chen   National Sun Yat-Sen University, Taiwan

Hui Chen	Virginia State University, USA
Huirong Fu	Oakland University, USA
Janusz Szczepanski	Institute of Fundamental Technological Research, Poland
Jiannong Cao	Hong Kong Polytechnic University
Jieh-Shan George YEH	Providence University, Taiwan
Jiming Chen	Zhejiang University, China
Jim-Min Lin	Feng Chia University, Taiwan
Jing Deng	University of New Orleans, USA
Jin Kwak	Soonchunhyang University, Korea
Jinn-Ke Jan	National Chung Hsing University, China
Jordi Forne Munoz	University of Catalonia, Spain
Juha Jaakko Röning	University of Oulu, Finland
Jung-Taek Seo	The Attached Institute of ETRI, Korea
Junmo Yang	Samsung Electronics Co., Ltd.
Kazuto Ogawa	Japan Broadcasting Corporation, Japan
Kevin Butler	Pennsylvania State University, USA
Kin Keung Lai	City University of Hong Kong, Hong Kong
Kwok-Yan Lam	Tsinghua University, China
Luis Javier Garcia Villalba	Complutense University of Madrid, Spain
Marc Lacoste	France Télécom Division R&D, France
Matthias Reuter	CUTEC GmbH / TU-Clausthal, Germany
Mohammad Riaz Moghal	Ali Ahmad Shah-University, Pakistan
P.K. Mahanti	The University of New Brunswick, Canada
Paulo Bacelar Reis Pedreiras	University of Aveiro, Portugal
Poompat Saengudomlert	Asian Institute of Technology, Thailand
Ricky Y K Kwok	The University of Hong Kong
Sabrina De Capitani di Vimercati	University of Milan, Italy
Serge Chaumette	University of Bordeaux 1, France
Shiuh-Jeng Wang	Central Police University, Taiwan
Shou-Hsuan Stephen Huang	University of Houston, USA
SLIM Chokri	ISCAE, University of Manouba, Tunisia
Soon Ae Chun	City University of New York, USA
Sun-Yuan Hsieh	National Cheng Kung University, Taiwan
Tae (Tom) Oh	Rockwell Collins, Richardson, USA
Tei-Wei Kuo	National Taiwan University, Taiwan
Terry Todd	McMaster University, Canada
Viktor Yarmolenko	University of Manchester, UK
Vincenzo De Florio	University of Antwerp, Belgium
Vojislav B. Misic	University of Manitoba, Canada
Wei-Bin Lee	Feng Chia University, Taiwan
Witold Pedrycz	University of Alberta, Canada
Yeong-Deok Kim	Woosong University, Korea
Young B. Choi	James Madison University, USA
Zvi Meir Kedem	New York University, USA

External Reviewers

Chi-Shih Chao	Feng Chian University, Taiwan
Chyi-Ren Dow	Feng Chian University, Taiwan
Hong Sun	University of Antwerp, Belgium
Ning Gui	University of Antwerp, Belgium
Shijian Li	Zhejiang University, China
Shun-Ren Yang	National Tsing Hua University, Taiwan
Weili Han	Fudan University, China

Table of Contents

Active Vessel Navigation Monitoring
with Multi-media Message Service

Chun Yang, Qinyou Hu, Chaojian Shi, and Jinhai Chen

Merchant Marine College Shanghai Maritime University
qyhu@mmc.shmtu.edu.cn

Abstract. Many online vessel monitoring services have been developed, and most of them, however, are available only when a user is logging on them. A notification service that can send vessel navigation messages to offline sub-scribers was developed in this paper. Therefore an active vessel navigation monitoring service is implemented. Each message contains a background image and a mark showing a vessel's position and navigation status, which are derived from AIS reports. The background image is selected from the existing map tile databases based on the position of the vessel. More than one image may be se-lected, so a RBF network with two inputs, image information entropy and scrambling degree, is built to choose the proper background image. Experi-ments show the RBF network has a correct rate of 84%. The active vessel navigation monitoring service developed in this paper shall be helpful for the business of the offline users.

1 Introduction

At the end of the 1990s, a new type of ship-borne equipment called Automatic Identi-fication System (AIS) was developed, and now more and more AISs have been de-ployed on board ships according to the compulsory requirements of International Maritime Organization (IMO). Although AIS was originally designed for anti-collision between vessels, it can dramatically change the way of people tracking vessels. An AIS transponder uses maritime VHF frequency, broadcasts the static, dynamic and voyage related information continually. The AIS base station around can collect this kind of information and sent it to some traffic management center, where the information is overlaid on electronic charts to facilitate people to monitor the vessel traffic.

It is of great value for the public in the shipping industry field to obtain real time vessel navigation information in order to make proper business arrangements [1][2]. To share the vessel navigation information collected from the AISs, sev-eral online vessel monitoring systems [3][4][5][6] have been built, for example, AISLive[1], ShipXY[2], Lloydsmiu[3] and Portlive[4]. Most of them, however, work in a

---

[1] http://www.aislive.com
[2] http://www.shipxy.com
[3] http://www.lloydsmiu.com
[4] http://www.portlive.com

T.-h. Kim et al. (Eds.): FGCN 2008, CCIS 27, pp. 1–13, 2009.
© Springer-Verlag Berlin Heidelberg 2009

passive way. That means the vessel monitoring services are available only when the user is logging on them. Obviously, it brings users some inconvenience. For example, when users are traveling, they can not link the Internet so they can not track their vessels as a result. On the other hand, users are very busy so that they can't concentrate themselves on the screen of the monitoring system to track vessels. A notification email or a short message will be a better substitution sometimes.

This paper developed a message notification service that could send vessel navigation messages to the subscribers via email or mobile message service. Therefore, an active vessel navigation monitoring service will be developed. For the aim of visualization, each message contained a background image and a mark, which shows the position and navigation status of a vessel derived from AIS reports. The background image was selected from the existing massive electrical map or chart image database based on the position of the vessel. More than one image may be selected, so a RBF network with two inputs of image information entropy and scrambling degree is built to choose the most proper background image.

Some online systems, for example AISLive, also provide active notification service. However, these systems can only sent less visual text messages to the subscribers.

This paper is organized as follows: section 2 describes the system architecture; section 3 introduces the automatic image selecting method; section 4 illuminates the experiments and finally, the conclusion is presented.

2 Service System Architecture

The multi-media message service shall be developed based on two essential components: AIS information database and chart tile database. These components can be built as figure 1 shows.

Recently, there are more and more AIS shore-based stations have been developed along the coastal to collect navigation information from vessels sent by AIS transponder on board. The information then will be sent to some traffic service centers (VTS in short) via Internet by using TCP/IP connection. TCP/IP connection is a type of linked-oriented connection different from UDP connection, which need not set up connection with other peers before they began to transmit data. So the TCP/IP connection is safer than UDP connection that will ensure no data lost during their transmission. The AIS information database stores the updated AIS information, which will be indexed by the geographical information.

Raster charts, scanned from paper charts and originated from Electric Chart Display and Information System (ECDIS in short) are cut into multiple tiles which formed the data of chart tiles database. Also, the service system provides map tiles as the background image of the notification message. The map tiles are originated from LiveMap[5].

---

[5] http://maps.live.com/

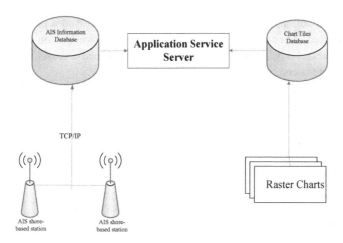

Fig. 1. AIS information database and chart tile database

The multi-media message service system can be divided into three components: users' subscribing module, message creating module and message outgoing module. Figure 2 shows its architecture. It also has a control unit called scheduler center, which will coordinate and control the procedure of the whole system. Chart tiles database provides the source of the background image of notification message. All these tiles are well organized and indexed in order to improve query speed. The candidate background images of the multi-media notification message will be selected out according to the vessels' navigation information provided by the AIS information database.

The system shall provide an interfaced that users can submit subscriptions and all of the subscriptions will be stored, which will form the subscription database. A subscription could be a timely notification request, which is triggered on a fixed time, or a regularly notification request, which is triggered between a fixed interval, or an arriving/leaving notification request, which is triggered when a vessel arrive or leave an area that users can define as well as some specific area such as anchorage, harbor limit, terminals or port and so on. That will be useful for users involved in logistics field, which need be reminded as soon as the vessel arrived at or departed from port.

The scheduler center can be developed by using Quartz[6] and it will query users' subscription database to obtain users' requirements, then trigger the message creating module to query the AIS information database to obtain vessels' navigation information. One copy of the information queried will be sent to the Background image creator. Then, the background image creator will choose some candidate background images from the chart tiles database according to the position of the vessel. And one proper image will be selected from the candidate images by using the automatic image selection method, which will be discussed in section 3. Another copy of vessel

---

[6] http://www.opensymphony.com/quartz/

navigation information will be sent to the Message creator. And a plain text message will be generated. Then the plain text message will be overlaid on the background image on the vessel's position accordingly, thus a multi-media vessel navigation notification message is created.

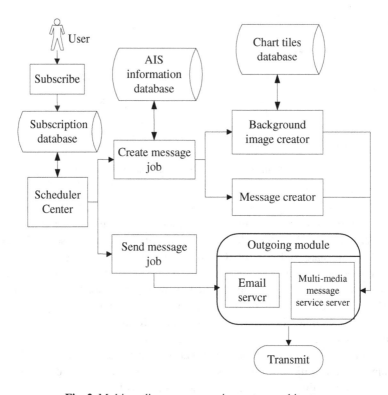

Fig. 2. Multi-media message service system architecture

Once the notification message is created, it will be handed to the message outgoing module. When the module is triggered by scheduler center, the notification message will be sent to users by email through email server or by Multi-Media Short Message (MMSM) through Multi-media message service server. The email or MMSM received by users will be demonstrated in section 4.

3 Automatic Background Image Selecting Method

A background image where the vessel's current position is marked shall contain adequate information so that it ensures the image can reflect the vessel's approximated geographical position and navigation environment. For each image, two properties namely image's information entropy and information scrambling degree are extracted. These properties decide whether an image meets the requirement of background image or not.

3.1 Image's Information Entropy

Information entropy is a concept comes from information theory and it describes the uncertainties of a stochastic system. For a random variable X, $s(X)$ is its value set, $p(x)$ is the distribution function. Then the information entropy $E(X)$ can be calculated by formula 1.

$$E(X) = - \sum_{x \in s(X)} p(x) \log(p(x)) \tag{1}$$

For an image, its pixel value can be regarded as a kind of random variable. Let $p_A(v)$ stands for the distribution function of the pixel whose value is v in image A (size: $n \times m$). Then the image's information entropy $H(V)$ can be calculated by formula 2.

$$H(V) = \sum_{v \in s(V)} p_A(v) \log(p_A(v)) \tag{2}$$

And $p_A(v)$ can be calculated by formula 3.

$$p_A(v) = \frac{f_A(v)}{n \times m} \tag{3}$$

Where $f_A(v)$ stands for the total numbers of the pixel whose value is v in image A.

Different colors on image stands for different objects or navigation aids. A more proper image will have more colors, that means it has more information entropy,

3.2 Image's Information Scrambling Degree

ll images have a same base color, and a selected image can be regarded as the result of the useful information scrambling on the bare image, which has only the base color. So the distribution of the information on the bare image, measured by scrambling degree, can be combined with Information Entropy to evaluate whether a background image is proper or not.

Scrambling degree evaluation of information has been studied in field of information hiding for many years and several methods have been developed [7] [8] [9]. Li Zhi-wei, Chen Yan-mei, et al, proposed image scrambling degree evaluation method based on the combination of image's SNR (signal-to-noise ratio) and its optimum partition [10].

An image can be treated as a matrix, let $f(x, y)$　$x, y \in \{0, 1, \ldots, N - 1\}$ stands for the original pixel value of the image, $g(x, y)$　$x, y \in \{0, 1, \ldots, N - 1\}$ stands for the pixel value after scrambling, then the noise $e(x, y)$ can be calculated by formula 4.

$$e(x, y) = f(x, y) - g(x, y) \tag{4}$$

The *SNR* of the image after scrambling can be calculated by formula 5.

$$SNR = \frac{\sum\limits_{x=0}^{N-1}\sum\limits_{y=0}^{N-1} g^2(x, y)}{\sum\limits_{x=0}^{N-1}\sum\limits_{y=0}^{N-1} e^2(x, y)} \tag{5}$$

Because the background image is a colored image, the *SNR* of the image should be calculated by formula 6.

$$SNR = \frac{\sum\limits_{i=0}^{N-1}\sum\limits_{i=0}^{N-1} (\overline{p_{ij}^R})^2 + (\overline{p_{ij}^G})^2 + (\overline{p_{ij}^B})^2}{\sum\limits_{i=0}^{N-1}\sum\limits_{i=0}^{N-1} (p_{ij}^R - \overline{p_{ij}^R})^2 + (p_{ij}^G - \overline{p_{ij}^G})^2 + (p_{ij}^B - \overline{p_{ij}^B})^2} \tag{6}$$

Where $p_{ij}^R, p_{ij}^G, p_{ij}^B$ are the values of the R,G,B color components in image's base color respectively while $\overline{p_{ij}^R}, \overline{p_{ij}^G}, \overline{p_{ij}^B}$ are their values after scrambling.

Meanwhile, we partitioned the color image into blocks. For each block, its *SNR* can be calculated by formula 6, and the average *SNR* of the color images is calculated by formula 7.

$$SNR = \frac{\sum\limits_{i=1}^{n} SNR_i}{n} \tag{7}$$

Where SNR_i is *SNR* of the ith image block.

3.3 Automatic Background Image Selecting Method

We have extracted two properties from image, and these two properties can be used together to decide whether the image meets the requirements of a background image or not, So the job of background image selection can be regarded as a classification calculation based on the two properties. Artificial neural network is a suitable tool to do this job. So we built a RBF network select out a most proper background image. RBF network is an effective feed-forward neural network. It has the best approximation and overall optimal performance and widely used in pattern recognition, function approximation and signal processing etc.

Firstly, we can choose a lot of images and calculate their information entropy and information scrambling degree. We read each image and decide whether it is qualified or not. For a qualified image, we assign its qualification value Q as true, otherwise false. Therefore, a sampling data set can be created. The RBF network is built by using Gaussian function as the kernel function of its hidden layer and trained by using a sampling data set. The symmetry center of the kernel function is decided by using fuzzy *K-means* algorithm [11]. This algorithm chooses k data from the sampling data set to act as the initial symmetry center $c_j(j=1,2,...k)$. The left data will be distributed to the c_j^{th} cluster scope approximately. In each scope, the average value of this scope will be calculated and the result will be relocated as the finally symmetry center.

After the symmetry center is fixed, the transformation width σ of the kernel function can be decided by using the following methods.

(a) Fixed method

The transformation width σ can be calculated by formula 8.

$$\sigma = \frac{d}{\sqrt{2M}} \tag{8}$$

Where d is the maximum distance between different cluster scopes of the sampling data set, M is the number of the symmetry center of the scopes.

(b) Average distance method

The reasonable estimated value of σ can be described by formula 9.

$$\sigma_i = \langle \| \mu_j - \mu_i \| \rangle \tag{9}$$

The above formula represents the Euclid distance between the cluster scope μ_i and scope μ_j.

In this paper, we decided the symmetry center and transformation width of the kernel function of the artificial neural network by the following steps.

Fist of all, assumed m as the iteration time, $c_1(m), c_2(m), ...c_k(m)$ as the cluster center after m times iteration and $w_1(m), w_2(m), ...w_k(m)$ as the cluster scope respectively.

(a). Choose some data from sampling set randomly act as the initial symmetry center, let $m=1$ and set threshold value ε $(\varepsilon > 0)$.

(b). Calculate the distance between the initial symmetry center of the all input training data X_j by formula 10.

$$d_j = \| X_j - c_i(m) \| \quad j=1,2,...n, i=1,2,...k \tag{10}$$

(c). Relocate the training data. The training data X_j will be relocated in cluster i when the symmetry center of i is the most nearest center to X_j.

(d). Re-calculate the symmetry center of each cluster center by formula 11.

$$c_i(m+1) = \frac{1}{N_i} \sum_{x \in w_i(m)} x \quad (i = 1,2,...k) \tag{11}$$

Where N_i represents the numbers of training data in the ith cluster scope $w_i(m)$.

(e). If $\| c_i(m+1) - c_i(m) \| < \varepsilon \quad (i = 1,2,...k)$, then c_i act as the finally symmetry center of cluster i, then switch to followed step, otherwise switch step b.

(f). The transformation width of each hidden layer of the neural network can be fixed by formula 12 according to the cluster center.

$$\sigma_i = \lambda d_i \tag{12}$$

Where d_i is the distance between the ith cluster center and its nearest adjacent cluster center while λ is the overlaid coefficient.

In this paper, we used JOONE[7] to build and train the neural network and the network was saved for further use. The background image selection procedure can be described as figure 2 shows.

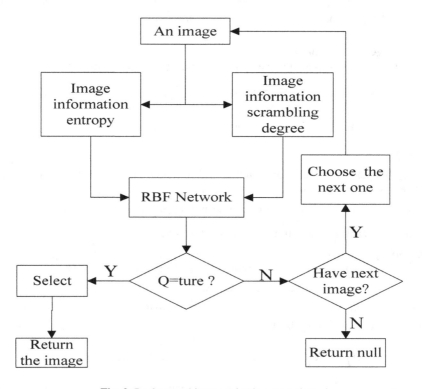

Fig. 2. Background image selecting procedure

---

[7] http://www.jooneworld.com

Images selected from map tile database will be arranged from largest scale to smallest scale. When an image was selected, its information entropy and information scrambling degree will be calculated and input into the RBF network. Then its qualification value Q will be output from the network. For qualified image, it will be selected and returned otherwise it will be discarded and the procedure began another loop if there have existed other images or return null if there haven't.

The correct rate of the RBF network while choosing a most proper background image will be tested in section 4.

4   Experiments

In this section, we will propose four experiments. First of all, we will build t the training data set for the artificial neural network and trained it. The network then will be tested after trained to evaluate its performance. The scheduler record will be recorded to show weather the scheduler center can manage those two jobs as shown in the system architecture figure. Finally, the multi-media notification message received at users' terminal will be given.

4.1   Neural Network Experiments

We have selected 421 images and calculated their image information entropy and information scrambling degree. After we read the images, we decided whether it was qualified or not. And then the training data set was formed. Table 1 is the part of the training data set. Then the RBF network built in section 3 was trained by this data set.

Table 1. The training data set (excerpted)

Entropy	Scrambling degree	Qualified?[8]
...	...	...
0.18015619	0.001191539	0
3.800539469	0.038937539	1
3.286869652	0.040878474	1
2.866505095	0.038707643	1
0.594572415	0.004982879	1
0.6709644	0.007873423	0
0.889521375	0.010041481	0
1.918290527	0.021568564	1
0.024153937	0.000126844	0
1.910414186	0.031503099	1
3.115887637	0.041123802	1
2.678651263	0.039506385	1
......	......	......

---

[8] "1" stands for true while "0" for false.

We have selected another 422 images by using the neural network and sent them out. After read these images, we found some of them did not meet the requirements of background image. There were totally 357 qualified images. The correct rate of image selection method is 84.59%. Table 2 shows part of the experiment result, the third column is the qualification value calculated by RBF network while the value in forth column is decided by reader.

Table 2. The neural network experiment result (excerpted)

Entropy	Scrambling degree	Qualified? (by RBF network)	Qualified? (by reader)
...	...	...	...
2.63762	0.028564	0.99973249	1
2.32571	0.035241	0.99999984	1
2.34853	0.031867	0.99999682	1
2.74257	0.036344	1	1
1.43897	0.037916	0.99999987	1
1.71602	0.028730	0.99999986	1
1.76334	0.019922	0.99999975	1
0.18250	0.000927	0.99999986	0
2.01415	0.023291	0.99999986	1
1.48078	0.019114	0.90151352	1
......	......	......	......

4.2 Scheduler Center Executing Records

The scheduler center was developed by using Quartz. Quartz is a full-featured, open source job scheduling system that can be integrated or used alongside virtually any Java applications - from the smallest stand alone application to the largest e-commerce system.

Figure 3 shows the scheduling records of a regular notification job triggered at the interval of one minute. From the records we can see that the scheduler center can coordinate message creating module and outgoing module.

The scheduler trigger can be easy defined by cron-expression. A cron-expression is a piece of code that defined the trigger interval. The following code (in Java) is presented as an example.

```
CronTrigger trigger = new CronTrig-
ger("triggername","triggergroup","jobname",scheduler's
ID,"0 0/1 * * * ?");

Scheduler.scheduleJob(job, trigger);
```

The cron-expression "0 0/1 * * * ?" means that the job will be triggered every one minute. So the cron-expression can be easily modified to meet the actual requirements.

```
------- Initializing ------------------
log4j:WARN No appenders could be found for logger (org.quar
log4j:WARN Please initialize the log4j system properly.
------- Initialization Complete -----------
------- Scheduling Jobs -----------
------- Starting Scheduler ----------------
------- Started Scheduler -----------------
OneMinuEmailJob execute: Fri May 30 10:07:09 CST 2008
SendMailJob execute: Fri May 30 10:07:13 CST 2008
OneMinuEmailJob execute: Fri May 30 10:08:09 CST 2008
SendMailJob execute: Fri May 30 10:08:13 CST 2008
OneMinuEmailJob execute: Fri May 30 10:09:09 CST 2008
SendMailJob execute: Fri May 30 10:09:13 CST 2008
OneMinuEmailJob execute: Fri May 30 10:10:09 CST 2008
SendMailJob execute: Fri May 30 10:10:13 CST 2008
```

Fig. 3. Scheduling records

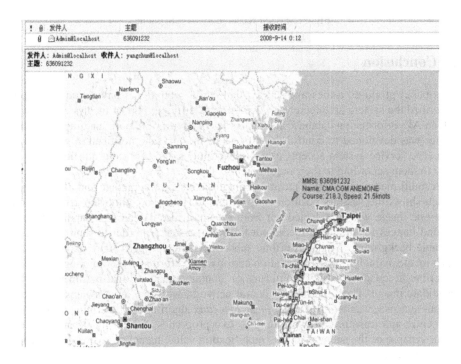

Fig. 4. An email notification message

4.3 Multi-media Notification Message

The message received by users in form of email is shown in figure 4 and the MMSM received by mobile phone was shown in figure 5.

The red triangle in figure 4 and figure 5 indicates the vessel's current position.

Fig. 5. MMSM received by mobile phone

5 Conclusion

This paper proposed a message service that could send vessel navigation messages, described the system architecture and function of different part of the system. First of all, an AIS information database and chart tiles database were built, and then a control center was developed to control the process of the message notification service system. The service system accepts users' subscriptions and sends out notification message to them according to their requirements.

A multi-media notification message contains a background image and a mark on it, which shows the vessel's position and navigation status, to offline subscribers. More than one image will be selected out from the chart tiles database as candidate background images for the multi-media notification message. In order to send out a more suitable background images to offline subscribers, two properties are extracted from each image, namely image information entropy and information scrambling degree, to describe the quantity of useful information contained and its distribution among the candidate image. Then an artificial neural network, with two input synapses and one output synapse, was built by using *fuzzy K-means* algorithm to determine its symmetry center and transformation width. The two properties of each image acted as the input synapse of the network and its qualification value, namely true or false, acted as the output of the network.

After the network trained and saved, it was tested in open mood. And the experiment result had shown that the neural network had a correct rate of 84%.

The active vessel navigation monitoring service was finally implemented. Vessel navigation messages can be sent via email and MMSM to the users according to their subscriptions. The vessel's position and navigation status can be indicated vividly by reading these multi-media notification messages.

Acknowledgement

This research was supported by Shanghai Education Committee with grant No. 08YZ107.

References

[1] Mingshi, W., Renying, Z.: Analysis of business value of AIS in shipping logistics industry. In: Port Science and Technology, June 2007, pp. 50–51 (2007) (in Chinese)

[2] Yifan, L.: Application of AIS in shipping brokerage business. In: Water Transportation Management, May 2006, vol. 25(5) (2006)

[3] Yong, L., Pin, Z., Jianjun, T.: Study of Shipping Monitoring and Management System Based on AIS and GIS. Microcomputer Information 23(6-1), 250–251 (2007)

[4] Yansong, G., Guojun, P., Xinggu, Z.: Web electronic sea map distribution system based on GeoBeans6.0. Ship and Ocean Engineering 36(5), 86–88 (2007)

[5] Guojun, P., Yuezong, W.: Web electronic chart system based on JavaApplet technique. Journal of Shanghai Maritime University 28(4), 26–29 (2007)

[6] HU, Q., Chen, J., Shi, C.: Bring Live AIS Information on the Web Sea Charts by Using Ajax. In: The proceeding of the2007 International Conference on Intelligent Transportation System and Telecommunication, Sophia Antipolis France, August 2007, pp. 455–459 (2007)

[7] Zou, J., Ward, R.K., Qi, D.: Some Novel Image Scrambling Methods Based on Chaotic Dynamical Systems. In: The proceeding of the 46th IEEE International Midwest Symposium on Circuits and Systems, December 2003, vol. 2, pp. 652–655 (2003)

[8] Sen, B., Chang-xiu, C.: A Novel Algorithm for Scrambling the Detail of Digital Image. In: The proceeding of the 4th World Congress on Intelligent Control and Automation, Shanghai China, June 2002, vol. 2, pp. 1333–1336 (2002)

[9] Sen, B., Changxiu, C.: Property of Sub-affine Transformation and Its Application. Journal of Computer Aided Design and Computer Graphics 15(2), 205–208 (2003)

[10] Zhi-wei, L., Yan-mei, C., Sheng-yuan, Z.: Digital Image Scrambling Degree Evaluation Method Based on SNR. Journal of Xiamen University (Natural Science) 45(4), 484–487 (2006)

[11] Nasser, S., Alkhaldi, R., Vert, G.: A Modified Fuzzy K-means Clustering using Expectation Maximization. In: The proceeding of 2006 IEEE international conference on Fuzzy Systems, Vancouver, BC, Canada, July 2006, pp. 231–235 (2006)

Improvement of Efficient Remote Mutual Authentication and Key Agreement

Han-Cheng Hsiang[1,2] and Wei-Kuan Shih[1]

[1] Department of Computer Science, National Tsing Hua University,
No. 101, Kuang Fu Rd, Sec. 2, 300 HsingChu, Taiwan, R.O.C.
shc@rtlab.cs.nthu.edu.tw, wshih@cs.nthu.edu.tw
[2] Department of Information Management, Vanung University,
No.1,Wanneng Rd., Zhongli City, Taoyuan County 320, Taiwan, R.O.C.
shc@vnu.edu.tw

Abstract. In an open networking environment, a server usually needs to identify its legal users for providing its services. In 2006, Shieh and Wang pointed
out the weakness of Juang's remote mutual authentication scheme using smart
card and further proposed an efficient remote mutual authentication and key
agreement scheme using smart card. Recently, Yoon and Yoo demonstrated that
Shieh and Wang's scheme does not provide perfect forward secrecy and is vulnerable to a privileged insider's attack. In this paper, we propose a security improvement to resolve the security problems. The proposed scheme not only
inherits the merits of their scheme but also enhances the security of their
scheme.

Keywords: Authentication, Password, Key agreement, Cryptanalysis, Smart
card.

1 Introduction

In ubiquitous computing, a user may use many computers at any time and any place,
while he does not need to know how to use these computers which could be thin servers and only have low computation and communication capacity. When a user enters
anywhere, if this user wants to use the allowed services provided by the connected
servers, he must pass the authentication of these servers [1].

In distributed computing environment, secure communication in insecure communication channels is a very important issue. Hence, user authentication and secret
key distribution become the most important security service for communication networks. Thus, authentication and key distribution protocols are necessary in distributed
environments.

Remote user authentication scheme allows a server to check the legitimacy of a
remote user through insecure network. In addition, a smart card based remote mutual
authentication scheme is very useful to authenticate remote users [2, 3]. Since Lamport [4] proposed the first well-known password based remote user authentication
scheme in 1981. Since then, many researchers have proposed new schemes and
improved the efficiency and security of remote authentication [17-21].

T.-h. Kim et al. (Eds.): FGCN 2008, CCIS 27, pp. 14–24, 2009.

In 2000, Sun [5] proposed an efficient password based remote user authentication scheme by using smart cards. Sun's scheme requires only several hash operations instead of the costly modular exponentiations. In 2002, Chien et al. [6] proposed an efficient remote mutual authentication scheme using smart card allowing server and user to authenticate each other. The advantages in the scheme include freely chosen passwords, no verification tables, low communication and computation costs. In2004, Hsu [7] demonstrated that Chien et al.'s scheme is vulnerable to the parallel session attack. Thereafter, in 2004, Juang [8] proposed another scheme preserving all the advantages of Chien et al.'s scheme. Unlike Chien et al.'s scheme, Juang's scheme is nonce based authentication and key agreement scheme. Hence, no synchronized clocks are required in the scheme. In addition, Juang's scheme generates a session key for the user and server in their subsequent communication.

However, in 2006, Shieh and Wang [9] pointed out the weakness of Juang's scheme and then proposed another similar scheme to improve the weakness. Shieh and Wang claimed that their scheme not only preserves all the advantages of Juang's scheme but also improves its efficiency. Recently, Yoon and Yoo [10] demonstrated that Shieh and Wang's scheme does not provide perfect forward secrecy [11] and is vulnerable to a privileged insider's attack [12,13]. Besides, we find that Shieh and Wang's scheme has the problem of user cannot change his password freely [15]. In this paper, we propose an improvement of Shieh and Wang's scheme to resolve the security flaws that Yoon and Yoo has demonstrated. The proposed scheme not only inherits the merits of their scheme but also enhances the security of their scheme.

The remainder of this paper is organized as follows: Section 2 briefly reviews Shieh and Wang's scheme. Section 3 demonstrates the security weaknesses of Shieh and Wang's scheme. Our improved scheme is proposed in Section 4. The security analysis of the proposed improved scheme is presented in Section 5. The conclusion is given in Section 6.

2 Review of Shieh-Wang's Remote Scheme

This section briefly reviews Shieh and Wang's a remote mutual authentication and key agreement scheme using smart card with secure one-way hash function [9]. Some of the notations used in this paper are defined as follows:

- $h(\cdot)$: secure one-way hash function

- x: the secret key maintained by the server

- p : a large prime number

- g : a primitive element in $GF(p)$

- $\oplus$: exclusive-or operation

- $\|$: string concatenation operation

Shieh-Wang's scheme consists of two phases: the registration phase, and the login and key agreement phase. The scheme works as follows:

2.1   Registration Phase

Assume a user U_i submits his identity ID_i and password PW_i to the server over a secure channel for registration. If the request is accepted, the server computes $R_i = h(ID_i \oplus x) \oplus PW_i$ and issues U_i a smart card containing R_i and $h(\cdot)$. Figure 1 shows the Registration phase.

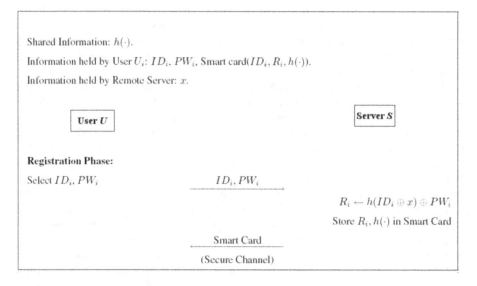

Fig. 1. The Registration phase of Shieh and Wang's scheme

2.2   Login and Key Agreement Phase

When the user U_i wants to login to the server, he first inserts his smart card into a card reader then inputs his identity ID_i and password PW_i. The smart card then performs the following steps to begin an access session:

1. Compute $a_i = R_i \oplus PW_i$.
2. Acquire current time stamp T_u, store T_u temporarily until the end of the session, and compute $MAC_u = h(T_u \| a_i)$.
3. Send the message (ID_i, T_u, MAC_u) to the server and wait for response from the server. If no response is received in time or the response is incorrect, report login failure to the user and stop the session.

After receiving the message (ID_i, T_u, MAC_u) from U_i, the server performs the following steps to assure the integrity of the message, respond to U_i, and challenge U_i to avoid replay:

1. Check the freshness of T_u. If T_u has already appeared in a current executing session of user U_i, reject U_i's login request and stop the session. Otherwise, T_u is fresh.

2. Compute $a'_i = h(ID_i \oplus x)$, $MAC'_u = h(T_u|| a'_i)$, and check whether MAC'_u is equal to the received MAC_u. If it is not, reject U_i's login and stop the session.
3. Acquire the current time stamp T_s. Store temporarily paired time stamps (T_u, T_s) and ID_i for freshness checking until the end of the session. Compute $MAC_s = h(T_u|| T_s|| a_i)$ and session key $K_s = h((T_u|| T_s) \oplus a\_i)$. Then, send the message (T_u, T_s, MAC_s) back to U_i and wait for response from U_i. If no response is received in time or the response is incorrect, reject U_i's login and stop the session.

On receiving the message (T_u, T_s, MAC_s) from the server, the smart card performs the following steps to authenticate the server, achieve session key agreement, and respond to the server:

1. Check if the received T_u is equal to the stored T_u to assure the freshness of the received message. If it is not, report login failure to the user and stop the session.
2. Compute $MAC'_s = h(T_u|| T_s|| a_i)$ and check whether it is equal to the received MAC_s. If not, report login failure to the user and stop. Otherwise, conclude that the responding party is the real server.
3. Compute $MAC''_u = h(T_s||(a_i + 1))$ and session key $K_s = h((T_u|| T_s) \oplus a_i)$, then send the message (T_s, MAC''_u) back to the server. Note that, in the message (T_s, MAC''_u), T_s is a response to the server.

When the message (T_s, MAC''_u) from U_i is received, the server performs the following steps to authenticate U_i and achieve key agreement:

1. Check if the received T_s is equal to the stored T_s. If it fails, reject U_i's login request and stop the session.
2. Compute $MAC'''_u = h(T_s ||(a_i + 1))$ and check whether it is equal to MAC''_u. If it is not, reject U_i's login request and stop the session. Otherwise, conclude that U_i is a legal user and permit the user U_i's login.

At this moment, mutual authentication and session key agreement between U_i and the server are achieved. From now on, the user U_i and the server can use the session key K_s in their further secure communication until the end of the access session. The Login and key agreement phase is shown in Figure 2.

3   Security Flaws on Shieh and Wang's Scheme

In this section, we review Yoon and Yoo's attacks on the Shieh and Wang's remote mutual authentication and key agreement protocol, and show that Shieh and Wang's scheme does not provide perfect forward secrecy [11] and is vulnerable to a privileged insider attack [12, 13].

3.1   Perfect Forward Secrecy Problem

For evaluating a strong protocol, perfect forward secrecy is considered to be an important security issue. A protocol providing perfect forward secrecy means that even if one entity's long-term secret key is compromised, it will never reveal any old

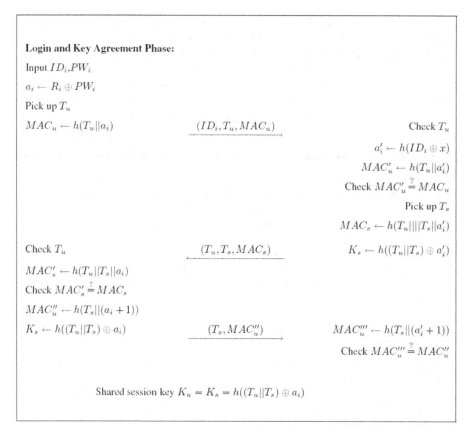

Fig. 2. The Login and key agreement phase of Shieh and Wang's scheme

short-term keys used previously. For example, the well-known Diffie-Hellman key agreement scheme can provide perfect forward secrecy [11, 16].

However, Shieh and Wang's scheme does not provide it because once the secret key x of the server is disclosed; all previous fresh session keys K_s will also be opened and thus previous communication messages will be found as follows:

1. If an attacker Eve obtains the secret key x from the compromised server and intercepts transmitted values (ID_i, T_u, T_s), from an open network. It will be easy to obtain the information since it is exposed over an open network.
2. Eve can compute $a_i = h(ID_i \oplus x)$ by using ID_i, and can compute the shared session key $K_S = h((T_u \| T_s) \oplus a_i)$ by using a_i, T_u and T_s.
3. Once Eve obtains the shared session key K_S, by using the K_S, Eve can get all previous communication messages.

Clearly, Shieh-Wang's scheme does not provide perfect forward secrecy.

3.2 Privileged Insider's Attack

In real environments, a user uses the same password to access several servers for his convenience. If a privileged insider of the server has learned the user's password, he may try to impersonate the user to access other servers. In the registration phase of Shieh and Wang's scheme, U_i's password PW_i will be revealed to the remote server S because it is transmitted directly to S. Then, the privileged insider of S may try to use PW_i to impersonate U_i to login the other servers that U_i has registered with outside this system. If the targeted outside server adopts the normal password authentication scheme, it is possible that the privileged insider of the server can successfully impersonate U_i to login it by using PW_i.

Clearly, Shieh and Wang's scheme is vulnerable to a privileged insider attack.

4 Our Improved Scheme

In this section, we propose an improvement to Shieh-Wang's scheme that can withstand the security flaws described in previous sections. The flowchart of the new protocol is shown in Figure 3. Our improved scheme enhances the security of Shieh and Wang's scheme; the proposed scheme performs as follows.

4.1 Registration Phase

The system selects two large prime numbers p and q, such that q divides $p - 1$. One generator g with order q in the Galois field $GF(p)$ [14], where $GF(p)$ is the set of integers $\{0,1, \ldots ,p\text{-}1\}$ with arithmetic operations defined modulo p, used in our scheme.

Assume a user U_i selects a random number b, password PW_i and computes $h(b \oplus PW_i)$. He submits his identity ID_i and $h(b \oplus PW_i)$ to the server over a secure channel for registration. If the request is accepted, the server computes $a_i = h(ID_i \oplus x)$, $R_i = a_i \oplus h(b \oplus PW_i)$ and $N=h_{a_i}(h(b \oplus PW_i))$. Then issues U_i a smart card containing R_i, N, p, g and $h(\cdot)$. U_i enters b into his smart card so that he does not need to remember b anymore.

4.2 Login and Key Agreement Phase

When the user U_i wants to login to the server, he first inserts his smart card into a card reader then inputs his identity ID_i, password PW_i, and a large random integer $y < p\text{-}1$. The smart card then performs the following steps to begin an access session:

1. Compute $a_i = R_i \oplus (b \oplus PW_i)$.
2. Acquire current time stamp T_u, store T_u temporarily until the end of the session, and compute $MAC_u = h(T_u \| a_i)$.
3. Compute $C = g^y \oplus a_i$.
4. Smart card generates a random number r, and computes $C_i = a_i \oplus h(r \oplus b)$.
5. Send the message $(ID_i, T_u, MAC_u, C, C_l)$ to the server S and wait for response from the server. If no response is received in time or the response is incorrect, report login failure to the user and stop the session.

After receiving the message $(ID_i, T_u, MAC_u, C, C_1)$ from U_i, the server S performs the following steps to assure the integrity of the message, respond to U_i, and challenge U_i to avoid replay:

1. Check the freshness of T_u. If T_u has already appeared in a current executing session of user U_i, reject U_i's login request and stop the session. Otherwise, Tu is fresh.
2. Compute $a_i' = h(ID_i \oplus x)$, $C' = a_i' \oplus C_1$, $MAC_u' = h(T_u \| a_i')$, and check whether MAC_u' is equal to the received MAC_u. If it is not, reject U_i's login and stop the session.
3. S chooses a large random integer $z < p-1$ and computes $g^z(\bmod\ p)$. S retrieves g^x by computing $g^x = C \oplus a_i'$. After all parameters are known, S computes $g^{yz}(\bmod\ p) = (g^y)^z = (g^z)^y = g^{yz}$.
4. Acquire the current time stamp T_s. Store temporarily paired time stamps (T_u, T_s) and ID_i for freshness checking until the end of the session. Compute $MAC_s = h(T_u \| T_s \| a_i)$, $C_2 = g^z \oplus a_i'$ and $C_3 = g^{yz} \oplus C_1' \oplus K_s$, which K_s is the session key. Then, send the message $(T_u, T_s, MAC_s, C_2, C_3)$ back to U_i and wait for response from U_i. If no response is received in time or the response is incorrect, reject U_i's login and stop the session.

On receiving the message $(T_u, T_s, MAC_s, C_2, C_3)$ from the server, the smart card performs the following steps to authenticate the server, achieve session key agreement, and respond to the server:

1. Check if the received T_u is equal to the stored T_u to assure the freshness of the received message. If it is not, report login failure to the user and stop the session.
2. Compute $MAC_s' = h(T_u \| T_s \| a_i)$ and check whether it is equal to the received MAC_s. If not, report login failure to the user and stop. Otherwise, conclude that the responding party is the real server.
3. Compute $g^z = C2 \oplus a'i$ and derive gxy (mod p) by raising the received gz to y. Next, retrieve session key Ks by computing Ks = gyz $\oplus$ h(b $\oplus$ r) $\oplus$ C3.
4. Compute $MAC_u'' = h(T_s \| (a_i' + 1))$, then send the message (T_s, MAC_u'') back to the server. Note that, in the message (T_s, MAC_u''), T_s is a response to the server.

When the message (T_s, MAC_u'') from U_i is received, the server performs the following steps to authenticate U_i and achieve key agreement:

1. Check if the received T_s is equal to the stored T_s. If it fails, reject U_i's login request and stop the session.
2. Compute $MAC_u''' = h(T_s \| (a_i' + 1))$ and check whether it is equal to MAC_u''. If it is not, reject U_i's login request and stop the session. Otherwise, conclude that U_i is a legal user and permit the user U_i's login.

At this moment, mutual authentication and session key agreement between U_i and the server are achieved. From now on, the user U_i and the server can use the session key K_s in their further secure communication until the end of the access session.

4.3 Password Change Phase

This phase is invoked whenever a user U_i wants to change his password PW_i with a new one, say PW_{new}.

1. U_i inserts his smart card into card reader, enters ID_i and PW_i, and requests to change password.

2. U_i's smart card computes $a_i = R_i \oplus h(b \oplus PW_i)$ and $N^* = h_{a_i}(h(b \oplus PW_i))$.

3. Check whether N^* equals to the stored N or not. If not, reject the password change request, otherwise U_i chooses a new password PW_{new}.

4. Compute $R_{new} = a_i \oplus h(b \oplus PW_{new})$ and $N_{new} = h_{a_i}(h(b \oplus PW_{new}))$, then stores R_{new}, N_{new} into the user's smart card and replaces the old values R_i, N respectively. The new password is successfully updated and this phase is terminated.

5 Security Analysis

In this section, we analyze the security of our scheme as following:

The proposed scheme inherits the security features of Shieh-Wang's remote user authentication and key agreement protocol [9]. Challenge tokens C, C_2 and C_3 are used to ensure authenticity of the server S and the freshness of the communication and prevent replay attacks. Under these circumstances, the messages in the scheme are fresh and replays of old messages can be detected. Moreover, the protocol can withstand the attacks presented by Yoon-Yoo [10].

Claim 1. The proposed scheme can provide perfect forward secrecy.

Proof. Our scheme is based on the following well-known hard problem, which is believed infeasible to solve in polynomial time. Given a prime p, a generator g, and two numbers $g^y \bmod p$ and $g^z \bmod p$, try to find $g^{yz} \bmod p$, it is computationally infeasible due to the Diffie–Hellman problem [14]. We assume that the user U_i's password PW_i, he server S's secret key x are all known by an attacker. Then the attacker can decrypt C to obtain g^y, and decrypt C_2 to obtain g^z. But he cannot calculate g^{yz} because the difficulty is similar to solve the Diffie–Hellman problem. So the attacker does not have any opportunity to get the session key K_S. Thus the session key is still secure.

Claim 2. The proposed scheme can resist privileged insider's attack.

Proof. In the registration phase of Shieh-Wang's scheme, a user U_i selects a random number b, password PW_i and computes $h(b \oplus PW_i)$. He submits ID_i and $h(b \oplus PW_i)$ to the remote server S. If the privileged insider of S may try to use PW_i to impersonate U_i to login the other servers, he will fail. Since U_i registers to S by presenting $h(b \oplus PW_i)$ instead of PW, the insider of S can not directly obtain PW. Moreover, as b is not revealed to S, the privileged insider of S can not obtain PW by performing an off-line guessing attack on $h(b \oplus PW_i)$. Thus, the improved scheme can resist the privileged insider attack [12, 13].

Claim 3. The user can freely change his/her password.

Proof. In our scheme, each user can choose her/his favorite password in the registration phase. It will make users easy to remember their own passwords. The proposed scheme also provides the mechanism of changing password. When any user wants to change password, the user's smartcard will compute $N^* = h_{a_i}(h(b \oplus PW))$, and verify N^*

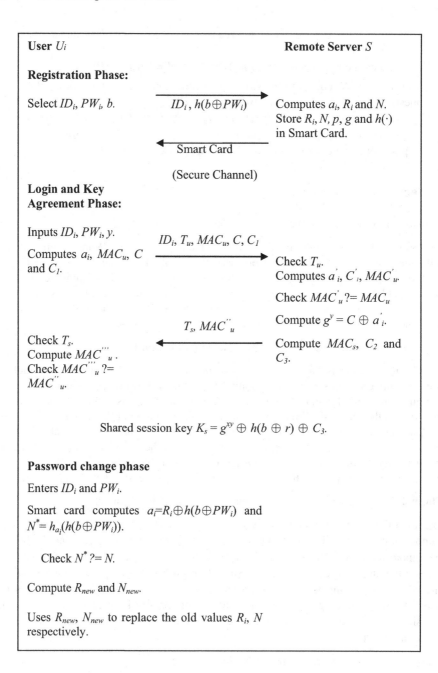

User U_i   **Remote Server S**

Registration Phase:

Select ID_i, PW_i, b. ID_i, $h(b \oplus PW_i)$ Computes a_i, R_i and N.
                                                 Store R_i, N, p, g and $h(\cdot)$
                                                 in Smart Card.

                              Smart Card

                          (Secure Channel)

**Login and Key
Agreement Phase:**

Inputs ID_i, PW_i, y. ID_i, T_u, MAC_u, C, C_1
Computes a_i, MAC_u, C Check T_u.
and C_1.   Computes a'_i, C'_1, MAC'_u.

                                                 Check MAC'_u ?= MAC_u

                                                 Compute $g^y = C \oplus a'_i$.
                              T_s, MAC''_u
Check T_s.   Compute MAC_s, C_2 and
Compute MAC'''_u. C_3.
Check MAC'''_u ?=
MAC''_u.

Shared session key $K_s = g^{xy} \oplus h(b \oplus r) \oplus C_3$.

Password change phase

Enters ID_i and PW_i.

Smart card computes $a_i = R_i \oplus h(b \oplus PW_i)$ and
$N^* = h_{a_i}(h(b \oplus PW_i))$.

   Check N^* ?= N.

Compute R_{new} and N_{new}.

Uses R_{new}, N_{new} to replace the old values R_i, N
respectively.

Fig. 3. The flowchart of our proposed scheme

compares with the stored N in smart card, respectively. If they are equal, i.e., $N^* = N$, the password change action will be executed. Otherwise, the smartcard rejects the password change request. Thus, the proposed scheme could effectively provide the mechanism of password change.

After above discussion, we summarize the comparisons of our scheme with Shieh and Wang's scheme in Table 1.

Table 1. Comparisons of various security attributes

	Shieh-Wang's scheme	Our scheme
Anonymity	Yes	Yes
Replay attack resistance	Yes	Yes
Parallel session attack resistance	Yes	Yes
Insider attack resistance	No	Yes
Forward secrecy	No	Yes
Mutual authentication	Yes	Yes
Secure password change	No	Yes

6 Conclusion

In 2006, Shieh and Wang proposed an efficient remote user authentication scheme using smart card. Recently, Yoon-Yoo demonstrated that Shieh and Wang's scheme does not provide perfect forward secrecy and is vulnerable to a privileged insider's attack. In this paper, we review Shieh and Wang.'s scheme and Yoon and Yoo's attacks. Then, we presented an improvement to prevent the attacks. The proposed scheme not only inherits the merits of their scheme but also enhances the security of their scheme. Moreover, the perfect forward secrecy and the privileged insider's attack are completely solved.

Acknowledgements. The authors would like to thank the anonymous reviewers for their valuable suggestions and comments in improving our manuscript.

References

1. Juang, W.: Efficient User Authentication and Key Agreement in Ubiquitous Computing. In: Gavrilova, M.L., Gervasi, O., Kumar, V., Tan, C.J.K., Taniar, D., Laganá, A., Mun, Y., Choo, H. (eds.) ICCSA 2006. LNCS, vol. 3983, pp. 396–405. Springer, Heidelberg (2006)
2. Peyret, P., Lisimaque, G., Chua, T.Y.: Smart Cards Provide Very High Security and Flexibility in Subscribers Management. IEEE Trans. Consum. Electron. 36(3), 744–752 (1990)
3. Sternglass, D.: The Future Is in the PC Cards. IEEE Spectrum 29(6), 46–50 (1992)

4. Lamport, L.: Password Authentication with Insecure Communication. Commun. of the ACM 24, 770–772 (1981)
5. Sun, H.M.: An Efficient Remote User Authentication Scheme Using Smart Cards. IEEE Trans. Consum. Electron 46(4), 958–961 (2000)
6. Chien, H.Y., Jan, J.K., Tseng, Y.H.: An Efficient and Practical Solution to Remote Authentication: Smart Card. Comput. Secur. 21(4), 372–375 (2002)
7. Hsu, C.L.: Security of Chien et al's Remote User Authentication Scheme Using Smart Card. Comput. Stand. Interfac. 26(3), 167–169 (2004)
8. Juang, W.S.: Efficient Password Authenticated Key Agreement Using Smart Cards. Compu. Secur. 23, 167–173 (2004)
9. Shieh, W.G., Wang, J.M.: Efficient Remote Mutual Authentication and Key Agreement. Compu. Secur. 25, 72–77 (2006)
10. Yoon, E.J., Yoo, K.Y.: Two Security Problems of Efficient Remote Mutual Authentication and Key Agreement. In: 2007 International Conference on the Future Generation Communication and Networking (FGCN 2007), Korea, pp. 66–70 (2007)
11. Menezes, A.J., Oorschot, P.C., Vanstone, S.A.: Handbook of Applied Cryptograph. CRC Press, New York (1997)
12. Ku, W.C., Chuang, H.M., Tsaur, M.J.: Vulnerabilities of Wu-Chieu's Improved Password Authentication Scheme Using Smart Cards. IEICE Trans. Fundamentals E88-A(11), 3241–3243 (2005)
13. Ku, W., Chen, S.: Weaknesses and Improvements of an Efficient Password based Remote User Authentication Scheme using Smart Cards. IEEE Trans. Consum. Electron 50(1), 204–207 (2004)
14. Diffie, W., Hellman, M.: New directions in cryptography. IEEE Trans. Info. Theory 22(6), 644–654 (1976)
15. Wang, X.M., Zhang, W.F., Zhang, J.S., Khan, M.K.: Cryptanalysis and improvement on two efficient remote user authentication scheme using smart cards. Comput. Stand. & Interface 29, 507–512 (2007)
16. Sun, H.M., Yeh, H.T.: Password-based authentication and key distribution protocols with perfect forward secrecy. J. Comput. Sys. Sci. 72, 1002–1011 (2006)
17. Lee, C.C., Li, L.H., Hwang, M.S.: A remote user authentication scheme using smart cards. ACM Operating Systems Review 36(4), 23–29 (2002)
18. Messerges, T.S., Dabbish, E.A., Sloan, R.H.: Examining smart-card security under the threat of power analysis attacks. IEEE Trans. Comput. 51(5), 541–552 (2002)
19. Mi, L., Takeda, F.: Analysis of the robustness of the pressure-based individual identification system based on neural networks. Int. J. of Innovative Computing, Inform. & Control 3(1), 97–110 (2007)
20. Mitchell, C.: Limitations of challenge-response entity authentication. Electron. Letters 25(17), 1195–1196 (1989)
21. Peyret, P., Lisimaque, G., Chua, T.Y.: Smart Cards Provide Very High Security and Flexibility in Subscribers Management. IEEE Trans. Consum. Electron 36(3), 744–752 (1990)

QTL Analysis of Ascochyta Blight
Resistance in Chickpea

A. Taleei[1,*], H. Kanouni[2], and M. Baum[3]

[1] Professor in the Department of Agronomy & Plant breeding, Faculty of Crop
& Animal Sciences, College of Agriculture and Natural Resources,
University of Tehran, Karaj, P.O. Box 31587-11167, Iran
[2] Seed and Plant Improvement Institute (SPII),
4119-31585, Karaj, Iran
[3] International Centre for Agricultural Research in the Dry Areas (ICARDA),
Aleppo, Syria
ataleei@ut.ac.ir

Abstract. Ascochyta blight, caused by *Ascochyta rabiei*(Pass.) Lab. is a devastating disease of chickpea (*Cicer arietinum* L.) worldwide. Resistant germplasm has been identified and the genetics of resistance has been the subject of
numerous studies. Besides, microsatellites have become markers of choice for
molecular mapping and marker assisted selection of key traits such as disease
resistance in many crop species. The aim of this study was to construct a genetic linkage map and analysis of quantitative trait loci (QTLs) for Ascochyta
blight resistance in chickpea (*Cicer arietinum* L.), as well as quantify the contribution of each QTL to observed phenotypic variation. Fifty-eight SSR
markers and one morphological marker (flower color) were mapped on F_2 individuals and $F_{2:3}$ families derived from the cross ICC 12004 (resistant)
×Bivanij (susceptible local variety) at the International Center for Agricultural
Research at Dry Area (ICARDA). The linkage map comprised eight linkage
groups, excluding flower color which didn't assign to any linkage group. Area
under disease progress curve (AUDPC) was used to evaluate the F_2 population
and F_3 families. Using composite interval mapping, three genomic regions
were detected, which were in association with reaction to ascochyta blight.
These QTLs on LG3, LG4 and LG6 accounted for 46.5% of the total estimated
phenotypic variation for reaction to ascochyta blight. Fine mapping of the
QTLs identified in this study would lead to the identification of markers that
could be used for marker-assisted selection of chickpea genotypes with resistance to Ascochyta blight. These findings are particular pertinent considering
that we used *Ascochyta rabiei* pathotype III and ICC 12004 (resistant to
pathotype III) for the first time.

Keywords: Chickpea (Cicer arietinum L.), *Ascochyta rabiei*, Disease
resistance, SSR, Linkage map, QTL.

---

* Corresponding author.

T.-h. Kim et al. (Eds.): FGCN 2008, CCIS 27, pp. 25–40, 2009.

1 Introduction

Chickpea (*Cicer arietinum* L.), a self-pollinating diploid annual, with 2x=2n=16 chromosomes. It is the third most important grain legume in the worldafter common bean (*Phaseolus vulgaris* L.) and pea (*Pisum sativum* L.)[19]. Primarily, chickpeas are grown in the Indian subcontinent, West Asia, North Africa, Ethiopia, Southern Europe, Mexico, Australia, North-Western United States and in the Brown and Dark Brown soil zones on the Canadian parties [8]. Average yield of chickpeas worldwide is about 700 kg/ha which is much below its potential [8], [16]. Yields are seen as low and unstable compared to other crops due to adverse effects of a number of biotic and abiotic stresses [8]. One of the greatest biotic stresses reducing potential yield in chickpea is ascochyta blight, caused by the fungus *Didymella rabiei* (Kovachevski) v. Arx. (anamorph: *Ascochyta rabiei* (Pass.) Labrousse) is the most devastating worldwide, causing up to 100 per cent yield losses in severely affected fields [7]. *Ascochyta rabiei* is heterothallic, thus when two compatible mating types are present genetic recombination can occur resulting in ascospore production [20], [21], [27]. Isolates of both mating types found in Iran indicating the occurrence of sexual recombination. Recombination could potentially lead to greater genetic and pathogenic variability in populationsof *A. rabiei*. Pathogenic variability in *A. rabiei* populations has been reported in almost all chickpea growing regions in the world, including India, Iran, Pakistan, Turkey, Syria, the Palouse region of north-western United States and Canada [3], [6], [8], [12], [23]. Chongo et al. (2004) also confirmed the presence of genetic variability among *A. rabiei* isolates collected in the 1998 and 1999 growing seasons based on RAPD molecular markers [3]. Despite recognition of destructiveness of *A. rabiei* in chickpea production world-wide, very little head way on controlling the disease through resistance breeding has been made in the past century. Resistance in breeding lines of chickpea to ascochyta blight is not durable due to the high variability of *A. rabiei* populations wherever chickpeas are grown [8], [12], [14], [15], [23]. Resistance break down is possibly the greatest challenge in breeding for resistance to ascochyta blight in chickpea [13]. Cultivars available in ICARDA, lack complete resistance to *A. rabiei*. Partial resistance in cultivars adapted to the western Iran tends to break down after the onset of flowering. Partially resistant cultivars contribute to the development of new pathotypes of the disease by imposing selection pressure, possibly resulting in increased virulence or aggressiveness within the pathogen population [17]. With a genetically diverse population of *A. rabiei*, it is important not only to develop cultivars with durable forms of resistance, but also to monitor changes in the population structure to anticipate resistance breakdown in existing cultivars. Among current understanding of the genetics of ascochyta blight resistance (ABR) in chickpea strongly suggests polygenic inheritance of the trait. In an interspecific genetic background, Santra et al. (2000) mapped two QTLs which conditioned ABR over two years of field screening [9]. Likewise, preliminary QTL mapping in a wide-cross between *C. arietinum* and *Cicer echino-spermum* (resistance source) revealed two to three QTLs for seedling resistance in controlled glasshouse bioassays [14]. Tar'an et al. (2007) identified one QTL on each of LG3, LG4 and LG6 accounted for 13%, 29% and 12% respectively, of the total estimated phenotypic variation for the reaction to ascochyta blight [18]. Although the genetic mechanism of ABR has been studied in identified resistant accessions of *C. arietinum*, the number and genomic locations of the genes or QTLs conditioning resistance has yet to be verified. Objectives of this study was to identify and map quantitative trait loci for resistance to ascochyta bight (pathotype III) in a population of chickpea derived from a cross between ICC12004 (resistance) and Bivanij (susceptible local) using micro-satellite markers.

2 Materials and Methods

The plants studied consisted of an intraspecific F_2 population and $F_{2:3}$ families derived from a cross between the Iranian local variety 'Bivanij' (maternal parent) and an Indian accession ICC12004. Bivanij is a high-yielding cultivar of *Kabuli* type with beige, relatively large seeds (400 mg), highly susceptible to *D. rabiei* and semi-erect growth habit. ICC12004 is resistant to the blight, with typical *Desi* small seeds (250 mg) and an erect growth habit. Phenotyping was done during two successive generations, for F_2 plants using detached leaf assay (Buchwaldt et al., 2007) and for $F_{2:3}$ families by 1-9 scoring method (Reddy and Singh, 1984) at controlled condition in a growth chamber. Isolate No. 13 of pathotype III (Udupa et al., 1998) was used for inoculation in both methods [1], [8], [25]. This isolate was cultured at room temperature under florescent light [2]. For F_2 population, the inoculation method was based on Buchwaldt et al., 2007, consisting in depositing a drop of spore suspension on detached leaves (10μL) [1]. Seven plants of each $F_{2:3}$ families were evaluated in the controlled environment. The parents, as well as the chickpea lines ILC1929 and ILC263 (susceptible), and ILC3279 (resistant to pathotypes I and II), were included as control genotypes. In this trial, the experimental design was a randomized complete block. Test plants were sown in a pair of seedling trays. Each pair of trays constituted one experimental block or replicate, and contained an individual plant of each of the $F_{2:3}$ families and control genotypes. Disease reactions were scored weekly after inoculation and AUDPC was calculated using the formula: $AUDPC = \sum [(x_i + x_{i+1})/2] (t_{i+1} - t_i)$. Isolate No.13 (PIII), was grown at room temperature under continuous fluorescent light. The suspension was filtered and adjusted to a final concentration of 2×10^5 conidia/mL using a hemacytometer. Genomic DNA of fresh leaves of young F_2 plants was extracted using CTAB protocol according to Weising et al., 1998 [26]. DNA of parental lines was screened for polymorphisms using 149 SSRs (Table 1) [11], [28]. The amplified DNA fragments were analyzed using ALFexpress DNA Sequencer [22] and DNA fragments were visualized via silver staining, using a silver staining kit

Table 1. Lists and characteristics of specific SSR markers for detecting Ascochyta blight resistance in chickpea

Locus	pairs of primers (5' → 3')	Replication	size (bp)	No. of alleles
TA1	TGAAATATGGAATGATTACTGAGTGAC/ TTGAAATAGGTCAGGCTTATAAAAATA	$(TAA)_{32}$	243	5
TA2	AAATGGAAGAAGAATAAAAACGAAAC/ TTCCATTCTTTATTATCCATATCACTACA	$(TAA)_{16}TGA(TAA)_{19}$	175	8
TA3	AATCTCAAAATTCCCAAAT/ ATCGAGGAGAAGAGAACCAT	$(TAA)_{11}$	287	3
TA5	ATCATTTCAATTTCCTCAACTATGAAT/ TCGTTAACACGTAATTTCAAGTAAAGAT	$(TTA)_{29}$	205	5
TA8	AAAATTTGCACCACAAAATATG/ CTGAAAATTATGGCAGGGAAAC	$(TAA)_{44}$	246	6
TA14	TGACTTGCTATTTAGGGAACA/ TGGCTAAAGACAATTAAAGTT	$(TAA)_{22}ATGA(TAA)_4T(A)_3TGAT(AAT)_5ATT(A)_3TGATAA$ $TAAAT(GAT)_4(TAA)_5$	250	4
TA18	AAAATAATCTCCACTTCAAATTTTC/ ATAAGTGCGTTATTAGTTTGGTCTTGT	$(TAA)_{24}$	147	6
TA22	TCTCCAACCCTTTAGATTGA/ TCGTGTTTACTGAATGTGGA	$(ATT)_{40}$	228	2
TA28	TAATTGATCATACTCTCACTATCTGCC/ TGGGAATGAATATATTTTGAAGTAAA	$(TAA)_{37}GAA(TAA)_{30}$	300	6
TA34	AAGAGTTGTTCCCTTTCTTTT/ CCATTATCATTCTTGTTTTCAA	$(AAT)_{34}$	230	6
TA42	ATATCGAAATAAATAACAACAGGATGG/ TAGTTGATACTTGGATGATAACCAAA	$(TA)_{19};(TAA)_{41}$	209	5
TA59	ATCTAAAGAGAAATCAAAATTGTCGAA/ GCAAATGTGAAGCATGTATAGATAAAG	$(TAA)_{29}$	258	4
TA71	CGATTTAACACAAAACACAAA/ CCT ATCCATTGTCATCTCGT	$(AAT)_{32}$	225	5
TA72	GAAAGATTTAAAAGATTTTCCACGTTA/ TTAGAAGCATATTGTTGGGATAAGAGT	$(ATT)_{36}$	256	7
TA78	CGGTAAATAAGTTTCCCTCC/	$(TTA)_{30}$	205	4

Table 1. (*Continued*)

Locus	pairs of primers (5' → 3')	Replication	size (bp)	No. of alleles
TA80	CATCGTGAATATTGAAGGGT / CGAATTTTACATCCGTAATG/	$(TTA)_{23}$	211	8
TA89	AATCAATCCATTTGCATTC / ATCCTTCACGCTTATTAGTTTTACA/	$(TAA)_2TAT(TAA)_{24}$	233	5
TA106	CAAGTAAAAGAGTCACTAGACCTCACA / CGGATGGACTCAACTTTATC/	$(TAA)_{26}$	248	7
TA110	TGTCTGCATGTTGATCTTGTT / ACACTATAGGTATAGGCATTTAGGCAA/	$(TTA)_{22}$	220	6
TA117	TTCTTTATAAATATCAGACCGGAAAGA / GAAAATCCCAAATTTTTCTTCTTCT/	$(ATT)_{52}$	248	5
TA125	AACCTTATTTAAGAATATGAGAAACACA / TTGAAATTGAACTGTAACAGAACATAAA/	$(TAA)_{33}$	235	8
TA146	TAGATAGGTGATCACAAGAAGAGAATG / CTAAGTTTAATATGTTAGTCCTTAAATTAT /ACGAACGCAACATTAATTTATATT	$(TTA)_{29}$	161	5
TA176	ATTTGGCTTAAACCCTCTTC/ TTTATGCTTCCTCTTCTTCG	$(TAA)_{40}(GAA)_9$	233	2
TA179	CAGAAGACGCAGTTTGAATAACTT/ CGAGAGAGAGAAAGGAAGGAAGAG	$(TAA)_{46}(TAAA)_8$	218	3
TA185	TGGTTGGAAATTGATGTTTT/ GTGGTTGTTGAGCATAATTCAA	na	235	1
TA194	TTTTTGGCTTCTTAGACTGACTT/ TTGCCATAAAATACAAAATCC	$(TTA)_{21}$	132	4
TR1	CGTATGATTTTGCCGTCTAT/ ACCTCAAGTTCTCCGAAAGT	$(TAA)_{31}$	224	5
TR19	TCAGTATCACGTGTAATTCGT/ CATGAACATCAAGTTCTCCA	$(TAA)_{27}$	227	5
TR20	ACCTGCTTGTTTAGCACAAT/ CCGCATAGCAATTTATCTTC	$(TAA)_{18}$	172	6
TR29	GCCCACTGAAAAATAAAAAG/	(TAA)TAGTAATAG	220	7

Table 1. (*Continued*)

Locus	pairs of primers (5' → 3')	Replication	size (bp)	No. of alleles
	ATTTGAACCTCAAGTTCTCG	$(TAA)_{32}$		
TR59	AAAAGGAACCTCAAGTGACA/ GAAAATGAGGGAGTGAGATG	$(TA)_3(TAA)_{17}T(TAA)_4$	174	6
TS19	TTTCTTTTGTTAGAGTTAAAAAAATT/ TCTCATGTTTTGCTTTTATTATTATTA	$(TAA)_{27}$	117	-
TS43	AAGTTTGGTCATAACACATTCAATA/ TAAATTCACAAACTCAATTATTGGC	$(ATT)_{33}$	212	5
TS45	TGACACAAAATTGTCTCTTGT/ TGTTCTTAACGTAACTAACCTAA	$(TAA)_8(A)_3(TAA)_{18}$	244	7
TS53	GATCNTTCCAAAAGTTCATTTNTATAAT/ TTAAAGAACTGATACATTCCATTATTT	$(TTA)_{65}$	267	7
TS54	TACAAGTTAAAAATGAATAAAATATTAATA /GAAATTTAGAGAGTCAAGCTTTAC	$(TAA)_3TAG(TAA)_{32}(CAA)_6$	209	2
TS72	CAAACAATCACTAAAAGTATTTGCTCT/ AAAAATTGATGGACAAGTTATTATG	$(ATT)_{39}$	264	7
TS83	AAAAATCAGAGCCAACCAAAAA/ AAGTAGGAGGCTAAATTATGGAAAAGT	Compound of $(TAA)_x(TTA)$	250	5
TS104	TCAAGATTGATATTGATTAGATAAAAGC/ CTTTATTTACCACTTGCACAACACTAA	$(ATT)_{40}$	214	5
TAA55	GGAACAACAACAACTCAAATG/ TGCTATTAAGTGTGACCGCAAA	$(AAT)_{66}$	299	5
TAA60	TCATGCTTGTTGGTTAGCTAGAACAAA/ GACATAATGGAGTTAAAGAAAA	$(CTT)_{6.5}(CTT)_9$	295	2
TAA137	CATGATTTCCAACTAAATCTTGAAAGT/ TCTTGTTTCGTTTAAACAATTTCTTCT	$(TAA)_{21}$	223	6
GA20	TATGCACCACACCTCGTACC/ TGACGGAATTCGTGATGTGT	$(CT)_{23}$	174	2
GA21	CCCCAGGTGAATTCCTCATA/ CTCAACCTTTGTTCAGCAACAC	$(CT)_{14}$	238	2

Table 1. (*Continued*)

Locus	pairs of primers (5' → 3')	Replication	size (bp)	No. of alleles
GA26	GATGCTCAAGACATCTGCCA/ TCATACTCAACAAATTCATTTCCC	$(CT)_{28}$	234	5
H1A10	TTGGAAGTTTAAGTGTTTGCTTC/ TTCATAAAGAGAAACACTTGTTCAAT	na	na	na
H1B06	GACTCACTCTCCAAATGGAACC/ AAGCCCATGAAAACCATATATTC	na	na	na
H1B09	GGTTTCATGACCTGCACCTA/ AAGAACCGAAAACACTTGTGA	na	na	na
H1B17	ATTCGAGGTGGTACCTCTAGTGA/ GAGGAACCGACGATGATATCTATT	na	na	na
H1C092	CAATAAAACACTTTGTTCCTTT/ TGTAGAAAGAAAGCTAGCATGG	na	na	na
H1C22	ATTTATACAAAGTTTTTGAAGTCG/ CTTGTAAGTAGATAGTTTCACCAAA	na	na	na
H1F22	TAATGTAATTTGTCTTTAACGTTTCC/ ATTGTGTTGTGTTATTTTAACTTTTGG	na	na	na
H1G16	GTTTGCTTTCAACACCGAGA/ CCCATGAAGGCCTGAATTAT	na	na	na
STMS24	AAAGACAGGTTTAATCCAAAA/ CTAATCTTTCTTCTTCTTTTGTCAT	$(AG)_{12}GG(AG)_3$	195	2

[22]. The polymorphic primer pairs were further tested on population. Mapmaker/Exp version 3.0 (Lincoln et al. 1993) was used to create a linkage map when the LOD value obtained was >3 [5]. Using the linkage map (F_2) genotype data and family-mean AUDPC of the $F_{2:3}$ families, putative QTLs for resistance to ascochyta blight were identified by single-point analysis or one-way ANOVA at P≤0.05 using the GLM procedure of SAS (SAS Institute Inc. 1996), and verified by composite interval mapping (CIM—Windows QTL Cartographer version 1.30; Wang et al. 2002) [10], [24].

3 Results and Discussion

The frequency distribution of the disease reaction of the F_2 and $F_{2:3}$ mapping populations to ascochyta blight were approximately normal (Figure 1) consistent with the polygenic control of resistance. Leaf size and reaction to ascochyta blight were highly significantly affected by F_2 plants (Table 2).

Table 2. One way ANOVA of the AUDPC of disease severity on F2 sibs derived from a cross between Bivanij and ICC12004 chick pea varieties

S.O.V.	D. F.	Mean Square	
		Leaf size	Reaction to AB
F_2 sibs	82	31.73**	96.303**
Error	166	8.28	79.05

Coefficient of Variation= 17.34%

Significantly ($P < 0.01$) higher disease scores were recorded in F_3 families (Table 3). Figure 2 shows the relationship between AUDPC of ascochyta bight $F_{2:3}$ families and their variances in the populations derived from a cross between

Table 3. One way ANOVA of the AUDPC of disease severity between F3 families derived from a cross between Bivanij and ICC12004 chick pea varieties

S.O.V.	D. F.	Mean Square	EMS
Between F_3 families	82	4865.7**	$\sigma^2\omega+7\sigma^2\beta$
Within F_3 families	498	2713.8	$\sigma^2\omega$

$\sigma^2\beta = 307.4.$

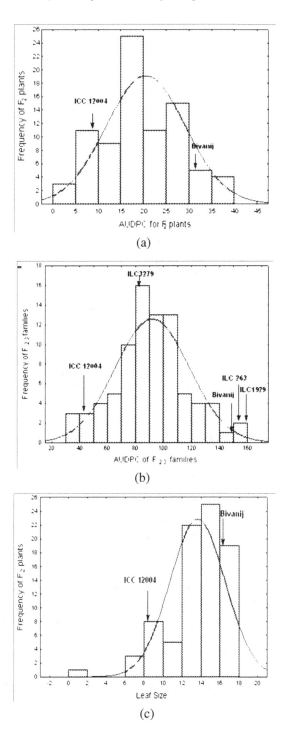

Fig. 1. Frequency distribution for leaf area, AUDPC for F_2 and $F_{2:3}$ families, respectively

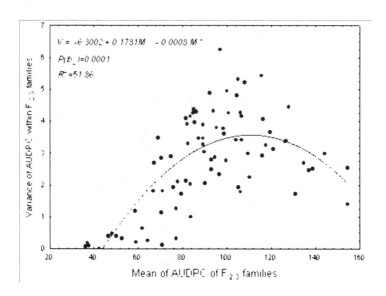

Fig. 2. Relationship between AUDPC of ascochyta bight $F_{2:3}$ families and their variances in the populations derived from a cross between ICC12004 and Bivanij

ICC12004 and Bivanij. There were not significant relationships between mean AUDPC for F_2 and F_3 generations due to Phenotyping based on mean scores of families for $F_{2:3}$ generation.

Mean blight scores of the resistant parent (AUDPC-F_2=32.2±6.2 and AUDPC-$F_{2:3}$ =148.4±0.2) were significantly different from that of the susceptible parent (AUDPC-F_2=8.1±3.14 and AUDPC-$F_{2:3}$= 44.1±0.32). To the best of our knowledge, this is the first study to identify and map QTLs confer resistance to payhotype III of ascochyta blight in an intraspecific population of chickpea. Out of 149 microsatellite markers tested, 58 markers revealed polymorphism between the parents ICC12004 and Bivanij, and 57 of them were mapped on the genome. The linkage map comprised eight linkage groups, excluding flower color which didn't assign to any linkage group. The SSRs that were common between the current map and previous maps (Winter et al., 2000; Udupa and Baum, 2003; Tar'an et al., 2007) were placed on the same linkage group but with slightly different orientation and distance [18], [22], [29]. Using composite interval mapping, significant association between SSR markers and putative QTLs for ascochyta blight reaction were found on three linkage groups. These QTLs on LG3, LG4 and LG6 determined 11, 17 and 19 percent, respectively and together these loci accounted for 47% of the total estimated phenotypic variation for reaction to ascochyta blight (Table 4).

The QTLs on LG3, LG4 and LG6 are flanked with TA125 and TA34, TA2 and TA72, and GA26 and TA80 respectively (Figures 3 and4), on the current map and

Table 4. Putative QTLs for ascochyta blight resistance in F_2 and $F_{2:3}$ generations by Composite Interval Mapping (CIM) method

Parameter	Linkage group	Interval (cM)[a]	Flanking markers	Position of QTL (cM)[b]	LOD[c]	Genetic effects[d]		Gene action[e]	$R^2(\%)$[f]
						Additive	Dominance		
AUDPC-F_2	LG3	14.1	TA125-TA34	0.81	2.50	-4.82	1.96	PD	10.98
AUDPC-$F_{2:3}$	LG4	29.8	TA2-TA72	23.8	4.15	-6.42	-14.43	OD	16.96
	LG6	6.7	GA26-TA80	45.7	4.57	2.69	19.39	OD	18.61

[a] interval between two flanking markers(cM)
[b] QTL position from the left flanking marker(cM)
[c] Peak value of LOD test statistic observed for the QTL in question
[d] Additive and dominance gene effects
[e] A = additive gene action (ld/al<0.2) , PD = partial dominance (0.2<ld/al<0.8) , D = dominance (0.8<ld/al<1.2), and OD = over dominance (ld/al>1.2)
[f] proportion of phenotypic variance explained by the QTL.

are co-localized with the QTLs reported by other investigators (Figures 5, 6 and 7) (Udupa and Baum, 2003; Tar'an et al., 2007) [18], [25]. None of the loci on LG2 was associated with resistance to ascochyta blight in our population. This result is in contrast to the findings of Cho et al., (2004) and Udupa and Baum (2003), which suggested that a major gene located on LG 2 controlled quantitative resistance to *D. rabiei* [3], [25]. This was not surprising; since current population was evaluated for its quantitative reaction to one isolate belong to pathotype III of ascochyta blight. Fine mapping of the QTLs identified in this study would lead to the identification of markers that could be used for marker-assisted selection of chickpea genotypes with resistance to ascochyta blight.

These findings are particular pertinent considering that we used *Ascochyta rabiei* pathotype III and ICC 12004 (resistant to pathotype III) for the first time.

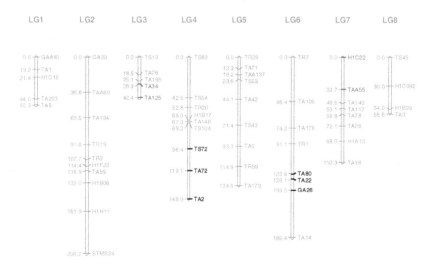

Fig. 3. SSR linkage map of chickpea showing detected QTLs for leaf size and ascochyta blight resistance for F_2 and $F_{2:3}$ families in the populations derived from a cross between ICC12004 and Bivanij

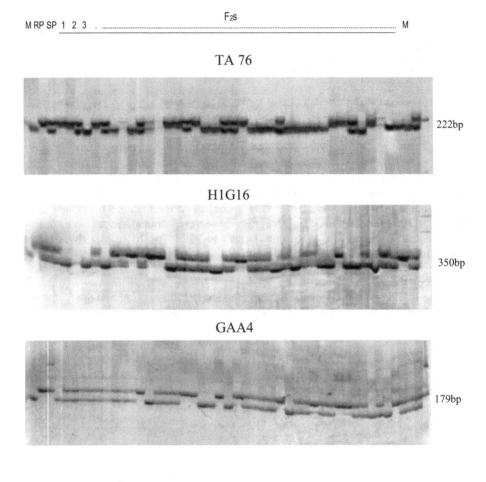

Fig. 4. Sequence Characterized 3 Microsatellite markers for few sibs of F_2 population; M: marker size, RP: resistant parent (ICC12004), SP: susceptible parent to ascochyta blight (Bivanij)

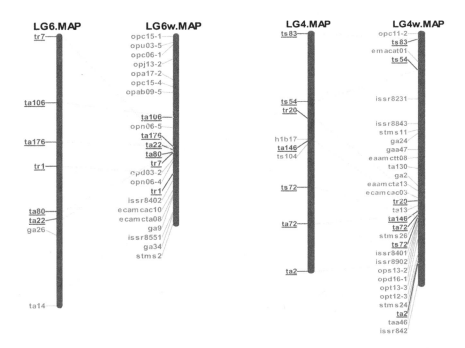

Fig. 5. SSR markers common between this map and those of (Winter et al., 2000, Udupa and Baum, 2003; Tar'an et al., 2007) with slightly difference in location and distance within linkage groups [18], [22], [29]

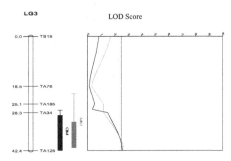

Fig. 6. Graph of LOD score for resistance to pathotype III of ascochyta blight in the F₂ population derived from a cross between Bivanij (Iranian susceptible local) and ICC12004

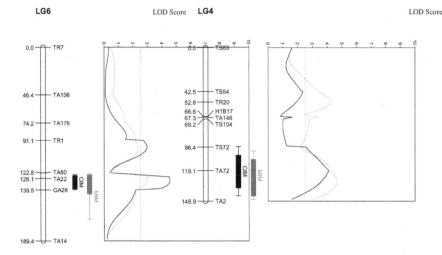

Fig. 7. Interval mapping (CIM) graphs for resistance to pathotype III on linkage groups 4 and 6 of $F_{2:3}$ families derived from a cross between 'Bivanij' (Iranian susceptible local) and ICC12004

Acknowledgment. This project was supported jointly by the University of Tehran and Agricultural Research, Education and Extension Organization (AREEO), Iran.

References

1. Buchwaldt, L., Booker, H., Gali, K.: A detached leaf assay for phenotyping of chickpea-ascochyta interaction. In: Agriculture and Agri-Food Canada, Saskatoon, Saskatchewan, S7N0X2 (2007)
2. Chen, W., Muehlbauer, F.J.: An Improved Technique for virulence assay of *Ascochyta rabiei* on chickpea. International chickpea and pigeonpea Newsletter 10(2003), 31–33 (2003)
3. Chongo, G., Gossen, B.D., Buchwaldt, L., Adhikari, T., Rimmer, S.R.: Genetic diversity of *Ascochyta rabiei* in Canada. Plant Disease 88(1), 4–10 (2004)
4. Collard, B.C.Y., Pang, E.C.K., Ades, P.K., Taylor, P.W.J.: Preliminary investigation of QTLs associated with seedling resistance to ascochyta blight from *Cicer echinospermum*, a wild relative of chickpea. Theor. Appl. Genet. 107, 719–729 (2003)
5. Lincoln, S.E., Daly, M.J., Lander, E.S.: MAPMAKER/EXP version 3.0: A Tutorial and Reference Manual, 3rd edn. Whitehead Institute for Biomedical Research, Cambridge (1993)
6. Kaiser, W.J., Muehlbauer, F.J.: Occurrence of *Ascochyta rabiei* on imported chickpeas in eastern Washington. Phytopathology 74, 1139 (1984)
7. Nene, Y.L.: A review of Ascochyta blight of chickpea (*Cicer arietinum L.*). In: Saxena, M.C., Singh, K.B. (eds.) Ascochyta blight and winter sowing of chickpea, pp. 17–34. Martinus Nijhoff/Dr. W. Junk Publisher, The Hague, the Netherlands (1984)
8. Reddy, M.V., Kabbabeh, S.: Pathogenic variability in *Ascochyta rabiei* (Pass.) Lab. In: Syria, Lebanon (eds.) Phytopathology Mediterranean, vol. 24, pp. 265–266 (1984); Reddy, M.V., Singh, K.B.: Evaluation of a world collection of chickpea germplasm accessions for resistance to Ascochyta blight. Plant Dis. 68, 900–901 (1985)

9. Santra, D.K., Tekeoglu, M., Ratnaparkhe, M., Kaiser, W.J., Muehlbauer, F.J.: Identification and mapping of QTLs conferring resistance to Ascochyta blight in chickpea. Crop. Sci. 40, 1606–1612 (2000)

10. SAS Institute Inc.: SAS/STAT user's guide. Version 9.12. SAS Institute, Cary, North Carolina (2000)

11. Sethy, N.K., Shokeen, B., Bhatia, S.: Isolation and characterization of sequence-tagged microsatellite site markers in chickpea (*Cicer arietinum L.*). Mol. Ecol. Notes 3, 428–430 (2003)

12. Singh, G.: Identification and designation of physiologic races of *Ascochyta rabiei* in India. Indian Phytopathology 43, 48–52 (1990)

13. Singh, K.B., Reddy, M.V.: Advances in disease resistance breeding in chickpea. Advanced Agronomy 45, 191–222 (1991)

14. Singh, K.B., Reddy, M.V.: Resistance to Six Races of Ascochyta rabiei in the world germplasm collection of chickpea. Crop. Science 33, 186–189 (1993a)

15. Singh, K.B., Reddy, M.V.: Sources of resistance to ascochyta blight in wild Cicer species. Netherlands Journal of Plant Pathology 99, 163–167 (1993b)

16. Singh, K.B., Malhotra, R.S., Halila, M.H., Knights, E.J., Verma, M.M.: Current status and future strategy in breeding chickpea for resistance to biotic and abiotic stresses. Euphytica. 73, 137–149 (1994)

17. Singh, K.B., Reddy, M.V., Haware, M.: Breeding for resistance to ascochyta blight in chickpea. In: Singh, K.B., Saxena, M.C. (eds.) Disease resistance breeding in chickpea, ICARDA, Aleppo, Syria, pp. 23–54 (1992)

18. Tar'an, B., Warkentin, T.D., Tullu, A., Vandenberg, A.: Genetic mapping of ascochyta blight resistance in chickpea (*Cicer arietinum L.*) using a simple sequence repeat linkage map. Genome 50, 26–34 (2007)

19. Tekeoglu, M., Santra, D.K., Kaiser, W.J., Muehlbauer, F.J.: Ascochyta blight resistance in three chickpea recombinant inbred line populations. Crop. Sci. 40, 1251–1256 (2000)

20. Trapero-Casas, A., Kaiser, W.J.: Development of Didymella rabiei, the teleomorph of Ascochyta rabiei, on chickpea straw. Phytopathology 82, 1261–1266 (1992a)

21. Trapero-Casas, A., Kaiser, W.J.: Influence of temperature, wetness period, plant age, and inoculum concentration on infection and development of ascochyta blight of chickpea. Phytopathology 82, 589–596 (1992b)

22. Udupa, S.M., Baum, M.: Genetic dissection of pathotype-specific resistance to ascochyta blight disease in chickpea (*Cicer arietinum L.*) using microsatellite markers. Theor. Appl. Genet. 106, 1196–1202 (2003)

23. Vir, S., Grewal, J.S.: Physiological specialization in *Ascochyta rabiei*, the causal organism of gram blight. Indian Phytopathology 27, 265–266 (1974)

24. Wang, S., Basten, C.J., Zeng, Z.B.: Windows QTL Cartographer 2.0. Department of Statistics, North Carolina State University. Raleigh N.C (2004), http://statgen.ncsu.edu/qtlcart/WQTLCart.htm

25. Udupa, S.M., Weigand, F., Saxena, M.C., Kahl, G.: Genotyping with RAPD and microsatellite markers resolves pathotype diversity in the ascochyta blight pathogen of chickpea. Theor. Appl. Genet. 97, 299–307 (1998)

26. Weising, K., Winter, P., Huttel, B., Kahl, G.: Microsatellite markers for molecular breeding. J. Crop. Prod. 1, 113–143 (1998)

27. Wilson, A., Kaiser, W.: Cytology and genetics of sexual incompatibility in *Didymella rabiei*. Mycolgia 87, 795–804 (1995)

28. Winter, P., Pfaff, T., Udupa, S.M., Hüttel, B., Sharma, P.C., Sahi, S., Arreguin-Espinoza, R., Weigand, F., Muehlbauer, F.J., Kahl, G.: Characterization and mapping of sequence-tagged Microsatellite sites in the chickpea (*Cicer arietinum L.*) Genome. Mol. Gen. Genet (1999)

29. Winter, P., Benko-Iseppon, A.M., Huttel, B., Ratnaparkhe, M., Tullu, A., Sonnante, G., Pfaff, T., Tekeoglu, M., Santra, D., Sant, V.J., Rajesh, P.N., Kahl, G., Muehlbauer, F.J.: A linkage map of the chickpea (*Cicer arietinum L.*) Genome based on the recombinant inbred lines from a C. arietinum xC. reticulatum cross: localization of resistance genes for *Fusarium* races 4 and 5. Theor. Appl. Genet. 101, 1155–1163 (2000)

A Context-Aware Adaptation Model
for Efficient Web Browsing on Mobile Devices

Ronnie Cheung

Hong Kong Polytechnic University,
Hong Kong SAR,
China
csronnie@gmail.com

Abstract. A mobile environment is characterized by low communication bandwidth and poor connectivity. Efficient Web access over a wireless network is challenging because of the varying characteristics of different devices constituting the wireless environment and the adverse interactions among HTTP, TCP and the wireless network. These lead to problems that significantly degrade the user-experienced performance of the web accessed through the wireless network. We have developed techniques to visualize web access in a mobile environment – the proxy-agent mobile document clustering architecture (PMDC). The PMDC architecture allows the mobile users to visualize and navigate through the Web structure without having to download all related links in a Web site. The Proxy-Agent model provides facilities for adaptation in a mobile environment.

Keywords: Mobile Environments, Adaptation, Efficient Web Access.

1 Introduction

The underlying technologies driving the World Wide Web are largely based on the assumption of wired communications and powerful desktop hardware. This is not true when a user is access the Web pages and documents using a PDA and moving from wireless network in a mall to a neighboring office environment. Taking into consideration of the information needs of the user, we have developed visualization techniques for document cluster graph model for the mobile users. A document cluster graph represents the high level structure for providing the navigation models for the mobile user. Based on the user requirements, a document cluster can be adjusted to a reasonable size. From the resulted document cluster (Figure 1), not only the underlying structure of the root document is presented but also the degree of closure among them can be studied. Based on the access requirements, current activity, and contextual information, the user can specify the adaptation model in a configuration file. The parameters for the document cluster graph model can be adjusted to suit the information needs of the user. We have developed techniques to implement the PDMC architectures using an agent-proxy model [4]. A configuration file is stored at the mobile device. It can be edited by the user at any time to suit the current information needs.

T.-h. Kim et al. (Eds.): FGCN 2008, CCIS 27, pp. 41–54, 2009.

The local copy is synchronized with the server configuration file dynamically. This is performed by using a pair of agents called the proxy-master agent and the client agent. The system is able to detect and adapt to rapid changes in contextual information according to the adaptation model stored in the configuration file.

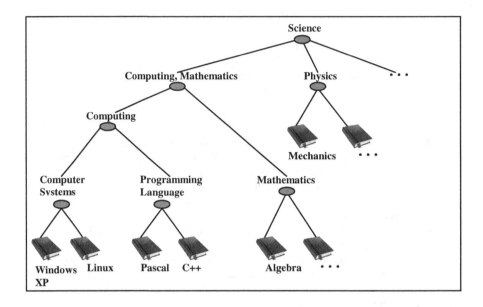

Fig. 1. A general scenario of document cluster structure

2 Related Work

We consider a mobile environment in which mobile clients navigate web documents via common web browsers. A mobile environment is weakly-connected, characterized by its low communication bandwidth and poor connectivity. In a conventional environment, users navigate the web pages using some search engines [1, 2, 7]. The documents are either in proprietary format (such as word or excel) or in html format, or "native" html documents. Those documents that are in proprietary format are very likely to be local files that can be completely downloaded to the client. Those "native" html documents are often buried deep in a website and require considerable navigation, in order to be retrieved completely. Even a complete technical document in html format (for example a document about mobile web browsing) may be represented as a large number of html files that requires separate download for each individual component.

In a mobile environment, the major issue is the problem of locating relevant web pages without making many unnecessary traversals. A roadmap provided by some carefully designed website may partly serve the purpose. However, as websites are usually updated dynamically, the roadmap may become outdated. In a mobile environment, it is necessary to provide a high level structure of the web pages that is available to the mobile user, with the relationship between the pages. In [10], the web structure is analyzed and web pages are classified in into various categories, such as head, organizational home page, index and content pages. Spreading activation is adopted to pump activation into networks connecting the nodes representing the pages so that the asymptotic behavior of the network reflects the relationship between various nodes. Pages relating to the current browsing page can be discovered. However, the matrices involved in the activation computation can be large and the number of iterations required for the activations to converge can be substantial.

Leong [9] proposed a multi-resolution transmission paradigm for mobile users. In the paradigm, higher content bearing portions of a web document are transmitted to a mobile client before the other portions. A document is partitioned into multiple organization units at various levels of detail according to the HTML or XML structure [3]. The information contents associated with organization unit is noted. Units with higher information content is transmitted earlier during a web browsing session, allowing documents to be transmitted at a coarser resolution, with the details to be filled in progressively. The client is able to explore the more content bearing portions of the documents earlier and to determine if the current document is of any interest. However this approach is only applicable in the context of technical documents.

The objective of this project is to develop technologies to help a mobile user to visualize, search, organize and find information useful to their daily work effectively by providing a high level navigation map without having to traverse all the links. We mainly follow the approach proposed by Leong [8, 9]. The web pages are organized into document clusters, which again can be grouped together into larger clusters. The clusters normally reside on a local side, but they can also be spanned across different sites. The document clusters are extracted and captured in a meta-data structure, in the form of XML documents [3], to be associated with the cluster members as a kind of navigation map. This would be the first entity to be transmitted to the mobile client for the user to get a feeling of the document and its related documents before hand. This XML structure also provides access frequency information of the relevant pages. The whole structure can be visualized by using a three dimensional document cluster graph [11].

3   The Proxy-Agent Model

We have previously described the Proxy-Agent platform – WebPADS – a Web Proxy for Active Deployable Service [4, 5]. The WebPADS platform is an object-oriented system that is based on an active-service deployment architecture, which comprises some components of the system and service objects called *mobilets*. Core components of the system provide essential services for the deployment of an agent-proxy that forms a unit of service, which executes under the WebPADS execution environment. Among the system's components, the event register allows objects to locate and register for event sources. When an event occurs, the objects that have registered for that event source are notified. Event sources include various changes in the status of a network, machine resources and connectivity. Furthermore, the composition of the services of the WebPADS server can be dynamically reconfigured to adapt to the vigorous changes in the characteristics of a wireless environment.

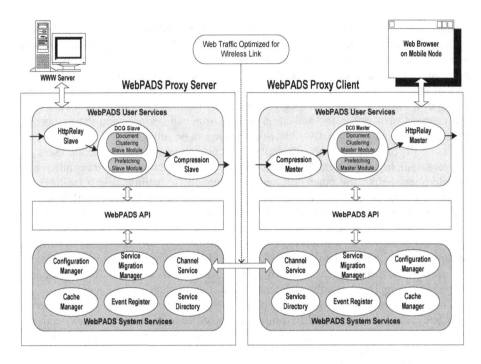

Fig. 2. The WebPADS system architecture

The unit of service is implemented as an agent-proxy mobilet that provides value-added services to a wireless environment. The system's components also provide generic facilities that serve the mobilets, which in turn provide services that enhance a user's Web-browsing experience. A series of mobilets can be linked together to form a processing-service composition, allowing WebPADS to benefit from the aggregated functionality of a group of services. Services provided by the WebPADS system can be migrated from one WebPADS server to another to track the mobility of a mobile node and serve the mobile node continuously. Services can also be added, removed and updated dynamically without interrupting the service provision to other mobile nodes. Furthermore, the composition of the services of the WebPADS server can be dynamically reconfigured to adapt to the vigorous changes in the characteristics of a wireless environment.

The unit of service in WebPADS is implemented as an agent-proxy mobilet that provides value-added services to a wireless environment. The system's components also provide generic facilities that serve the mobilets, which in turn provide services that enhance a user's Web-browsing experience. A series of mobilets can be linked together to form a processing-service composition, allowing WebPADS to benefit from the aggregated functionality of a group of services. Services provided by the WebPADS system can be migrated from one WebPADS server to another to track the mobility of a mobile node and serve the mobile node continuously. Services can also be added, removed and updated dynamically without interrupting the service provision to other mobile nodes. Furthermore, the composition of the services of the Web-PADS server can be dynamically reconfigured to adapt to the vigorous changes in the characteristics of a wireless environment.

4 The Document Cluster Graph (DCG) Model

With the advent of mobile computing, it is common for users to access the Web through various mobile devices such as mobile phone, hand-held PC and PDA etc. Each mobile device has different characteristics. A user using a PDA has only 240 x 320 resolution and Web access through the mobile device is normally performed through a few proxy servers, either through a home wireless network or a wireless gateway installed in a mobile user's office. To provide adaptation to suit the requirements of mobile users, we have developed a proxy-agent mobile document clustering architecture (PMDC) to improve the browsing efficiency of a mobile web client. As shown in figure 3, a PMDC architecture supports a number of mobile clients communicating with a base station via wireless channels. The base station maintains a web proxy server as a concentrator of web traffic for the clients, enabling the sharing of common hot web pages needed by individual clients. The notion of document clusters and personalized document clusters are modeled in the form of a directed graph, called document cluster graph.

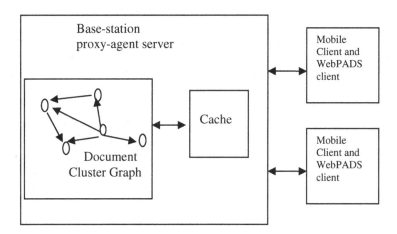

Fig. 3. Proxy-mobile Document Clustering Architecture

When a mobile client requests for an uncached document P from a remote server, the proxy server generates a document cluster using the document P as seed. A document cluster is a collection of web pages that are highly common in some shared properties (such as the distance from the root). It is generated and stored in the cache by optimizing the following gain function proposed by Leong [8]:

$\rho(V, E) = \Sigma W_{i,j} / h^{\gamma} |V|$ for all links $l_{i,j} \in E$ where :

V   -   a set of web pages to be evaluated

E   -   a set of hyperlinks to be evaluated, most of the links are related to the set of web pages in V.

$W_{i,j}$ -   weight of a link from web page (i) to web page (j), which is calculated from the probability of accessing a particular link using the log file from the web server

H   -   the maximum of the shortest distance between any two pages in the cluster (the depth of the graph G).

γ -   An adjustable parameter which is a non-negative value that is greater than zero ($\gamma >= 0$)

$l_{i,j}$ -   Hyperlink from web page (i) to web page (j)

In the above equation, $W_{i,j}$ denotes the weight of a link from web page (i) to web page (j).Hence, the higher the weight of the link from web page (i) to web page (j) will give a higher cost to the cluster. The size of the cluster cannot be too large as the value function is an inverse function of the depth of the graph. An increment of the depth will lead to a smaller value on each link and hence for the overall weighting. If the weight of the link is sufficiently large to cover the loss, it will be identified as a related page to the root document. The weight of a link indicates the relationship between the web pages. It can be calculated for considering the conditional access probability, which indicates the probability of a referenced page (j) to be visited after the reference page (i) being accessed. It can be estimated by the hit count (in the log file of the web server) of the corresponding link. In case if there are no statistics available in the log file of the web server, all hyperlinks for page (i) should have equal accessing probabilities. With current value from the equations, the denser the links within a cluster, the more closely related are the documents in the cluster.

If there does not exist any document cluster information available at the remote web server for the document, the proxy server starts from the seed document, follow the hyperlinks that lead to new documents and tries to include documents whose presence will improve the value for the gain function incrementally. The cycle is repeated until the gain function is maximized for the given parameters, and the cluster yields an optimal value for the gain function.

When a cluster with an optimal value for the gain function is found, the system generates an XML document that encapsulates the document cluster graph so that a web surfer can easily identify where he/she is when navigating through the web. In our

XML representation, we indicate either the weight of a link or the conditional access probability of a link in the document cluster graph through the intensity of the link. A naive surfer may follow the link with a high weight, which is more likely to have a close relationship with the current browsing page. To improve the user interface for the user, we have developed facilities for viewing the document cluster in the three-dimensional space, allowing users to browse the structure in different angles. An example of a document cluster graph implemented using a PDA is shown in figure 4.

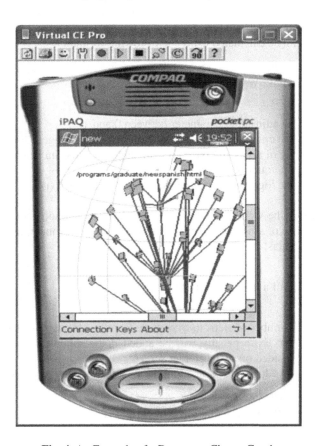

Fig. 4. An Example of a Document Cluster Graph

5   Weight Adjustment for Document Links

In this project, we use web mining techniques to adjust the weight of links to the documents. There are a large number of links in a web document. In a mobile environment, it would be difficult for the user to select among a large number of inactive links. By analysing the access logs the Web Server, it is possible to adjust the weight of a link so that in-active links or those links that are rarely accessed are filter out. The weight $W_{i,\,j}$ denotes the weight of a link from web page (i) to web page (j).

Hence, the higher the weight of the link from web page (i) to web page (j) will give a higher cost to the cluster. The size of the cluster cannot be too large as the value function is an inverse function of the depth of the graph. An increment of the depth will lead to a smaller value on each link and hence for the overall weighting. If the weight of the link is sufficiently large to cover the loss, it will be identified as a related page to the root document. The weight of a link indicates the relationship between the web pages, being governed by two factors: the web distance and the access pattern for accessing a particular link. In the following formula, we include a parameter α for adjusting the weight by considering web log access patterns and the weight for considering the web distance between the web document and the root document. The weight of a link can be calculated using the following formula:

The weight of a link: $W_{i,j} = \alpha P_{i,j} + (1 - \alpha) D_{i,j}$

α   -   an adjustable parameter between 0 and 1
$P_{i,j}$ -   the conditional probability from page (i) to page(j), i.e. the probability of accessing page (j) from page (i). This can be calculated by the hit count of the link from i to j.
$D_{i,j}$ -   the logical distance between page(i) and page (j)

In above equation, the weight of a link is determined by the adjustable parameter α. The logical distance of a link $D_{i,j}$ and the conditional access probabilities are given by the following formulas:

Logical distance of a link: $D_{i,j} = 1 / \theta d$

D   -   Number of steps to transverse from the directory of page (i) to page (j). Extra penalty will be added if the source and target pages are resided on two different server
θ   -   an adjustable parameter with a value greater than zero ($\theta > 0$)

Conditional Access Probability of a link: $P_{i,j} = H_{i,j} / H_i$

$H_{i,j}$ -   hit rate of accessing page(j) from page (i)
H_i -   total hit count for page (i)

Conditional Access Probability is just a simple probability value which indicates the probability of a referenced page (j) to be visited after the reference page (i) being accessed. In short, it will be represented by Pi, j. It can be estimated by the hit count of the corresponding link using the proposed formula. If there are no statistics available for the access patterns, all hyperlinks for the web document are assigned with equal probabilities for being accessed.

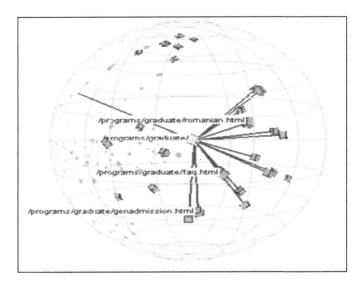

Fig. 5. A Document Cluster Graph with depth level = 2

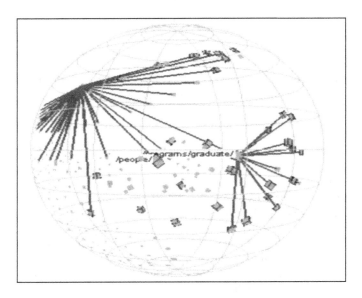

Fig. 6. A Document Cluster Graph with depth level = 3

In the proxy-agent mobile document clustering architecture, we have enhanced Leong's model [8] by providing a three-dimensional implementation for viewing the document cluster. All the links from the root to the nodes are enclosed in a three-dimensional sphere. The amount of links visible in the sphere can be adjusted by tuning the parameters. The number of levels displayed in the links can also be adjusted.

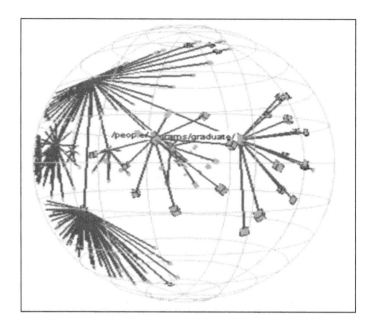

Fig. 7. A Document Cluster Graph with depth level = 4

Figure 5 to figure 7 shows the documents cluster graphs corresponding to depth levels 2, 3 and 4. In our implementation of the adaptation model, the depth parameters can also be adapted according to the display characteristics of the screen.

6 The H3 Viewer

As this project aims at developing a viewer for the document cluster, we utilize the H3 Viewer [11] to visualize the result clustered files. The H3 Viewer library provides the layout and interactive navigation model of node-link graphs in 3D hyperbolic space. The library can handle large graphs of up to 100,000 edges quickly and with minimal visual clutter. The hyperbolic view allows the user to see a great deal of the context around the current focus node. The cluster model is described with Cube and links. The cube object represents the web page item and the line is for the hyperlink among those web page items. All the links in the web space can be interpreted as 3D objects inside the volume of a ball. In the interactive system the scene is disambiguated as soon as the user sees the objects rotate inside the ball.

The H3 viewer is developed under the hyperbolic space. Hyperbolic methods are very effective at providing global overviews and displaying many nodes at once. There are three classes for drawing nodes: main/labeled, peripheral, and fringe. What we call peripheral nodes is small but still distinguishable as individual entities upon close inspection. Fringe nodes are not individually distinguishable, but their aggregate presence or absence shows significant structure of far-away parts of the graph. Each class can fit roughly an order of magnitude more than the last. The H3 and Palo Alto Research Center (PARC) browsers can both show up to 50 main/labeled nodes. The

PARC layout does not have peripheral nodes as such, since nodes are not drawn as discrete entities. The H3 layout can show up to 500 peripheral nodes. The H3 fringe can show information about thousands of nodes, whereas the PARC fringe shows information about hundreds of nodes.

The advantage of moving from a 2D tree to a 3D graph is the ability to see non-tree links in context. One of the greatest strengths of the H3 approach is the ability to see relationships between a part and the far-flung reaches of the whole. Although the details of the non-tree link destinations are usually distorted, a rough sense of their direction helps the user construct and maintain a mental model of the overall graph structure. The details become clear in a smooth transition when that area of the structure is brought towards the center. It might be possible to extend a 2D browser to support graph display, but non-tree links would have to be drawn in the same plane as the main spanning tree links, necessarily intersecting them. In the 3D system the non-tree links can follow paths, which are unlikely to intersect the surrounding spanning tree links.

7   Adaptation in a Mobile Environment

Table 1 lists the contextual information that will be identified for each device. The information collected is used to adjust the settings of the display for the document graph. In particular, the user can alter the settings by choosing various options in order to best suit their actual information needs.

Table 1. Contextual information reported by the WebPADS client

Unit Type	Contextual Information
Processor	CPU type, clock rate, utilization
Storage	RAM size, free space, Secondary Storage size, free space
Network	Network type, capacity, data rate, delay, error rate
Power	Battery maximum lifetime, remaining lifetime
Display	Color type, depth, Screen resolution
Audio	Type of sound supported
Operating System	OS name, version
Browser	Browser name, version

Table 2 lists the major options and their possible values. As shown in the table, the adaptation options are used for providing different formats for the results.

Table 2. The options available for accessing document graphs

Option	Possible Values
Device adaptation option	
Text Compression	None, Low, Medium, High
Image Compression	None, Low, Medium, High
Color Scheme	B&W, Color, High Color
Result Details	Document graph depth : 1, 2, 3, 4, 5, 6, 7, 8, 9, 10
Advanced options	
Brightness level	Low, High, Medium
Proxy cache size	Low, Medium, Large
Screen layout	Horizontal, Vertical

To regulate the service configuration policies, the WebPADS system maintains a configuration description file utilizing XML. To dynamically adapt to the changes in the environment, WebPADS employs the environment monitor and event system to monitor and communicate the changes. An environment element consists of one or more conditions, where each condition specifies an event and a relational value that will fulfill that condition.

When a WebPADS client starts, a default service composition is created that is based on the description of the XML configuration file. At the same time, a number of alternative reconfiguration service chain maps are also created. Each map is attached to an environment monitor, which regulates the time and conditions for the service reconfiguration to take place. When all the conditions monitored by a specific environment monitor are fulfilled, the current service composition will be reconfigured to the service chain map attached to that environment monitor.

The configuration file is used for constructing the user adaptation model. Table 3 shows examples of adaptations that can be modeled according to the information in the configuration file and the information from the environment monitor.

Table 3. Examples of the Adaptation Model

Condition (event)	Adaptation Action
Bandwidth = low	Graphic_image_resolution = low
Secondary_storage_space = low	compression = yes
Battery = low	Brightness_level = low
Screen resolution = high	Document_cluster_graph_size = high
Location = office	Proxy_cache_size = large

8 Conclusion

The underlying technologies driving the world wide web are largely based on the assumption of wired communications and powerful desktop hardware. This is not true when a user is access the Web pages and documents using a PDA and moving from wireless network in a mall to a neighboring office environment. We have developed WebPADS using an agent-proxy model for wireless access. WebPADS provides contextual information such as mobile device characteristics as well as dynamic event status. Taking into consideration of the information needs of the user, we have developed visualization techniques for document cluster graph model for the mobile users. A document cluster graph represents the high level structure providing the navigation model for the user. Based on the access requirements, current activity, and contextual information, the user can specify the adaptation model in a configuration file. The parameters (specifying the detail level) for the document cluster graph model can be adjusted to suit the information needs of the user. The system is implemented using an agent-proxy model. There are a number of advantages in using the proxy-agent model. Firstly the configuration file can be store at the mobile device and edited by the user at any time to suit the current information needs. The local copy of the configuration file is synchronized with the server configuration file dynamically. This is performed by using a pair of agents called the proxy-master agent and client proxy agent in Web-PADS. Secondly, WebPADS is able to detect and adapt to rapid changes in contextual information according to the adaptation model stored in the configuration file. Thirdly, WebPADS is able to maintain on-going service provision as the mobile node movies across different domains (e.g. from a home network to an office network in a wireless environment).

A major concern about our implementation is that the adaptation for Web access is computationally intensive. The adaptation model for access document using a cluster graph also requires a lot of processing. In our experiments, it was noticed that the execution of the WebPADS client did not increase the CPU loading of the mobile device significantly [4, 5]. This is because a lot of computations like compression mobilet and DCG computation are performed at the proxy server. Our experiment has shown that in addition to context adaptation, user adaptation can also be implemented effectively. Future directions of research include using AI techniques to improve flexibility in adaptation. Experiments can be carried out to evaluate the effectiveness using different mobile platforms.

Acknowledgment

This project is supported by RGC CERG grant no. PolyU 5200E/04 of the HKSAR.

References

1. Belkin, N., Croft, W.B.: Information Filtering and Information Retrieval: Two Slides of the Same Coin? Communications of the ACM 35(12), 38–39 (1992)
2. Bharadvaj, H., Joshi, A., Auephanwiriyakul, S.: An Active Transcoding Proxy to Support Mobile Web Access. In: Proceedings of the 17th IEEE Symposium on Reliable Distributed Systems, pp. 118–123 (1998)

3. Bradley, N.: The XML Companion. Addison Wesley, Reading (1998)
4. Chuang, S.N., Chan, A.T.S., Cao, J., Cheung, R.: Dynamic Service Reconfiguration for Wireless Web Access. In: Proceedings of the Twelve International World Wide Web Conference, Budapest, Hungary, pp. 58–67. ACM Press, New York (2003)
5. Chuang, S.N., Chan, A.T.S., Cao, J., Cheung, R.: Actively Deployable Mobile Services for Adaptive Web Access. IEEE Internet Computing, 26–33 (2004)
6. Fensel, D.: The Semantic Web, Tutorial notes. In: 9th IFIP Conference on Database Semantics – Semantic Issues in e-Commerce Systems (2001)
7. Frakes, W., Baesa-Yates, R.: Information Retrieval: Data Structures and Algorithms. Prentice-Hall, Englewood Cliffs (1992)
8. Leong, H.V.: Browsing Document Clusters on Mobile Web. In: Proceedings of the ACM Digital Library Workshop on Organizing Web Space, California, pp. 76–88 (1999)
9. Leong, H.V., McLeod, D., Si, A., Yau, S.M.T.: Multi-Resolution Transmission and Browsing in Mobile Web. In: Proceedings of the CIKM 1998 Workshop on Web Information and Data Management, pp. 12–16 (1999)
10. Pirolli, P., Pitkow, J., Rao, R.: Silk from a Sow's Ear: Extracting Usable Structures from the Web. In: Proceedings of Conference on Human Factors in Computing Systems, CHI 1996, pp. 118–125 (1996)
11. Laying Out Large Directed Graphs in 3D Hyperbolic Space, http://www-graphics.stanford.edu/papers/h3/

Data Gathering Based on Nodes' Credit in Wireless Sensor Network

Farnaz Dargahi[1], Amir Masoud Rahmani[1], and Sam Jabbehdari[2]

[1] Islamic Azad University science and research branch, Tehran, Iran
farnazdargahi@gmail.com, rahmani@sr.iau.ac.ir
[2] Islamic Azad University North Tehran branch
sjabbehdari@gmail.com

Abstract. For data gathering in wireless sensor networks, sensors extract useful information from environment; this information has to be routed through several intermediate nodes to reach the destination. How information can effectively disseminate to the destination is one of the most important tasks in sensor networks. Problem arises when intermediate nodes fail to forward incoming packets. Due to limited power and slow processor in each node, algorithms of sensor networks must be designed carefully. Directed Diffusion (DD) is a typical data-centric algorithm which has been used to provide efficient data transmission. We enhance this algorithm based on nodes' credit by using five factors. Simulation results show that our proposed algorithm is more energy efficient and reliable than DD and has the ability of traffic load distribution.

Keywords: Directed Diffusion, Data gathering, Nodes' Credit, Sensor network.

1 Introduction

A sensor network is a group of wireless nodes randomly distributed in a region. In most data gathering applications, information produced by one or more sources usually has to be routed through several intermediate nodes; these wireless nodes have the ability of packet forwarding, i.e. relaying incoming packets to one of its neighbor nodes. Problem arises when intermediate nodes fail to forward incoming packets. Sensor nodes have many failure modes. Each failure decreases the performance of data gathering procedure. Our approach is designed by considering that nodes maybe not available during the dissemination procedure. Directed Diffusion [1] is a routing mechanism for data gathering in which data consumer (sink) search for the data sources by sending interest packets and find the best route to receive the data. Many researches have been done to meet specific need of wireless sensor network applications [6, 8, 11, 12].

Yu et al. [9] discussed the use of geographical information while disseminating queries to appropriate regions. The protocol, called Geographical and Energy Aware Routing (GEAR), uses energy aware and geographically-informed neighbor selection heuristics to route packets towards the destination region. By doing this, GEAR can conserve more energy than directed diffusion. Each node in GEAR keeps a cost. The

T.-h. Kim et al. (Eds.): FGCN 2008, CCIS 27, pp. 55–62, 2009.
© Springer-Verlag Berlin Heidelberg 2009

cost is a combination of residual energy and distance to destination. Raicu et al. proposed E3D diffusion (Energy-efficient Distributed Dynamic Diffusion routing algorithm) in [13], in which each node keeps a list of neighbors and chooses the next hop neighbor based on the location information, power and load towards the base station. In this scheme, when a receiver's queue is full, or its power is lower than the sender's power or when it is below a threshold, it will tell its sender to stop forwarding packets.

HDA [2] (hierarchical data aggregation) is proposed for enhancing DD.In HDA, nodes between the sink and the source are arranged in different levels (i.e. hierarchy).packets are only transmitted between two nodes in neighboring level. This new feature can save energy significantly.

In this paper, a new reliable and energy efficient DD algorithm is introduced.

The rest of the paper is organized as follows. In section 2 we briefly review the original directed diffusion algorithm and its limitations. Section 3 presents our algorithm in details .Simulation based performance studies are conducted in section 4. Finally; we conclude our work in section 5.

2 Review: Directed Diffusion

In this section, we first review the original directed diffusion in brief, and then point out its limitations.

2.1 Basic Scheme

Directed Diffusion [1] consists of three phases: a) interest propagation, b) Initial gradients setup, and c) Data delivery reinforced path as shown in Fig. 1. Sink node send out its query whenever it wants to obtain some information from sensor   nodes. This

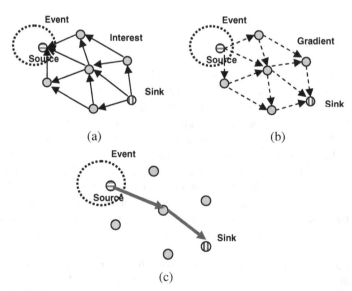

Fig. 1. Directed Diffusion. (a) Interest Propagation. (b) Initial gradients setup. (c) Data delivery reinforced path.

query is carried by interest packet. When a node receives an interest packet, the packet is cached and broadcast to other neighbors to ensure every node in the network will receive it. Propagation of interest packets also setup the gradient in the network for delivering data to the sink .Gradient is a reply link to a neighbor form which the interest was received. When a node matches an interest, it generates a sample sensed data, which is called exploratory data and sends individually to the neighbors from which the gradient established before. As these exploratory data reach the sink from some neighbors, several paths are established between sink and source.

The sink reinforces one of these paths by increasing the data rate in the interest packet. Usually this path is the one which has the least delay. Eventually only one path remains while other paths are torn down. Finally the real data will send from the source, following the selected path.

2.2 Limitations

When the sink starts selecting one particular neighbor in order to reinforce the path, it chooses the neighbor from whom it first received the latest event matching the interest. In this way, each node/sink has limited information about its neighbors to choose them, for example a node can only know which neighbor is nearest with it based on the sequence of interest it receives, without considering the neighbor queue is full or not, energy level and neighbor ability to transmit the data to the base station. This will result in some limitations in term of the amount of traffic generated and hence energy inefficiency. Moreover, if there are multiple sources and one sink, the sink only selects the path based on which neighbor send back exploratory data sooner [2].So in- network aggregation will not effectively be done. If the selected node covers more sources, in network aggregation can do more effectively as shown in Fig. 2 [2].

3   The Proposed Algorithm

Unlike location centric algorithm each sensor node in Directed Diffusion needs not to know its position information, all its decisions about data transmission are based on its knowledge about the neighbor nodes. The main reason of limitations mentioned, is that this knowledge of nodes about their neighbors is insufficient. Each node chooses that neighbor from whom it first received the last event matching the interest, without considering other parameters, such as energy level, traffic load and neighbor ability to aggregate data more efficiently. To solve such problems, we enhance this knowledge based on credit of nodes. Computation of nodes' credit is done by using five factors; at each node. This credit is computed according to Eq.1.Each node selects one of its neighbors which have a higher credit.

$$V = \alpha_1 \times V_s + \alpha_2 \times V_E + \alpha_3 \times V_B + \alpha_4 \times V_R + \alpha_5 \times V_C.$$
$$\alpha_1 + \alpha_2 + \alpha_3 + \alpha_4 + \alpha_5 = 1.$$

$$(1)$$

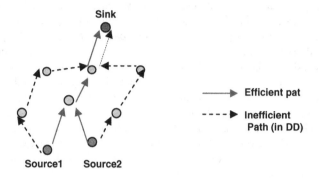

Fig. 2. Inefficient data aggregation

Each of the parameters of above formula has specific coefficient (α) that is amount between [0,1].Different alternatives have been considered for finding the best value of coefficients in order to provide desired result.

The first parameter (Vs) is the number of successful or unsuccessful transmission and how nodes succeeded to deliver packets in the past. A low amount of this parameter of a node means that the node failed to route message in the past. This parameter is increased with each successfully routed packet and decrease with each failing in routing packets.

The second parameter (VE) is the residual energy in candidate node's battery. Eq.2 is used for calculating this parameter. This parameter has an important effect on increasing the network lifetime.

$$V_E = \frac{\text{existing energy}}{\text{capacity of battry}} \tag{2}$$

The third parameter (VB) is traffic load at each node (Figure 3).This parameter is computed according to Eq.3

$$V_B = \frac{\text{free spac of buffer}}{\text{all space of buffer}} \tag{3}$$

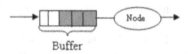

Buffer

Fig. 3. Scheme of traffic load in buffer

If there would be high traffic load in candidate node end to end delay will increase in sink node, in addition this high traffic load will cause more spending energy in candidate node.

The forth parameter (VR) is the distance of candidate node to destination (sink). Interest message of sink node is able to count and record the number of hops that passes through it. This allows nodes to discover the neighbor with minimum number of hops to the sink.

The fifth factor (VC) is how many sources can cover by each node. When the exploratory data pass through a node the node will record such source ID's. The number of these sources ID represents how many sources are covered by this node. This factor let us to do better in-network aggregation and as a result increasing lifetime of network.

Each node computes its credit based on these factors according to Eq.1. In our proposal, there is also an additional field in the exploratory data that identifies nodes credit. Since each node has computed the credit, it utilizes exploratory message to inform its neighbor about its own credit, by adding a field in the message to denote it. After each neighbor receives this credit, it will record it. When the sink receives the exploratory data, it will respond with the reinforcement message. Since each node has recorded its neighbor's credit, selects higher credit between them. So the sink will select the best path according to this credit to the source. Once a source receives the reinforcement message, it sends out the actual data.

4   Performance Evaluation

In this section, we compare our proposed algorithm with Directed Diffusion. we implement algorithm in NS-2 simulator and use the following model for our simulation study.

- The number of nodes which are distributed randomly over a rectangular area of 900m×900m is 100.
- The radio transmission rang R is 50 m.
- a sensor node's transmitting, receiving and idle listening power consumption rate are 0.660W, 0.395W and 0.035W respectively.
- Initial power is 5000 joules.
- The size of data packet is 64 byte.

The value of α1, α2, α3, α4, and α5 are set to 0.2, 0.3, 0.15, 0.25, and 0.1 respectively.

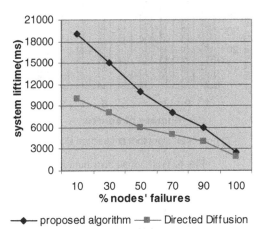

Fig. 4. System lifetime

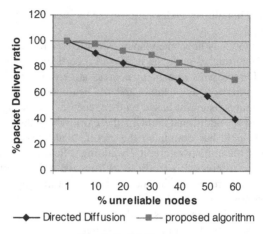

Fig. 5. Reliability

Three metrics are chosen for evaluating and comparing the performance of our algorithm with DD: system lifetime, reliability of path and load distribution.

System lifetime is used as the measure of energy consumption. The system lifetime is the total time which a wireless sensor network experiences. Fig. 4 shows the system lifetime in terms of nodes' failures. As simulation result shows, using suggested policy causes to increase system lifetime under variant nodes' failure.

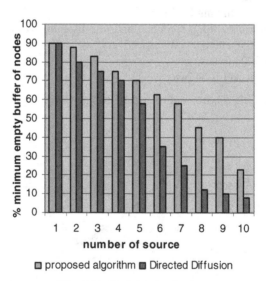

Fig. 6. Traffic load distribution

Next we analyze our algorithm for finding reliable paths. For this purpose data delivery percentage is selected to delegate reliability of paths. Data delivery is defined as the ratio of the number of data packets successfully received by the sink to the number of data packets send by the data source.   Fig. 5 shows that, as the unreliable nodes increase, DD's performance decreases faster than our proposal. This is because of giving higher priority to the reliable nodes in our proposed algorithm.

Finally, the traffic load distribution on surface of network is one of the metrics of our simulation, Fig. 6 shows the simulation result and its ability to distribute traffic load in terms of increasing source nodes.

5 Conclusion

In this paper, a new mechanism is presented for selecting intermediate nodes for transferring data. The aim of this paper is making the directed diffusion of data centric algorithm of sensor networks in a good order. For this purpose, desired parameters in this policy include number of successful or unsuccessful transmissions, number of existence processing loads in candidate node, amount of energy in selective node's battery, location and the distance between selective candidate node and destination node (sink) and number of sources that candidate node covers. Each of these parameters has specific coefficient which has influence on selecting node. Finally, between several candidate nodes, nodes with higher preference will choose. The proposed approach is deduced an energy efficient and reliable algorithm with supporting traffic load distribution.

References

[1] Intanagonwiwat, C., Govindan, R., Estrin, D., Heidemann, J., Silva, F.: Directed Diffusion for wireless sensor networking. Networking 11(1), 2–16 (2003); Digital Object Identifier 10.1109 /TNET. 2002. 80 8417

[2] Zhou, B., Ngoh, L.H., Lee, B.S., Peng, C.: HDA: A hierarchical data aggregation scheme for sensor networks. Computer Communications 29(9), 1292–1299 (2006)

[3] Schurgers, C., Srivastava, M.B.: Energy Efficient Routing in Wireless Sensor Network. Electrical Engineering Department University of California UCLA. CA (2006)

[4] Yanrong, C., jaheng, C.: An improved Directed Diffusion for Wireless Sensor Networks. In: International Conference on Wireless Communications Networking and Mobile Computing, 2007, September 21-25, pp. 2380–2383 (2007), DOI: 10.1109/WICOM. 2007. 593

[5] Machado, M.d.V., Loureiro, A.A.F., Nogueira, J.M.: Data Dissemination Using the Energy Map. In: Proceedings of the Second Annual Conference on Wireless On-demand Network Systems and Services (WONS 2005), pp. 23–34 (2005)

[6] Chang, J.-H., Tassiulas, L.: Maximum Lifetime Routing in Wireless Sensor Networks. IEEE/ACM Transactions on Networking 12(4), 609–619 (2004)

[7] Han, Q., Mehrotra, S., Venkatasubram, N.: Application-aware integration of data collection and power management in wireless sensor networks. Journal of Parallel and Distributed Computing 67(9), 992–1006 (2007)

[8] Hsiao, P.-H., Hwang, A., Kung, H.T., Vlah, D.: Load-balancing routing for wireless access networks. In: INFOCOM 2001. Twentieth Annual Joint Conference of the IEEE Computer and Communications Societies. Proceedings, April 22-26, vol. 2, pp. 986–995. IEEE, Los Alamitos (2001)

[9]   Yu, Y., Estrin, D., Govindan, R.: Geographical and energy aware routing: A recursive data dissemination protocol for wireless sensor networks. Technical Report TR-01-0023, UCLA Computer Science Department Technical Report (May 2001)

[10] Raicu, I., Schwiebert, L., Fowler, S., Guipta, S.K.S.: Local load balancing for global efficient routing in wireless sensor networks. International Journal of Distributed Sensor Networks 1, 163–185 (2005)

[11] Fasolo, E., Rossi, M., Widmer, J., Zorzi, M.: In-network aggregation techniques for wireless sensor networks: a survey. Wireless Communications 14(2), 70–87 (2007)

[12] Wu, S., Selçuk Candan, K.: Power-aware single and multipath geographic routing in sensor networks Ad Hoc Networks. 5(7), 974–997 (September 2007)

[13] Chen, M., Kwon, T., Choi, Y.: Energy-efficient differentiated directed diffusion (EDDD) in wireless sensor networks. Computer Communications 29(2), 231–245 (2006)

A Privacy Preserved Model for Medical Data Sharing in Telemedicine*

Wong Kok Seng[1], Myung Ho Kim[1], Rosli Besar[2], and Fazly Salleh[2]

[1] Department of Computer, Soongsil University, 156-743 Sangdo-dong,
Dongjak-Gu, Seoul, Korea
{kswong,kmh}@ssu.ac.kr
[2] Faculty of Engineering, Multimedia University, Jalan Ayer Keroh Lama,
75450 Bukit Beruang Melaka Malaysia
{rosli,fazly.salleh.abas}@mmu.edu.my

Abstract. In the converged Information and Communication Technology (ICT) era, medical data sharing has emerged as an important element in the healthcare industry. Hospitals within a Telemedicine system would like to share their private local databases with other hospitals. However, they do not agree to keep a copy of their database into a central server. The central repository (data warehouse) model is not secure because too much control will be granted to the central site. In order to fully utilize the distributed and heterogeneous resources, a secure and privacy preserved model should be used to reach the balance between knowledge discovery and data privacy protection at the same time. We proposed a privacy preserved model to securely share the data for Telemedicine system.

Keywords: Data Sharing, Privacy Preserving, Telemedicine.

1 Introduction

Medical databases are considered valuable to many parties including hospitals, practitioners, researchers, insurance company, and etc. Hospitals and practitioners used their patients' medical records to support their services, while researchers used these data to validate their research findings. Medical data for a single patient could be found in several hospitals in the case where he or she visited to different hospitals at different times. Since the data were distributed in several locations, the data gathering process becoming a daunting task.

Sharing of patient's medical records is not a new approach. From paper based format to electronic format, patient's medical records are shared among physicians, medical staffs and etc. The benefits of medical data sharing are significant. It helps to improve access to doctors, nurses, and other healthcare practitioners from anywhere, and anytime. Medical data sharing can reduce time, cost and risk of travel for patients, families, and healthcare personnel.

* This work was supported by the Soongsil University Research Fund.

T.-h. Kim et al. (Eds.): FGCN 2008, CCIS 27, pp. 63–75, 2009.
© Springer-Verlag Berlin Heidelberg 2009

The data sharing in healthcare industry is different from other domains such as finance, banking and e-learning. Medical data are useful, but also harmful to a patient if it's not accurate or real. Medical data received from other collaborators can bring a big impact to the practitioner's decision making. The level of trust among collaborators must be as high as possible in order to guarantee the mutual benefits for all parties as well as for patients.

Conventionally, the medical data sharing can be held by using the trusted third party [3, 12]. A copy of database from each collaborator will be gathered at one place to construct a central repository (data warehouse). Collaborator or data miner will then use the repository to mine their required data. Unfortunately, due to the security and privacy concern, many collaborators were afraid to share their patients' medical records in this way. Without the usage of centralized repository, how can each hospital securely share their private database while the privacy is preserved?

1.1 Organization

The rest of this paper is organized as follows: The literature review for this research is discussed in Section 2. We describe the problem definition in Section 3 followed by the proposed solution in Section 4. We then demonstrate how to implement our proposed model in Section 5. We give our discussions and conclusion in Section 6.

2 Literature Review

Data sharing process can be considered as the backbone for many other operations. It is a necessary pre-requisite process for data integration and data mining operations. For data integration methods [6, 17], an effective data sharing technique can produce more accurate union set. At the same time, it is the basic requirement for any privacy preserving solutions.

The proliferation and misuse of medical data is now a subject of global interest. Cryptographic and security research communities paying a closed attention in medical data sharing. Techniques such as sovereign information sharing [2] have been proposed to solve the above mentioned problem. The database contents for each collaborator will not be revealed under this technique.

In order to obtain a complete dataset for a single patient, data sharing or information sharing is necessary to ensure that all available data from multiple sites can be gathered. Under distributed environment, much works have been focused on designing a specific information sharing protocols [1]. However, the privacy of the shared data becoming a challenging issue. Privacy is addressed as preventing dissemination rather than integrating privacy constraints into the data sharing process [5].

Database operations such as intersection, equijoin, and aggregation are important operations that being used to protect the privacy of shared data. Operations in privacy preserving set operations such as set union [4, 14] and set intersection [7, 8, 11, 13] are essential to prevent extra information being revealed in the data sharing process.

Secure multi-party computation which was introduced in [18], is another techniques used in cryptography and distributed computing. It is used to protect the collaborators from revealing additional information which is not needed to be shared.

Under this approach, a group of collaborators want to compute a function with their private inputs while keeping their inputs privately. Only the answer (output) to the query will be learned by the data miner, and nothing else can be revealed [9, 10].

Database operations such as union or intersection computation, equijoin, and aggregation are important operations that can be used to support the secure data sharing process. For example, intersection computation is used to find the common value for different distributed datasets while revealing only the intersection [15]. However, the computation of these database operations involve anonymity and security concerns [11]. Anonymity means the identity of the data owner shouldn't be identified.

2.1 Issues in Medical Data Sharing

Medical data can be divided into few categories. Medical records consist of raw data, test result, X-ray, diagnosis images and etc. All medical data will be used by physicians to make decisions. What kind of data should be shared? What kind of information should be retrieved remotely? If raw data are shared, data mining techniques can be applied to find novel, hidden and useful information. When medical images such as X-ray films are shared, image processing techniques should be performed to digitize those images into medical data. All shared medical data should be standardized into the same format.

In the converged Information and Communication Technology (ICT) era, domains such as finance and business shared data with their partners or competitors to gain the mutual benefits. Data sharing or information sharing is necessary for distributed systems. The level of trust among parties must be as high as possible in order to guarantee the mutual benefits for all. However, due to the privacy and security concern, some of the data owners are not willing to share all information required. Data might be modified or perturbed by the data owner before it is being shared with others. The following questions are some of the issues focused in medical data sharing:

1. What kind of information should be shared?
2. Who had the permission to use the shared data?
3. How to ensure the privacy protection for data being shared?

2.2 Data Sharing in Telemedicine

Data sharing is a process where one party is given permission to access data from other parties. This process is easy and simple if there is no privacy or security concern. In Telemedicine, data sharing needs to be handling carefully. . Medical data sharing or information sharing has emerged as an important element in healthcare industry to ensure the quality of health services. Medical data is useful, but also harmful at the same time if it's not accurate or real. Compared to other domains, the level of correctness for shared medical data must be 100% accurate. Data owners (hospitals) should provide all information required without hiding or changing them. All received data from other parties can influent the decisions made by the practitioners.

Data sharing in other domains mostly required data miner to distribute the gained information or results to everyone at the end of the sharing process. One might disagree if the output or results is not delivered to them. However, the data sharing in Telemedicine is different from this approach. The results gained from the data sharing process will not distribute or send to other parties.

3   Definition

3.1   Problem Definition

N hospitals, $\{H_a, H_b, ..., H_N\}$ with a private local database $\{D_a, D_b, ..., D_N\}$ respectively would like to share their private local database. Data miner with query (Q) spanning the tables in all databases to compute the answer to Q without revealing extra information apart from the query result.

Solution 1
Each hospital sends a copy of their entire database to the data miner. The data miner will process the Q on the local copy of the databases.

Solution 2
Each hospital sends a subset of their database to the data miner. The data miner will process the Q on the local copy of the subset databases.

Solution 3
Each hospital sends a copy of their entire database to the central server. The data miner will process the Q on the central repository.

Solution 4
Each hospital sends a subset of their database to the central server. The data miner will process the Q on the central site.

Solution 1 and 2 are not practical because the data miner needs a great cost to store all databases. At the same time, the communication costs for both solutions will be increased when the database size is large.

In solution 3 and 4, the level of trust required for each party is too high. Too much additional information which is not needed to answer Q will be revealed. Due to this concern, some of the parties might refuse to share their data.

3.2   Privacy and Security

The tradeoff between privacy and security is an interesting topic. A secure system cannot guarantee that the privacy of the shared data is being preserved. However, a privacy preserved system normally can ensure that it had a series of secure mechanisms for privacy protection.

Privacy is an issue that is frequently undervalued during the development of information systems. Generally, security and privacy are two inter-related issues that must be solved at the same time. Each of them will become a treat for another. There are many definition have been defined for privacy. In telemedicine system, data miner is one of the collaborators within the collaborative framework. Identity of both data miner and other collaborators should be protected. In summary, here listed some of the information that assumed to be private and should not be revealed:

- Number of collaborators who shared their local database.
- Identity of the collaborators.
- Size of each database.
- Answers to the query.

If any of the party obtains this information, it can perform malicious attack easily and gain unauthorized access to the data source. Without construct a central repository, a temporary union dataset should be used in order to support the data sharing mechanism.

3.3 Privacy in Telemedicine

Telemedicine is an emerging technology that being applied into health industry. Ideally, the implementation of Telemedicine System is to guarantee a better health services regardless of distance and locations of the patient. However, the privacy concern in Telemedicine is more serious compared to other domains. Telemedicine is not only concern about security, but also privacy and confidentiality of patients' data.

4 Proposed Model

Based on the above definition, we present a solution which can be used as the model for secure data sharing. The following criterion gives a brief description of our proposed framework:

1. No central server is allowed to store databases from all collaborators. A temporary union dataset is used instead of central repository.
2. No collaborator can conclude how many collaborators contributed their dataset into the union dataset.
3. Prevent any collaborator to identify the owner of the datasets (anonymity concern).
4. Third party engine is required to form the union dataset and generate the results to the data miner.
5. No dataset owners can determine any origin records other that its own.
6. Two kinds of queries will be used in this model to facilitate the data sharing goals.
7. The proposed system is secure and privacy protected.

The secure data sharing model contains the following five steps:

Step 1
Data miner generates a pair of commutative encryption key-pair (E_{pk}, D_{pk}). Only encryption key, E_{pk} is sent to the encryption engine. The decryption key, D_{pk} will be sent and stored at the computation engine.

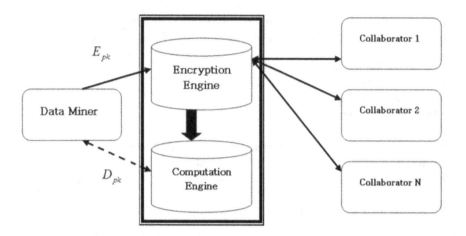

Fig. 1. General Architecture Design

Step 2

Encryption engine broadcasts the same encryption key, E_{pk} to all collaborators. A count, N will be generated to compute the frequency of successful delivered encryption keys. Primary queries will be sent to the collaborators once the connection has been established.

Step 3

Each collaborator will encrypts the requested data with E_{pk}, and send the encrypted data ("ciphertext") to the encryption engine.

Step 4

Encryption engine will make sure all collaborators responded to the query. It will send all received "ciphertext" to the computation engine after additional operations are performed on the encrypted data.

Step 5

By using the private key (received from data miner), the computation engine decrypts the ciphertext and form the union dataset. Data miner uses the union dataset by sending the secondary queries.

4.1 Components

There are four main components in our proposed model. Each component plays their own roles to ensure the security and privacy of shared data is being preserved.

1. *Data miner* is one of the hospitals (collaborators) within the framework. All hospitals involved in the Telemedicine system can be the data miner. As the data miner, it must generate a pair of commutative cryptography key. The encryption key will be broadcast to other collaborators through encryption engine while the decryption

key will be sent and use by the computation engine. Under this model, data miner will receive the requested dataset without knowing who the contributors are. At the same time, the number of sources will not be revealed.

2. *Encryption engine* is the only party which had the direct communication with data miner, computation engine, and all collaborators. It served as the central hub for all parties. Upon receiving the encryption key from the data miner, the encryption engine will broadcasts the key to all collaborators in order to establish an active connection. At this stage, the number of successful delivered key will be stored in a count, N. When the requested dataset is returned to the encryption engine, the encryption engine must make sure that the number of received encrypted dataset is equal to the count, N before sending them to the computation engine. This is to ensure that all collaborators already responded to the queries and no other incoming dataset are in the queue. Encryption engine can learn the number of sources available, identity of data miner and all collaborators. At the same time, it can know the primary queries made by the data miner. However, it will not be informed about the contents of the requested data because all data were encrypted by the collaborators.

3. *Computation engine* plays an important role in this model. By holding the decryption key received from data miner, it responsible to decrypt all encrypted dataset received from the encryption engine. Decrypted dataset will be combined to form a union dataset. This union dataset is a temporary shared repository for a specific primary query. It will be used as the replacement for the central repository and support all secondary queries from the data miner.

4. *Collaborator* needs to response to the encryption engine to initiate an active connection. All collaborators will share their private local database in this framework by answering the primary queries made by the data miner. These primary queries were delivered by the encryption engine to each collaborator. Based on the primary queries, each of the collaborators will encrypt the requested dataset with the encryption key. If the requested dataset is not found, an empty dataset will be sent to prevent the encryption engine to know which collaborator does not contribute to the union dataset. In this model, no direct communication among collaborators. They do not know the number of collaborators involved as well as identity of each collaborator.

4.2 Communications between Components

Communications between components in this proposed model is very important. It is used to ensure that the privacy of all parties can be protected while no extra information to be concealed. In our model, the communications between parties have been restricted to one-way and two-way communication. Under one-way approach, only a single direction is allowed and no fall-back communication can be performed. As shown in Fig. 2., there are four communication channels used in our model.

Communication Channel 1: The communication between data miner and encryption engine is restricted to one-way communication only. Encryption engine is not allowed to response to the data miner in any form. There is no direct communication between data miner and other collaborators. The communication is established indirectly by using the encryption engine.

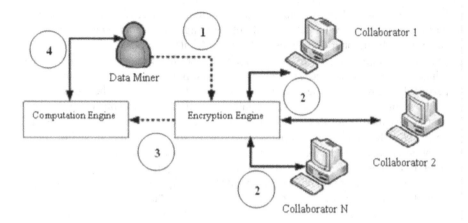

Fig. 2. Overview of Communications between Components

Communication Channel 2: Encryption engine is designed to have two-way communication with all collaborators. It is responsible to broadcast the encryption key to all collaborators and receive the encrypted message from them. However, there is no interaction between collaborators (except data miner) involved in this model. They do not have any direct or indirect communication via any channel.

Communication Channel 3: Communication between encryption engine and computation engine is designed to be one –way. Computation engine can only receive the encrypted message from the encryption engine. Computation engine is not allowed to send or communication to the encryption engine in another way.

Communication Channel 4: Two-way communications will be established between data miner and the computation engine. The results at computation engine will be sent to data miner. Further operations (such as data mining process) can be performed directly to the dataset at computation engine by the data miner.

Table 1. Communications between Components

	Data Miner	Encryption Engine	Computation Engine	Collaborators
Data Miner	-	One-way	Two-way	No
Encryption Engine	One-way	-	One-way	Two-way
Computation Engine	Two-way	One-way	-	No
Collaborators	No	Two-way	No	No

As summarized in Table 1, some of the parties will not have communication with others. For example, collaborators do not have direct communication (one-way and two-way) with the computation engine as well as the data miner. The design can prevent any extra information being revealed during the sharing process.

5 Implementation

In this section, we will demonstrate on how to use our proposed model to perform the secure SUM operation. Secure SUM can be used to demonstrate the difficulty and subtlety involved in making and proving a protocol secure [5]. We will use the following additive homomorphism proposed by Paillier [16] in our secure computation:

$$E_{pk}(m_1) + E_{pk}(m_2) = E_{pk}(m_1 + m_2) \tag{1}$$

Data miner will generate a pair of encryption key and a set of random number (with the size greater than N, number of collaborators which followed the Independent Identical Distribution). The size of the random number should be greater than N. The total summation of all random numbers is calculated.

Encryption engine will broadcast the public key and one random number to each collaborator. If the size of random numbers, |R| < N, the same number can be used more than one time. Each collaborator needs to perturb their secret value with the received random number, r. In the case where no secret value existed, the collaborator still required to use the random number to perturb a dummy value (zero). All encrypted "ciphertext" will be sent back to the encryption engine.

Upon receiving the $E_{pk}(v_i)$, encryption engine must ensure that:

$$n[E_{pk}(v_i)] = N \tag{2}$$

This is to confirm that all collaborators already responded and no other incoming "ciphertext" are in the queue. At this stage, additively homomorphic operation will be performed. We can efficiently compute $E_{pk}(V)$ because all secret values were encrypted by using the same public key.

$$E_{pk}(V) = E_{pk}(v_1 + v_2 + v_3 + ... + v_n) \tag{3}$$

The summation of unused random numbers will be calculated. Decryption can be performed at this stage to obtain the perturbed secret SUM.

$$D_{pr}[E_{pk}(V)] = (s_1 + s_2 + s_3 + ... + s_n + \sum r) \tag{4}$$

The final computation is performed as follow:

1. Total Used Random Numbers, $\sum r$
2. Total Random Numbers, $\sum_1^n R_i$
3. Total Unused Random Numbers, $\sum R_u$

$$\sum r = \sum_1^n R_i - \sum R_u \tag{5}$$

$$\sum_1^n s_i = \sum_{i=1}^n (v_i) - \sum r \tag{6}$$

Secure SUM, $S = \sum_1^n s_i + s_m$,where s_m is the secret value from the miner. (7)

The following is the sample algorithm for the secure SUM computation.

Algorithm 1. Secure SUM

```
Requirements:
```
$C_i = \{C_1, C_2, C_3,...., C_n\}$

(E_{pk}, D_{pr}), Homomorphic key pair

s_i : Secret value of C_i R_i : Random Number

```
1: Input:
```
2: $E_{pk}(v_i)$: Encrypted secret value from collaborators

```
3: Output:
4: Answer P: Secure SUM, S
5: /*Initial Phase*/
```
6: Data miner generates (E_{pk}, D_{pr}) and $\{R_i \mid i = 1,...,n\}$, where

$n \geq N$

7: Compute $\sum_1^n R_i$

8: Sends E_{pk} and R_i to encryption engine

```
9: /*Distribution Phase*/
```
10: Broadcast E_{pk} and r ($r \in R_i$) to each collaborator

11: **for** i =1; i $\leq$ $|C_i|$; i++

12:    **for** all C_i **do**

13:     **if** $s_i == 0$ **then**

14:      $v_i = r$

15:            **else**

16:               $v_i = r + s_i$

17:            **end if**

18:          **end for**

19:          Encrypt v_i with the public key $\Rightarrow E_{pk}(v_i)$

20:          Send $E_{pk}(v_i)$ to Encryption Engine

21: **end for**

22: /*Computation Phase1 by Encryption Engine*/

23: Receive $n[E_{pk}(v_i)] = N$

24: **for** all $E_{pk}(v_i)$ **do**

25:        $E_{pk}(v_1) + E_{pk}(v_2) + E_{pk}(v_3) + ... + E_{pk}(v_n)$

$$= E_{pk}(v_1 + v_2 + v_3 + ... + v_n) = E_{pk}(V)$$

26: **end for**

27: Send R_u (unused random numbers) and $E_{pk}(V)$ to computation engine

28: /*Computation Phase2 by Computation Engine*/

29: Compute $\sum R_u$

30: Compute Answer $= D_{pr}[E_{pk}(V)] = \sum_{i=1}^{n}(v_i) = \sum_{1}^{n} s_i + \sum r$

31: return $\sum R_u$ and Answer to Data Miner

32: /*Final Computation by Data Miner*/

33: Compute $\sum r = \sum_{1}^{n} R_i - \sum R_u$

34: $\sum_{1}^{n} s_i = \sum_{i=1}^{n}(v_i) - \sum r$

35: Secure SUM, $S = \sum_{1}^{n} s_i + s_m$

     where s_m is the secret value from the miner.

6 Discussions and Conclusion

In our model, there are two types of queries made by the data miner. Primary query is sent to the collaborators via encryption engine. The answers for the primary query (Q_p) will be used to form the union dataset ($d_1, d_2, ..., d_n$) in the computation engine. Secondary query (Q_s) will be sent to the union dataset for further operations. Data miner will not gain any extra knowledge despite of the answer to its queries.

Algorithm 2. Primary Query

```
1: Input:
2: Qₚ: Primary Query [key(s), dataset]
3: Output:
4: Answer P: Encrypted (dataset)
5: Procedure:
```
6: **for** i =1; i ≤ | $D_a, D_b, ..., D_N$ | ; i++ **do**
7:     Search Q_p from $D_i = \{ D_a, D_b, ..., D_N \}$
```
8:          Add encrypted[i] to P
```
9: **end** for

Algorithm 3. Secondary Query

```
1: Input:
2: Qₛ: Secondary Query [process]
3: Output:
4: Answer S:
   Secure sum, Intersection, Union, Equijoin, and etc
5: Procedure:
```
7:     Search Q_s from $\{ d_1, d_2, ..., d_n \}$
```
8:      return S
```

In order to utilize the distributed and heterogeneous resources within the Tele-medicine system, a secure and privacy preserved model should be used. By using our proposed model, hospitals within the Telemedicine system do not need to construct a central repository to share their local databases. Encryption and computation engine used in this model can prevent the identity of the data miner and other collaborators being revealed to each other. The privacy of the shared data will still preserved even thought one of the engines is compromised. The protocols for database integration such as intersection and equijoin can be applied using this model.

References

1. Agrawal, R., Evfimievski, A., Srikant, R.: Information Sharing across Private Databases. In: 22nd ACM SIGMOD International Conference on Management of Data, pp. 86–97. ACM Press, New York (2003)
2. Agrawal, R., Terzi, E.: On honesty in sovereign information sharing. In: Ioannidis, Y., Scholl, M.H., Schmidt, J.W., Matthes, F., Hatzopoulos, M., Böhm, K., Kemper, A., Grust, T., Böhm, C. (eds.) EDBT 2006. LNCS, vol. 3896, pp. 240–256. Springer, Heidelberg (2006)
3. Ajmani, S., Morris, R., Liskov, B.: A trusted third-party computation service. Technical Report, MIT-LCS-TR-847, MIT (2001)
4. Brickel, J., Shmatikov, V.: Privacy-preserving graph algorithms in the semi-honest model. In: Roy, B. (ed.) ASIACRYPT 2005. LNCS, vol. 3788, pp. 236–252. Springer, Heidelberg (2005)
5. Clifton, C., Kantarcioglu, M., Doan, A., Schadow, G., Vaidya, J., Elmagarmid, A.K., Suciu, D.: Privacy preserving data integration and sharing. In: 9th ACM SIGMOD Workshop on Research Issues in Data Mining and Knowledge, Paris, pp. 19–26 (2004)
6. Dayal, U., Hwang, H.Y.: View definition and generalization for database integration in a multidatabase system. IEEE Transaction 10(6), 628–645 (1984)
7. Evfimievski, A., Gehrke, J., Srikant, R.: Limiting privacy breaches in privacy preserving data mining. In: PODS 2003: Proceedings of the twenty-second ACM SIGMOD-SIGACT-SIGART symposium on Principles of database systems, pp. 211–222. ACM Press, New York (2003)
8. Freedman, M., Nissim, K., Pinkas, B.: Efficient private matching and set intersection. In: Cachin, C., Camenisch, J.L. (eds.) EUROCRYPT 2004. LNCS, vol. 3027, pp. 1–19. Springer, Heidelberg (2004)
9. Goldreich, O.: The foundations of cryptography, vol. 2. Cambridge University Press, Cambridge (2004)
10. Goldreich, O., Micali, S., Wigderson, A.: How to play any mental game - a completeness theorem for protocols with honest majority. In: 19th ACM Conference on Theory of computing, pp. 218–229. ACM Press, New York (1987)
11. Huberman, B., Franklin, M., Hogg, T.: Enhancing privacy and trust in electronic communities. In: Proceedings of the 1st ACM conference on Electronic commerce, pp. 78–86. ACM Press, New York (1999)
12. Jefferies, N., Mitchell, C., Walker, M.: A proposed architecture for trusted third party services. In: Dawson, E.P., Golić, J.D. (eds.) Cryptography: Policy and Algorithms 1995. LNCS, vol. 1029, pp. 98–104. Springer, Heidelberg (1996)
13. Keefe, O., Yung, M., Gu, L., Baxter, R.: Privacy-preserving data linkage protocols. In: Proceedings of the 2004 ACM workshop on Privacy in the electronic society, pp. 94–102. ACM Press, New York (2004)
14. Kissner, L., Song, D.: Privacy-preserving set operations. In: Shoup, V. (ed.) CRYPTO 2005. LNCS, vol. 3621, pp. 241–257. Springer, Heidelberg (2005)
15. Naor, M., Pinkas, B.: Oblivious transfer and polynomial evaluation. In: 31st ACM Symposium on Theory of Computing, Atlanta, pp. 245–254 (1999)
16. Stefan, B., Sebastian, O.: Secure set union and bag union computation for guaranteeing anonymity of distrustful participants. Journal of Software 3(1), 9–17 (2008)
17. Wiederhold, G.: Intelligent integration of information. In: ACM SIGMOD Conference on Management of Data, Washington, pp. 434–437 (1993)
18. Yao, A.C.: How to generate and exchange secrets. In: 27th Annual Symposium on Foundations of computer science, pp. 162–167. IEEE Press, Los Alamitos (1986)

Wireless Network of Collaborative Physiological Signal Devices in a U-Healthcare System*

Joonyoung Jung[1], Jeonwoo Lee[1], Youngsung Kim[2], and Daeyoung Kim[3]

[1] Electronics and Telecommunications Research Institute, 161 Gajeong-dong, Yuseong-gu, Deajeon, 305-700, Republic of Korea
{jyjung21,ljwoo}@etri.re.kr
[2] Korea University, Anam-dong 5-ga ,Seongbuk-gu, Seoul, Republic of Korea
dragenda@gmail.com
[3] Chungnam National University, 220 kung-dong Yuseong-gu, Deajeon, 305-764, Republic of Korea
dykim@cnu.kr

Abstract. We designed and implemented collaborative physiological signal devices in a u-healthcare(ubiquitous healthcare) system. In this system, wireless body area network (WBAN) such as ZigBee is used to communicate between physiological signal devices and the mobile system. WBAN device needs a specific function for ubiquitous healthcare application. We show several collaborative physiological devices and propose WBAN mechanism such as a fast scanning algorithm, a dynamic discovery and installation mechanism, a reliable data transmission, a device access control for security, and a healthcare profile for u-healthcare system.

Keywords: Wireless Body Area Network, Healthcare, Physiological Signal Device.

1 Introduction

The number of elderly people is rapidly increasing around the world. The worldwide population of people over 65 years old will reach 761 million by 2025, more than double the 1990 figures [1]. Generally, providing more efficient utilization of physicians, shortened hospital stays, reducing the skill level and frequency of visits of home-care professionals, reducing hospital readmission rates, and promoting health education can all contribute to reduced healthcare costs [2]. The ubiquitous healthcare system enables medical professionals to remotely perform real-time monitoring, early diagnosis, and treatment for potential risky disease. Furthermore, the medical diagnosis and patient consultations can be delivered via wire/wireless communication channels. Thus, the ubiquitous healthcare system can provide a cheaper and smarter way to manage and care for patients suffering from age-related chronic diseases, such as

---
* This work was supported by the IT R&D program of MKE/IITA, [2008-S-034-01, Development of Collaborative Virtual Machine Technology for SoD].

T.-h. Kim et al. (Eds.): FGCN 2008, CCIS 27, pp. 76–88, 2009.

heart disease [3], because chronic diseases require continuous, long-term monitoring rather than episodic assessments.

In [4], they told that a continuous health monitoring system should be wearable and easy to use. So they propose a wearable, plug-and-play system using Bluetooth as the wireless communication protocol. In [5], they propose a mobile patient monitoring system, which integrates current personal digital assistant (PDA) technology and wireless local area network (WLAN) technology. This paper shows that the wireless PDA model is superior to the currently used monitors both in mobility and in usability and is better suited to patient transport. In [13], it encourages paradigm shift of moving a monitoring system for at-risk patient from the health facility to the patient's daily living environment (the locations where they happen to be during normal living).

Several technologies are needed for implementing a wearable healthcare system. That is, a physiological signal measurement technology to measure user's physiological signals continuously and wireless communication technology to construct a wireless body area network (WBAN).

In this paper, we show our physiological signal devices, WBAN and ubiquitous healthcare system. It enables continuous physiological signal monitoring and supports health consulting information anywhere and anytime.

2 Wearable Physiological Signal Devices

We developed several type wearable physiological signal devices as shown in figure 1. Our strategy is that every possible physiological signal instruments is built into a physiological signal device and a central processor supervise the operation of each component, analyzes the measured data and then rapidly transfer these data using

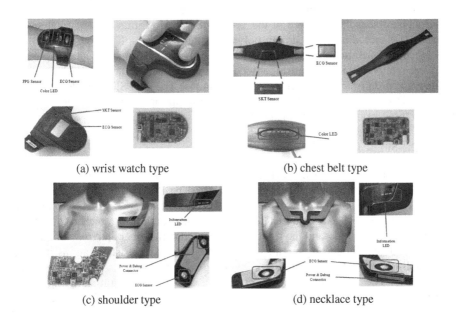

(a) wrist watch type

(b) chest belt type

(c) shoulder type

(d) necklace type

Fig. 1. Wearable Physiological Signal Devices

WBAN such as ZigBee. The technical challenge is to make the physiological device easy to operate and manage, reliable under various operating conditions, and affordable for most possible users.

I will explain wearable physiological signal devices with the wrist watch type.

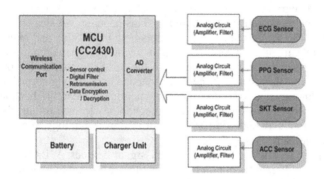

Fig. 2. Functional Block diagram of a Wrist Watch Type Wearable Physiological Signal Device

As shown in figure 2, the central unit of a micro-controller (CC2430-RF Chip, Chipcon-TI, USA) manages the operation of each measurement module. The hardware of the actual device is composed of a wrist body and a band attached its. Two PDMS electrodes for ECG(electrocardiogram) and a ribbon type temperature sensor are attached to the back of the body and a reflective flat type SpO2 sensor is mounted to the top of the wrist. The wrist watch type physiological signal device (W-PSD) contains three printed circuit boards, which include analog and digital circuitry and other onboard sensors. The size of the W-PSD is 60x65x15mm and the total system weighs 160g including one Lithium-polymer batteries. The software of W-PSD was developed for operational simplicity and efficiency. Considering the fact that possible users are relatively old and infirm, any complicated user interface would be counterproductive in daily life or in emergency situations. The W-PSD provides relatively small LED of current state for low power consumption, which indicate electrical function (power on/off, communicating, and battery charging).

2.1 ECG-Single Channel

For ECG Measurement on the wrist, we used only 2 PDMS electrodes for a single channel(Lead I), which record between each arm. The PDMS electrodes are made of flexible flat with a gold coating of polydimethylsiloxane surface, which has a surface resistance of $0.05\Omega\sim0.2\Omega$. One ECG electrode for the left arm is attached to the inner surface of the wrist body and the right hand must touch the other electrode at the outer layer of its body. The analog circuitry of the ECG module consists of an instrumentation amplifier, a notch filter and a non-inverting amplifier with a total gain and bandwidth 50Hz. The ECG signal is converted to a digital signal with sampling rate of 100Hz for heart rate detections. Performance evaluation of the developed ECG module was accomplished using a commercial ECG simulator(Patient Simulator 300B,

FLUKE Inc. Japan). For various simulated ECG outputs with range of 30~ 200bpm, the developed ECG module produced HR outputs within an error range of 1%.

2.2 PPG (Photopleth-Ysmography)

A PPG module was developed using a commercial reflective flat sensor mounted the wrist body, which includes the required electronic circuitry and program. The performance of the developed PPG module was verified using a commercial SpO2 simulator (Oxitest plus7, FLUKE, JAPAN). Over various pulse rate measured in PPG, the output showed an accuracy within an error range of 1%.

2.3 SKT (Skin Temperature)

The skin surface temperature module was fabricated using a ribbon type temperature sensor (S38F, MINCO, USA). It is gauzy, soft, consumes little power and is highly accurate. The sensor is attached to the inner surface of the wrist body with its sensing surface contacting the skin. To evaluate its performance, the developed module was tested inside a heated chamber at temperatures which were incremented over the range 25~40°C in one degree steps. The results obtained showed good linearity and accuracy within an error range of 1%.

2.4 Fall Detector (Using ACC Sensor)

We developed a simple fall detector using a 3-axis ACC (accelerometer) (KXP47, Kionix, USA). Once the acceleration sensor output exceeds the empirically determined threshold, then arithmetic value from each axis determines whether the W-PSD wearer has fallen or not. When the W-PSD detects a fall event, it confirms whether the wearer is conscious or not by raising a sound alarm. Then if there is no response from the wearer in a given time (ten seconds), the W-PSD starts the physiological signal measurements and provides the emergency occurrence to pre-assigned caregivers with the appropriate information.

2.5 SBP (Using ECG and PPG Sensor)

An indirect estimation of blood pressure is the pulse wave transit time(PTT), which is measured as the transmission time of the arterial pulse pressure wave from the aortic valve to the periphery. The main factors influencing PTT are heart rate and vessel compliance. As blood pressure increases, there is a reduction in arterial compliance why the pulse wave travels faster (PTT decreases) [6]. Thereby, devices such as electrocardiographs and pulse wave of PPG are used to measure in-directive systolic blood pressure. There are sensors that provide the data required to calculate blood pressures as described below. The wrist electro-potential sensor (ECG and PPG sensor where you place your finger is the one terminal while the back of the watch in contact with your wrist is other terminal) detects the electrical signals generated right about the time the heart contracts. This electrical signal is the starting point of the pulse wave transit time. The detection software calculates the time between the electrical signal generated by the heart beat and detection of the pulse wave at the fingertip placed on the wrist body to determine the pulse wave transit time. For all simulator outputs, the developed SBP (systolic blood pressure) module provided outputs within an error range of 7%.

2.6 Dongle and Mobile System

In the developed system, wireless-transferring was accomplished in two separate ways. The first involved an RF link between the W-PSD and the mobile system for short range transmission using Zigbee communication. The second involved the transmission of information to remote caregivers and/or a server computer through the commercial wide network. We used ZigBee chip CC2430 (1.2GHz, Chipcon-TI, USA) as RF transmission and reception modules, respectively, the latter is connected to the mobile system (BIP-5000, Bluebird, Korea) via an RS-232 connection. Recently, the mobile system equipped with a code division multiple access module has become available and provides more processing power as well as a local wireless function. This is especially helpful when a larger amount of data is collected and analyzed.

3 Wireless Body Area Network (WBAN)

The W-PSD performs all measurements and sends the measured data to pre-assigned caregiver using PDA as quickly as possible. Nowadays, Multiple wireless communication standards exist [7]–[9], each suited to certain applications, e.g. BluetoothTM, wireless LAN, radio frequency (RF) transceiver and a cellular phone. We compared the wireless communication methods to be used with a same type for emergency situation. Based on the results of the previous study and considering the system complexity, power consumption, size of body and reliability, we chose an ZigBee(IEEE 802.15.4) and the PDA(WLAN and CDMA) for short and long range wireless communication, respectively.

The goal of ZigBee(IEEE 802.15.4) was to provide a standard with ultra-low complexity, cost, and power for low-data-rate wireless connectivity among inexpensive fixed, portable, and moving devices [10]. The ZigBee Alliance is an association of companies working together to enable reliable, cost-effective, low-power, wirelessly networked, monitoring and control products based on an open global standard [11].

3.1 Scanning Algorithm

The physiological signal device (PSD) may always connect with the same mobile system (PDA). Thus, the PSD can know the address of the mobile system by using last or the most recent mobile system connected. However, according to the scanning algorithm of IEEE 802.15.4, the PSD that wants to connect with a mobile system should scan all channels, even if the PSD knows the address of the mobile system. Thus, establishing a connection may take a long time in certain situations.

In the proposed algorithm, the mobile system has a channel priority to select a channel for making a WBAN. The PSD can also know the channel priority of the mobile system by using the past connection information between the PSD and the mobile system. That is, the PSD can know the IEEE address and channel priority of the mobile system to which it is connected. Because the PSD knows the IEEE address and the channel priority of the mobile system, it does not need to scan all channels before establishing an association. If the PSD finds the mobile system during the scan and then tries to connect with it immediately, the duration of scanning time can be reduced greatly. We compared the scanning time of the proposed algorithm with the scanning time of the IEEE 802.15.4. We excluded the possibility of network error because the wireless network error is random and mostly effected by RF environment. Based on the IEEE 802.15.4 algorithm, the scanning time can be calculated with base superframe duration and scan duration [12]. Equation1 shows the equation about the length of scanning time in IEEE 802.15.4. aBaseSuperframeDuration is the number of symbols forming a superframe when the superframe order is equal to 0 and is consisted of aBaseSlotDuration × aNumSuperframeSlots. aBaseSlotDuration is the number of symbols forming a superframe slot when the superframe order is equal to 0 and the default value is 60. aNumSuperframeSlots is the number of slots contained in any superframe and the default value of it is 16. Scan Duration is a value used to calculate the length of time spent scanning each channel for scan.

$$\sum_{ch=first}^{ch=last}((S \times (2^n + 1))symbols) \qquad (1)$$

$$\text{where } S : \text{aBaseSuperframeDuration},$$
$$n : \text{Scan Duration } (0 - 14)$$

Equation2 shows the equation for scanning time in the proposed algorithm. The P_i is the probability that the PSD finds the mobile system at i channel.

$$\sum_{i=1}^{i=last} \{P_i \times [(i - \frac{1}{2}) \times (S \times (2^n + 1))](symbols)\} \qquad (2)$$

$$\text{where } S : \text{aBaseSuperframeDuration},$$
$$n : \text{Scan Duration } (0 - 14)$$
$$P_i : \text{i-th Channel Probability}$$

3.2 Dynamic Discovery and Installation

There are a lot of small devices in ubiquitous healthcare system. There is much difficulty in using a new small device if it is not discovered automatically. The small devices should be discovered and installed automatically to implement ubiquitous healthcare system. Nowadays, the middleware like an UPnP discovers the service between electronic devices but it does not fit for a small device like sensor. So, this paper proposes the dynamic discovery and installation algorithm suitable for the ubiquitous healthcare system.

PSDs are connected with the mobile system by ZigBee in ubiquitous healthcare system. The mobile system should recognize them to receive a physiological signal properly. If a patient buys a new PSD, the mobile system connects with it by zigbee and then receives the physiological signal of it. For this, a device provider system supports installation data to the mobile system. So, the mobile system discovers and

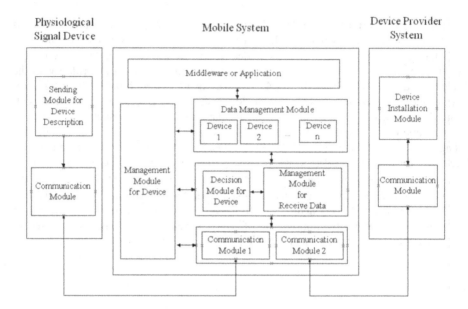

Fig. 3. Block Diagram for Dynamic Device Discovery and Installation

installs the new PSD. The algorithm about this automatic device discovery and installation is below. First of all, the PSD sends device description message when it is powered. The mobile system received the message decides whether the message is the device description message or not. If it is a device description message, the mobile system decides whether it is the device description message from a necessary PSD. If it comes from a necessary PSD, the mobile system decides whether the PSD is installed or not. If the PSD is not installed in mobile system, the mobile system requests the installation data from a device provider system. The device provider system sends installation data to the mobile system and then the mobile system installs the PSD. After installation, if the mobile system does not receive the device description message from the PSD, the mobile system uninstalls it to save the mobile system resource.

Figure 3 shows the block diagram for dynamic discovery and installation in the ubiquitous healthcare system. The PSD has the sending module for device description and communication module. The sending module sends the device description regularly. The communication module uses the zigbee to communicate with the mobile system. The device provider system has the device installation module and communication module. The device installation module receives the installation data request message from the mobile system and then sends the device installation data to the mobile system. The communication module uses the (W)LAN to communicate with the mobile system. The mobile system has the several modules as seen figure 3. The management module for receive data decides whether the received data from PSD is a device description message or not. It sends the data to the decision module for PSD if the received data is a device description message. It sends the data to the data management module if the received data is a physiological signal data. The decision module for PSD decides whether the received device description message come from a necessary PSD or not. The management module for PSD manages the PSD. This module decides to install or uninstall of PSDs. The data management module treats the physiological signal data properly and then sends the data to the middleware or application. In our ubiquitous healthcare system, the master device such as the mobile system can discover and install the new PSDs by using a network automatically. Therefore even if new PSDs are very small and plenty, the master device can manage the new PSDs very easily and conveniently.

3.3 Reliable Data Transmission

We made a reliable data transmission by using a retransmission scheme. The sensor device transmits the data with AR(Acknowledgement request). If the sensor device doesn't receive an acknowledgement within apscAckWaitDuration seconds from the mobile system, the sensor device repeats the process of transmitting the frame up to a maximum of apscMaxFrameRetries times. If an acknowledgement is not received after apscMaxFrameRetries retransmissions, the APS sub-layer shall assume the transmission has failed and notify the next higher layer of the failure [11]. In this case, the next higher layer retransmits the data until the buffer is overflowed. APS sub-layer Constants say that the apscAckWaitDuration is $0.05 \times (2 \times nwkcMaxDepth) +$ (security encrypt/decrypt delay) where security encrypt/decrypt delay is 0.1, nwkcMaxDepth is 0x0f. The apscMaxFrameRetries is 3.

3.4 PSD Access Control

We use the access control between PSDs and a mobile system for security. First of all, the user of a mobile system inputs and saves the device ID of PSD at a mobile system. A ZigBee dongle requests device ID table from mobile system when the ZigBee dongle is powered on. If the mobile system receives a device ID table request message from the ZigBee dongle, it sends the device ID table to the ZigBee dongle. If the ZigBee dongle receives the device ID table from the mobile system, it saves device ID table. We use the group ID to communicate between the mobile system and a PSD. If the group ID of the PSD is same with it of the mobile system, the PSD can communicate with the mobile system. A PSD requests group ID from the ZigBee dongle when the PSD is powered on. If the ZigBee dongle receives group ID request message, it decides whether there is the device ID that requests the group ID in the device ID table or not. If there isn't the device ID in the device ID table, the ZigBee dongle sends the fail message to the PSD. If there is the device ID in the device ID, the Zig-Bee dongle sends the group ID to the PSD. The PSD can communicate with the Zig-Bee dongle after receiving the group ID. The group ID of the PSA should be same with the group ID of the ZigBee dongle to communicate each other.

3.5 Ubiquitous Healthcare Profile

The ubiquitous healthcare system may use a lot of PSDs and environment sensor devices (ESDs) to get context information. We justify a devices specified in the ubiquitous healthcare (UH) profile. Device descriptions specified in this profile are summarized in Table 1 along with their respective Device IDs. A product that conforms to this specification shall implement at least one of these device descriptions. Devices are classified by the PSD for measuring a physiological signal and the control and monitor devices for controlling and/or monitoring the PSD and the ESD for measuring an environment context. As seen Table 1, PSDs are consisted of ECG for measuring ECG pulse rate, respiration for respiration rate, SpO2 for SpO2 value and so on. The plural device can measure two or more physiological signals simultaneously. It has physiological signals

Table 1. Devices specified in the UH profile

	Device	Description	Device ID
PSD	ECG	ECG pulse rate	0x0100
	Respiration	Respiration rate (RR)	0x0101
	SpO2	SpO2 value	0x0102
	PPG	ECG pulse rate	0x0103
	Blood Pressure	Blood Pressure value	0x0104
	Body Temperature	Body Temperature value	0x0105
	Blood Sugar	Blood Sugar value	0x0106
	Body Fat	Body Fat value	0x0107
	Weight	Weight value	0x0108
	Plural	Plural value of physiological signal	0x0109
	Reserved		0x010A - 0x1FF
Control & monitor Device	ECG/EKG	ECG/EKG Device Control & Monitoring	0x0200
	Respiration	Respiration Device Control & Monitoring	0x0201
	SpO2	SpO2 Device Control & Monitoring	0x0202
	PPG	PPG Device Control & Monitoring	0x0203
	Blood Pressure	Blood Pressure Device Control & Monitoring	0x0204
	Body Temperature	Body Temperature Device Control & Monitoring	0x0205
	Blood Sugar	Blood Sugar Device Control & Monitoring	0x0206
	Body Fat	Body Fat Device Control & Monitoring	0x0207
	Weight	Weight Device Control & Monitoring	0x0208
	Plural	Plural Device Control & Monitoring	0x0209
	Reserved		0x020A- 0x2FF
Environment Sensor Device	Temperature	Temperature value	0x0300
	Relative Humidity	Relative Humidity value	0x0301
	Oxygen rate	Oxygen rate value	0x0302
	Air pressure	Air pressure value	0x0303
	Wind speed	Wind speed value	0x0304
	Rain gauge	Rain gauge value	0x0305
	Toxic gas	Toxic gas value	0x0306
	Reserved		0x0307 - 0x3FF
Etc.	Accelerometer	Accelerometer value	0x0400
	Reserved		0x0401 - 0xFFFF

information about the number and the kind; for example, it has three physiological signals, ECG, PPG and body temperature. ESDs can measure environment such as temperature, relative humidity and so on. The context-aware ubiquitous healthcare system may know where the patient is by using sensor devices information. The control & monitoring device can control and monitor PSDs. For example, it can turn off PSDs and changes device status and so on. The accelerometer device in Etc. may be needed for detecting the falling down of a patient. This list will be added to in future versions of the profile as new clusters are developed to meet the needs of manufacturers. The reserved values shall not be used until the profile defines them.

4 Service Scenario and Application

A ubiquitous healthcare system infrastructure is shown in figure 4. This system consists of PSDs, a mobile system, a device provider system, a healthcare service provider system, a physician system and a healthcare personal system. PSDs measure the physiological signals of the patient and send the data to the mobile system using ZigBee. The mobile system can display the physiological signal data from PSDs and send them to a healthcare service provider system by using WLAN or CDMA. The device provider system provides device installation data to the mobile system. The healthcare service provider system is the portal server deciding all comprehensive tasks regarding health care. A physician logs in the healthcare service provider system and then can monitor and analysis the patient's physiological signals at the physician system. The patient logs in the healthcare service provider system and then can monitor own physiological signals at the healthcare personal system.

In our scenario, we developed 4 healthcare applications including the Self-Diagnosis Service, the Remote Monitoring Service, the Exercise Management Service and the Emergency as shown in figure 5.

The Self-Diagnosis Service shows the user's physiological data. When the user selects the Self-Diagnosis service in the user interface of the mobile system, the value and status of physiological data such as skin temperature, blood pressure, pulse and respiration are displayed.

If a medical doctor desires to monitor the physiological data of the user, the Remote Monitoring Service transfer user's physiological raw data to the remote heath care center. Thus the doctor can monitor the user's data in remote.

The Exercise Management Service shows the consumed user's calories in the mobile system.

If the state of the user is determined to be an emergency state, the Emergency State Management Service (ESMS) is invoked. The ESMS call the Short Message Service (SMS) transfer and transfer the user's physiological data to the remote healthcare center. Therefore, the medical doctor can monitor the emergency physical data of the patient.

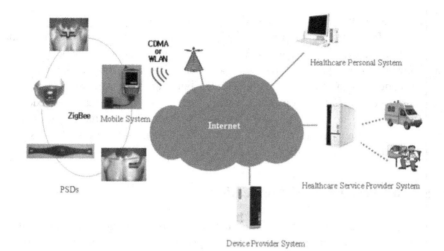

Fig. 4. Ubiquitous Healthcare System Infrastructure

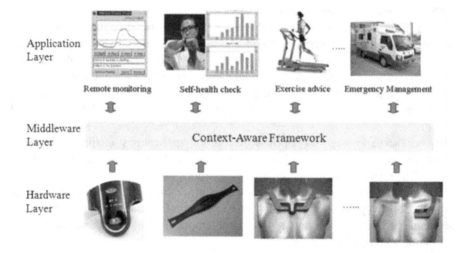

Fig. 5. Ubiquitous Healthcare Application

5 Conclusion

We developed a ubiquitous healthcare system that allows the patient to be managed and have their health monitored anytime and anywhere. We demonstrate that the developed PSDs provide convenient and comfortable multi-parameter health monitoring for a period of weeks or months, or even continuous monitoring in a very cost effective manner with acceptable reliability.

We use ZigBee communication within these PSDs and the mobile system in WBAN region. In a ubiquitous healthcare system, PSDs and the mobile system in WBAN region are personalized to a patient. Thus, PSDs will almost connect with the same mobile system. Therefore, we proposed a novel algorithm to improve the IEEE 802.15.4 scanning algorithm. If the personalized PSD finds the personalized mobile system during the scan, the personalized PSD tries to connect with it immediately. Therefore, the scanning time for connection can be reduced greatly.

In the ubiquitous healthcare system, there are a lot of tiny devices to sense a physiological signal and/or an environment data. The mobile system of a patient receives the data from sensing devices. The mobile system should discover and install the sensing devices to receive sensing data. In this paper, we propose discovery, installation and removal method of sensing devices automatically. This method and algorithm make an offer convenient and efficient when the mobile system manages sensing devices around.

One user's health monitoring system has a few ZigBee devices to measure one user's physiological data. Even if there are a lot of ZigBee devices nearby, the communication should be accepted between only one user's ZigBee devices. So, the access control should be implemented because there can be a lot of ZigBee devices nearby. We propose a group ID mechanism to implement an access control. The physiological data must not be lost but a wireless communication such as zigbee can lose a data. So, this paper proposes the reliable data transmission not to lose a physiological data in zigbee based health monitoring system. The access control and reliable data transmission can help to communicate between the PSD and the mobile system safely and reliably.

We propose the healthcare profile for Ubiquitous healthcare system. This profile involves PSD, environment sensor device and control/monitor device. It will help to improve interoperability between Ubiquitous healthcare devices.

However, we have a problem to solve. the PSD is a wearable device, so it has a small battery. Now, it can work for about 6 hours without recharging. We should improve this problem.

References

1. Ross, P.E.: Managing Care Through the Air. IEEE Spectrum, 14–19 (December 2004)
2. Schepps, J., Rosen, A.: Microwave industry outlook – wireless communications in healthcare. Microwave Theory and Techniques 50(3), 1044–1045 (2002)
3. Lubrin, E., Lawrence, E., Navarro, K.F.: Wireless remote healthcare monitoring with Motes. In: ICMB, July 2005, pp. 235–241 (2005)
4. Yao, J., Schmitz, R., Rarren, S.: A wearable point-of-care system for home use that incorporates plug-and-play and wireless standards. IEEE Transactions on Information Technology in Biomedicine 9(3), 363–371 (2005)
5. Lin, Y.-H., Jan, I.-C., Ko, P.C.-i., Chen, Y.-Y., Wong, J.-M., Jan, G.-j.: A wireless PDA-based physiological monitoring system for patient transport. IEEE Transaction on Information Technology in Biomedicine 9(4), 439–447 (2004)
6. Barschdorff, D., Erig, M.: Continuous blood pressure monitoring during stress ECG. Bio-Med. Tech. 43(3), 34–39 (1998)

7. PalowirelessWireless Resource Center. Palowireless Pty Ltd., http://www.palowireless.com/

8. Williams, S.: IrDA: Past, present and future. IEEE Pers. Commun. Mag., 11–19 (February 2002)

9. Shim, R.: HomeRF Working Group disbands. CNET News.com, http://news.com.com

10. Middleton, S.: IEEE 802.15 WPAN Low Rate Study Group PAR, doc. number IEEE P802.15-00/248r3 (submitted, September 2000) (2002)

11. ZigBee Alliance Home Page, http://www.zigbee.org

12. IEEE Std. 802.15.4-2003, IEEE Standard for Information Technology – Telecommunications and Information Exchange Between Systems – Local and Metroplitan Area Networks – Specific Requirements – Wireless Medium Access Control (MAC) and Physical Layer (PHY) Specifications for Low-Rate Wireless Personal Area Networks (LR-WPANs) (2003)

13. Rigby, M.: Applying emergent ubiquitous technologies in health: The need to respond to new challenges of opportunity, expectation, and responsibility. International Journal of Medical Informatics 76, 349–352 (2007)

Mobility and QoS Control Concern
in Next Generation Networks

Mahmoud Pirhadi[1], Seyed Mostafa Safavi Hemami[2], Ahmad Khademzadeh[3],
and Jahangir Dadkhah Chimeh[3]

[1] Islamic Azad University, Science and Research Branch, Tehran, Iran
[2] Amirkabir University of Technology, Tehran, Iran
[3] Iran Telecom Research Center, Tehran, Iran
mahmoud.pirhadi@itel.ir, msafavi@aut.ac.ir,
khademzadeh@itrc.ac.ir, dadkhah@itrc.ac.ir

Abstract. This paper presents an overview of mobility management and QoS Control in next generation networks. The NGN architecture is expected to provide generalized mobility for users while keeping the desired quality of service and providing required resources for different kinds of services. The approach taken is, initially, to overview the basic concepts and goals of mobility and QoS in the context of NGN. Following this, the overall architecture of NGN is presented and then the migration path toward the next generation mobile networks and the mobility management function in NGN is discussed. Also we take a closer look to QoS control and resource management in NGN and the related activities in standardization bodies. Finally the resource management architecture proposed by ITU and the mobility considerations in this architecture are presented.

Keywords: Next Generation Network, Mobility, Quality of Service, RACF.

1 Introduction

During recent years, great efforts have been initiated in order to converge various telecommunications networks. This has led to a new networking concept called Next Generation Network (NGN). According to ITU's definition, NGN is a packet-based network able to provide telecommunication services and able to make use of multiple broadband, QoS (Quality of Service)-enabled transport technologies and in which service-related functions are independent from underlying transport-related technologies. It offers unfettered access by users to different service providers [1].

The basic characteristics of NGN can be derived from the problems faced by the network operators: the need to provide services over broadband accesses; the need to merge diverse network services such as data, voice, telephony, multimedia, and emerging popular Internet services such as instant messaging and presence and broadcast type services; and the desire of customers to be able to access their services from anywhere. Rather than a network to provide a specific solution (e.g., the PSTN), what is needed for the 21st century is a converged network which can support a flexible platform for service delivery.

T.-h. Kim et al. (Eds.): FGCN 2008, CCIS 27, pp. 89–104, 2009.
© Springer-Verlag Berlin Heidelberg 2009

NGN should support both existing and "NGN aware" end user terminals. Hence terminals connected to NGN will include analogue telephone sets, fax machines, ISDN sets, cellular mobile phones, GPRS (General Packet Radio Service) terminals, SIP (Session Initiation Protocol) [2] terminals, soft phones, digital set top boxes, cable modems, etc.

At present, similar services are offered to users both on so-called fixed accesses and on mobile networks. However, these services are still considered, up to now, as different customers, with different service configurations and no bridging possible between the different services. A major feature of NGN will be *generalized mobility*, which will allow a consistent provision of services to a user, i.e., the user will be regarded as a unique entity when utilizing different access technologies, regardless of their types.

Generalized mobility means providing the ability of using different access technologies, at different locations while the user and/or the terminal equipment itself may be in movement allowing users to use and manage consistently their applications/customer services across existing network boundaries.

At present mobility is used in a limited sense such as movement of user and terminal and with or without service continuity to similar public access networks (such as WLAN, GSM, UMTS, etc.) and service discontinuity to some wireline access networks with strong limitations. In the future, mobility will be offered in a broader sense where users may have the ability to use more access technologies, allowing movement between public wired access points and public wireless access points of various technologies. This means that this movement will not necessarily force an interruption of an application in use or a customer service [1].

One of the most important features of NGN is the independence of different layers. This feature is inherited from the Internet. Because of this feature, NGN is an open environment. This means that it is much easier to develop new and better services comparing to legacy networks such as PSTN. The benefits of migration from the legacy networks to NGN are clear, but on the other hand this migration can cause some serious challenges.

One of the critical issues in Next Generation Networks (NGN) development is QoS provisioning and resource management. Services which have been offered in PSTN so far should be offered now in NGN with the same or even better quality while these two networks are quite different from a technical point of view. In PSTN/PLMN, QoS is guaranteed due to allocation of a dedicated circuit to each call, while in packet-based networks there is not any dedicated circuit and usually resources of the network are shared between all users. Different applications generate different types of traffic each of which has its own QoS requirements. Therefore, the network resources have to be managed so that each call gets enough resources to guarantee the quality of service.

This has made clear-sighted organizations such as ITU and ETSI to propose models and architectures for provision of resource management in NGN networks. The models and architectures include various elements in each layer and specified protocols are used between these elements. Some of these protocols have evolved and have become mature, while the others are still being developed [3].

An architecture which has been introduced by ITU-T for the sake of resource management is called RACF (Resource and Admission Control Function), which is introduced and presented in the next sections. ETSI has also recommended a model for resource and admission control in NGN that is envisaged as an instance of ITU RACF for fixed access networks [4].

This paper gives an overview of some mobility and QoS issues in NGN and related current standardization efforts. The rest of the paper is organized as follows. The next section is an overview of NGN architecture and its main layers and functions and their roles in the architecture. In section 3, the different aspects of mobility in NGN are discussed and the mobility management architecture and its functionalities are presented. Resource and admission control function in NGN and its mobility considerations is discussed in section 4 and finally, section 5 concludes the paper.

2 NGN Architecture

The main characteristic of NGN is its layered architecture in which service-related functions are independent from underlying transport-related technologies. The separation is represented by two distinct layers or strata of functionality. The transport functions reside in the *transport stratum* and the service functions related to applications reside in the *service stratum*. Figure 1 illustrates this architecture [5].

In general, any and all types of network technologies may be deployed in the transport stratum, including connection-oriented circuit-switched (CO-CS), connection-oriented packet-switched (CO-PS) and connectionless packet-switched (CL-PS) technologies. For NGN it is considered that IP (Internet Protocol) is the preferred protocol used to provide NGN services as well as supporting legacy services.

The services platforms provide the user services, such as a telephone service, a Web service, etc. The service stratum may involve a complex set of geographically distributed services platforms or in the simple case just the service functions in two end-user sites.

The NGN framework is expected to support advanced architecture objectives, to enable the offering of a comprehensive set of services over a unified IP layer network. The NGN is expected to support a multiplicity of access transport functions and a

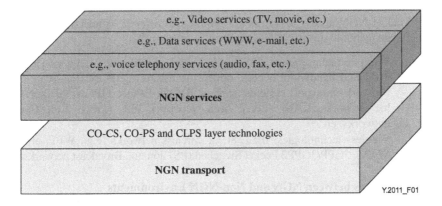

Fig. 1. NGN Overall Architecture

variety of mobile and fixed terminal types. Services are not limited to those provided by the "home network," but may be obtained from multiple service providers and third parties. Services are able to traverse multiple providers' networks. The functions that are supported by NGN are illustrated in Figure 2. The figure shows the main functions in each stratum and includes the interfaces between NGN and end-user functions, between NGN and other networks, and between NGN and Applications.

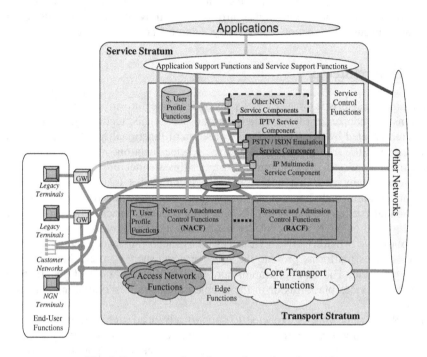

Fig. 2. Transport and service configuration of the NGN

All kind of NGN access networks are required to offer IP connectivity. Some of the candidate technologies in NGN access are as follows:

- Wireline technologies: xDSL (e.g., ADSL, SDSL and VDSL), PDH/SDH dedicated bandwidth access, optical access (e.g., xPON (Passive Optical Network) transport systems, such as BPON, EPON, GPON, GEPON), cable networks, LANs (Local Area Network), PLC (Power Line Carrier) networks, etc.
- Wireless technologies: IEEE 802.x wireless networks (e.g., Wi-Fi and Wi-MAX), 3GPP/3GPP2 Packet Switched (PS) domain, Broadcast networks, etc.

2.1 Interactions between NGN and Non-NGN Environments

Unlike an NGN, many existing networks and their services are vertically integrated, i.e., do not have a clear separation between services and packet transport.

It is clear that many services have to be operated across a hybrid combination of NGN and non-NGN technologies. In such cases interworking arrangements will be necessary. Interworking is a complex subject, involving arrangements between one or more layers of both the NGN and non-NGN architectures.

The NGN is required to support access to and from other networks that provide communications, services and content. Direct interconnection with the PSTN/ISDN will be supported by means of interworking functions (e.g., Media/Signaling gateways) implemented within the NGN. The followings are the Network-to-Network interconnection capabilities which have to be supported:

- Circuit based legacy networks: PSTN/ISDN, PLMN (Public Land Mobile Network)
- Other IP based networks: public Internet, Cable networks, Broadcast networks, other multimedia networks (3GPP/3GPP2 IMS) [6]

3 Mobility in NGN

The NGN architecture is expected to support all kind of mobility (i.e., generalized mobility) while providing the required resources to guarantee the quality of service for users. In the next subsections the migration path from existing mobile networks toward next generation networks is reviewed and then some aspects of the mobility management in 2G and NGN are presented.

3.1 Mobile Networks' Infrastructure Evolution

Many mobile operators are currently upgrading their second-generation networks to evolved 2G (2.5G) and third-generation systems. The major 2G mobile networks are based on four technologies: Global System for Mobile Communications (GSM), Personal Digital Cellular (PDC), Universal Wireless Communications 136 (UWC-136), and Code Division Multiple Access (CDMA).

The generally accepted 3G migration path is to upgrade the GSM network to the 2.5G General Packet Radio Service (GPRS). With a data transfer rate of up to 171 kilobits per second, more than 10 times current standards, GPRS provides more effective mobile data capabilities. The GSM/GPRS network will in turn evolve into EDGE (Enhanced Data Rates for Global Evolution) and finally into the Universal Mobile Telecommunications System (UMTS), with speeds in excess of 2 megabits per second [7].

Mobile users will be able to use the high capacity and bit rates that UMTS offers to send and receive sounds, images, and streaming video. UMTS will also use wide area network radio technologies such as wideband code division multiple access (WCDMA) to bridge Bluetooth networks, wireless local area networks (WLANs), high-performance radio local area networks (HiperLANs), and wireless personal-area networks (WPANs).

Existing mobile networks primarily use circuit switching to deliver voice and data, but multimedia services require more efficient packet-switched networks capable of sharing available transmission capacity for multiple user sessions. Separating service, control, and signaling functions enables real-time as well as non-real-time applications in one physical channel and facilitates the introduction of new services.

UMTS offers this capability through its Internet protocol Multimedia Subsystem (IMS). Approved by the Third Generation Partnership Project (3GPP) in March 2002 as part of UMTS Release 5, IMS provides packet-based transport for both data and voice services. Figure 3 illustrates the IMS architecture in UMTS and the main functions in each plane.

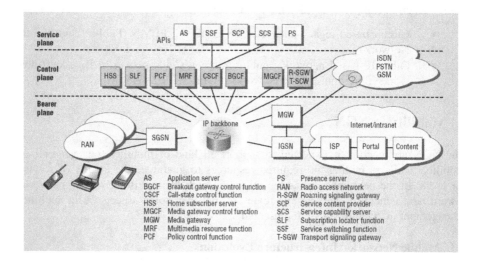

Fig. 3. IMS architecture in UMTS

Multimedia services typically require multiple sessions over one physical channel. Such capability will be possible with packet-switched networks. They share available physical transmission capacity for several sessions, either for one user or among all users leading to more efficient capacity utilization compared to the traditional circuit switching.

The common protocol set for this is IP. It allows distributed functionality, network intelligence, packet-based radio access and backbone, open platforms, and mediation technologies. Additionally, adding SIP into the UMTS IP multimedia subsystem separates signaling and control tasks from end-to-end user information exchange, letting the user manage several multimedia real-time and non-real-time sessions simultaneously.

The 3GPP and 3GPP2 developed a complete set of globally applicable standards for a 3G system when they began in 1998. 3GPP based the development on the evolved GSM core network and a new radio interface using the WCDMA technique. This radio interface covers two operation modes: frequency division duplex (FDD) and time division duplex (TDD) to make use of paired and unpaired frequency bands in the 2-GHz range. The first specification release was approved in 1999 (R99), then followed by Release 4 in 2000 and Release 5 in 2002. The work started from a network architecture comprising circuit-switched and packet-switched domains in Release 99 and Release 4.

The transition to all-IP is part of UMTS Release 5 and Release 6. It encompasses the end-user terminal, the radio and core network, and the gateway to external networks [8].

3.2 Mobility Management in 2G Networks

Mobility management in second-generation (2G) cellular networks is supported by two international standards: the Electronic/Telecommunications Industry Associations Interim Standard 41 (EIA/TIA IS-41) mostly used in the United States for the AMPS and IS-54/IS-136 networks, and the GSM Mobile Application Part (MAP) for GSM, DCS-1800, and PCS-1900. In both cases, the call processing and location management functions are based on Signaling System 7 (SS7). As shown in Figure 4, 2G networks are organized in cells, while the switching center responsible for a specific geographical or logical area is known as the mobile switching center (MSC). Location management is based on location databases, called home location register (HLR) and visitor location register (VLR). VLRs can be considered extra intelligence on each MSC, and contain temporal information for a specific area. HLRs are hierarchical higher databases that contain permanent information for each terminal. The entry of each subscriber is registered in one HLR, including a link to the VLR, which is responsible for the area the terminal is currently visiting [9].

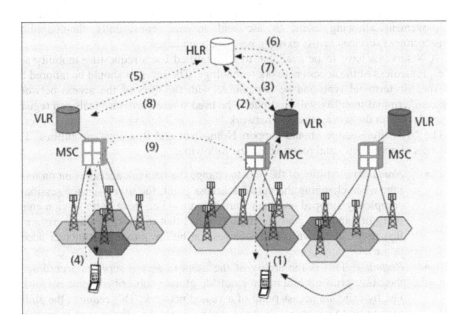

Fig. 4. Reference architecture of a 2G network

When a mobile terminal changes base station, it may roam to a cell that corresponds to a new serving VLR. In that case it has to update the information stored in the HLR. Therefore, the terminal initiates an update message (1), which via the base station and MSC is forwarded to the current associated VLR. The VLR checks its local records. If the terminal's Mobile Identification Number (MIN) is already stored there, no further action takes place, since the terminal has not changed location area. Otherwise, the terminal's MIN is stored locally and a new update message is forwarded to the HLR (2). The HLR in turn authenticates the terminal and replies with a positive registration acknowledgment to the new VLR (3). Additionally, the HLR may send a registration cancellation message to the old VLR, or a periodical mechanism may automatically update the VLR database and remove out-of-date entries.

Whenever a new connection is initiated (4) the VLR will check its local records again for the called mobile. If both calling and called parties are in the same servicing area, the call is directly routed to the terminal. Otherwise, the VLR of the calling terminal initiates a location request to the HLR (5). The HLR confirms that the terminal is located in this area and sends a route request message (6). This message is forwarded via the VLR to the serving MSC, which allocates a temporary local directory number (TLDN) for the specific terminal. The TLDN is returned to the HLR (7) and forwarded to the calling VLR (8). Using SS7, a path between the MSCs is established (9), and a paging or alerting message is sent to the called mobile terminal.

3.3 Mobility Management in NGN

Generalized mobility means providing the ability of using different access technologies, at different locations while the user and/or the terminal equipment itself may be in movement allowing users to use and manage consistently their applications/customer services across existing network boundaries.

NGN services have to be available to all qualified users requesting mobility services, regardless of the access network technology. The services should be tailored for the specific terminal type and be compatible with the QoS of the access network. Personal/terminal mobility will continue to be used where users/terminals can register themselves with the services/access network.

The NGN architecture should support Nomadism and Roaming capabilities. The concepts of nomadicity and roaming are the following:

- *Nomadism:* Ability of the user to change the network access point on moving; when changing the network access point, the user's service session is completely stopped and then started again – i.e., there is no session continuity or handover possible. It is assumed that the normal usage pattern is that users shutdown the service session before moving to another access point.
- *Roaming:* This is the ability of the users to access services according to their user profile while moving outside of their subscribed home network – i.e., by using an access point of a visited network. This requires the ability of the user to get access in the visited network, the existence of an interface between home network and visited network, as well as a roaming agreement between the respective network operators.

In the NGN, Nomadism and Roaming should not be restricted to a single administrative domain. [10].

Mobility Management Functionalities. Mobility Management (MM) in NGN will be realized by using basic mobility-related functionalities plus associated functionalities. The basic functionalities are concerned directly with mobility management for mobile users and terminals, whereas the associated functionalities are used for supporting MM or for exchanging related information for overall control and management purposes [11]. The basic MM functionalities include location and handover management.

Location management is performed to identify the current network location of a Mobile Terminal (MT) and to keep track of it as it moves. Location management is used for the control of calls and sessions terminated at the MT. Location information is given to the call or session manager for establishing a session. With the help of location management, the correspondent node is able to locate the MT and establish a session via appropriate signalling.

Location management consists of two basic functions: location registration and call delivery/paging. The location registration is the procedure to register the current location when MTs change the attachment point to the network. Call delivery is to deliver packets to the destined MTs and paging is used to search the MTs in dormant mode.

The LM function is used to keep track of the movement of a UE in the network and to locate the UE for data delivery. The LM function is used for supporting the prospective 'incoming' session (or call) to the mobile user. The LM functionality includes the following subfunctions: location registration/update and location query/response (for user data transport) that may be performed with a service control function for call/session establishment.

The location registration and update functions are used to keep track of the current location of a User Equipment (UE). When a UE is attached to the network, it will register its current location with the location database for LM. When the UE moves into the other network, the corresponding Location ID (LID) will be updated. In the location registration and update function, the information of mapping between User ID (UID) and LID for a specific UE will be managed and updated all the time. [12]

Handover management is used to provide MTs with session continuity whenever they move into different network regions and change their point of attachment to the network during a session. The main objective of seamless handover is to minimize service disruption due to data loss and delay during the handover. Most MM protocols perform handover management together with an appropriate location management scheme. According to the handover areas concerned, the handover types can be classified into "handover within an Access Network (AN)", where the MT moves within a region covered by the same AN in NGN, and "handover between different ANs or Core Networks (CN)", where the MT changes its concerned access system for ongoing sessions.

Requirements for Mobility Management. Followings are some general requirements for MM in NGN regardless of MM types.

- Harmonization with IP-based networks

The NGN is envisaged to be IP-based. Accordingly, the MM protocols for NGN should be IP-based or, at least, well-harmonized with IP technology for its efficient and integrated operation in such future networks.

- Separation of control and transport functions

The transport plane should be separated from the control plane for efficient mobility management and scalability. Such separation of control and transport planes provides the architectural flexibility that facilitates the introduction of new technologies and services. Open interfaces between the control plane functions and the transport plane functions are necessary to implement their separation.

- QoS support

The MM protocols must support QoS, which mobile users require, to support QoS-required services such as VoIP, streaming, and so on as well as convenient Internet best-effort services.

- Independence from network access technologies

It is expected that NGN will consist of an IP-based core network with several access networks that may use different access technologies. In this architecture, MM should provide mobility between either homogeneous or heterogeneous types of access networks that belong to the same or different operators. Accordingly, it is required that MM be independent of the underlying access network technologies such as 2/3G Cellular, WLAN, etc.

Mobility Management Control Function (MMCF). As a control function, the MMCF operates independently of the data transport scheme used in the network. The MMCF can further be divided into Location Management Function (LMF) and Handover Control Function (HCF) for location management and handover control, respectively.

The MMCF includes Location Management Function (LMF) and Handover Control Function (HCF). It is noted that the LMF and HCF functions represent the logical functions and thus those two functions can be implemented on either a single network component or different network components, which depends on implementation. The MM signalling operations may include interworking between LMF and HCF via an internal or external interface. MMCF shall be added to the existing NGN functional architecture.

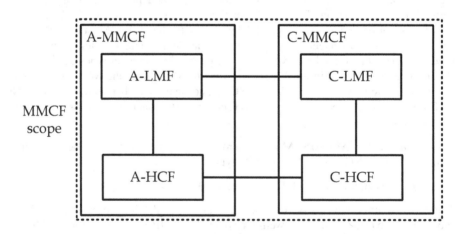

Fig. 5. Structure of MMCFs

Figure 5 illustrates the MMCFs in the NGN. The MMCFs can be classified into A-MMCF and C-MMCF, and each MMCF will contain the LMF and HCF. The MM framework will focus on the functionality and information flows associated with the MMCFs which will also interact with the other NGN functions or functional entities for MM [12].

4 Resource Management and QoS Control in NGN

As mentioned before, QoS provisioning and resource management is one of the most important issues in development of NGN. Over the past several years there has been a considerable amount of research within the field of QoS and resource management support for NGN. To date, most of the work has occurred within the context of architectural models and required protocols in different layers.

The main part of current international research activities in this field is being actively discussed in ITU-T, ETSI and IETF. In the next subsections we are going to overview these activities and efforts. First, the related work in ETSI and IETF is briefly discussed and then the ITU standardization progress and its proposed architecture for resource management in NGN are presented in detail.

4.1 Related Research Work by ETSI and IETF

ETSI NGN architecture is based on the IMS (IP multimedia subsystem) specification delivered by 3GPP (The 3rd Generation Partnership Project), which is the 3rd generation mobile network organization. Telecommunications and Internet converged Services and Protocols for Advanced Networking (TISPAN) as a technical and standardization body of ETSI, developed the IMS architecture to fit the specific requirements of fixed-line networks. TISPAN presented a functional architecture for network resource management in the access and aggregation networks called Resource and Admission Control Sub-system (RACS).

The RACS is responsible for elements of policing control, including resource reservation and admission control in the access and aggregation networks [13]. RACS can be viewed as a particular instantiation of ITU RACF which we are going to describe in the next subsection.

In the Internet Engineering Task Force (IETF), current QoS control work is focused on resource management and QoS signaling protocol completion, deployment, operation, and refinement.

Two framework QoS solutions were proposed by IETF: resource reservation (Integrated Services - IntServ) or service classification (Differentiated Services - Diffserv). QoS signaling mechanisms were developed inside these frameworks. Currently, the IETF QoS policy framework considers policies of the network operator aimed at automated DiffServ and IntServ configurations [14]. The IETF Policy Framework is aimed at representing, managing, sharing and reusing policies in a vendor independent, interoperable, and scalable manner ([15], [16]) and is based on the interactions of a policy management application, a policy repository, a policy decision and a policy enforcement point.

Most of the NGN/IMS protocols are standardized by IETF (e.g. the Session Initiation Protocol (SIP)). Some of these protocols will be introduced in sections 4 and 5.

4.2 Resource and Admission Control Functional Architecture

Figure 6 illustrates a simplified model of resource and admission control architecture recommended by ITU for supporting end-to-end QoS in NGN [17]. In this architecture RACF acts as the mediator between Service Control Functions (SCF) and transport functions for QoS-related transport. One of the basic functionalities of RACF is to make decisions according to defined policies based on resources status in transport layer and also based on utilization information, Service Level Agreements (SLA), network policy rules, and service priorities. The RACF presents a view of transport network infrastructure to the SCF so that service providers do not need to know the details of the transport layer such as network topology, connectivity, resource utilization, QoS mechanisms, etc. The RACF interacts with the SCF and transport functions for the applications that require resource control in the transport layer. SIP-based call flows presented in this paper are examples of such applications.

The SCF represents the functional entities of NGN service layer such as call servers and SIP proxies which can request QoS resource and admission control for media flows of a given service via its interface to RACF.

The RACF applies control policies to transport resources, e.g., routers, upon SCF requests, determines whether transport resource is available, and makes admission decisions. The RACF interacts with transport functions to control the following tasks in the transport stratum from the QoS point of view: bandwidth reservation and allocation, traffic classification, traffic marking, traffic policing, and priority handling.

As illustrated in Figure 6, functional entities of RACF are PD-FE (Policy Decision Functional Entity) and TRC-FE (Transport Resource Control Functional Entity).

The main functionality of PD-FE and TRC-FE is to make policy decisions and to determine network resources availability, respectively.

Dividing RACF into two distinct functions, i.e., PD-FE and TRC-FE, enables it to support variant networks within a general resource control framework. Also the PE-FE (Policy Enforcement Functional Entity) in the transport layer is a gateway at the boundary of different packet networks, e.g., edge routers, and/or between the CPE (Customer Premises Equipment) and access networks. Dynamic QoS is enforced in PE-FE.

The capabilities of transport networks and associated transport profiles of the subscribers are considered in RACF to support the transport resource control function. The interaction between RACF and Network Attachment Control Functions (NACF) includes network access registration, authentication and authorization, parameter configuration, etc., for checking transport subscriber profiles.

NACF encompasses a collection of functional entities that provide a variety of functions for network management and configuration to provide user access based on the user profiles.

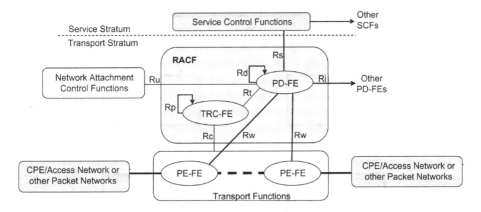

Fig. 6. Resource and admission control functional architecture in NGN

4.3 Mobility Considerations in RACF

The QoS control architecture in both RACF and RACS are closely related with the 3GPP effort. The 3GPP was originally founded for developing new service architecture over cellular networks, especially for the GSM network. During this effort, the 3GPP developed the IMS for controlling the IP multimedia services in the areas of session control, service control, and subscriber database management. Even though IMS was initially developed for the evolution of GSM cellular networks, its framework can be applied to any type of transport technology. The IMS architecture has been adopted by the other QoS control architectures, such as 3GPP2 multimedia domain (MMD), ETSI TISPAN, and ITU-T NGN. Thus, both RACS and RACF are interoperable with IMS. [18]

In order to support resource control for mobility, the RACF shall be able to install and revoke policy in the transport network. The following are the scenarios for mobility. In the next subsections two scenarios for mobility regarding resource control are presented.

Resource Control Scenario for Nomadism. In this scenario SCF sends the call requests to the RACF for nomadic users. There are two transport functions controlled by their own RACFs, and the two RACFs are connected with the same SCF as shown in Figure 7. The following is the scenario when a nomadic user moves from network 1 to network 2.

The user is registered in network 1 and is going to move to network2. The events are as follows:

(1) UE sends a deregistration message to SCF before moving to network 2.
(2) After receiving the message from UE, SCF send a request to RACF1 to revoke the installed policy for the services provided for the UE in network 1.
(3) RACF1 revokes the policy in transport function 1.
(4) The UE send a service request to SCF from network 2.
(5) SCF sends a request to RACF 2 with service information.
(6) The RACF2 enforce the policy in the transport function 2.

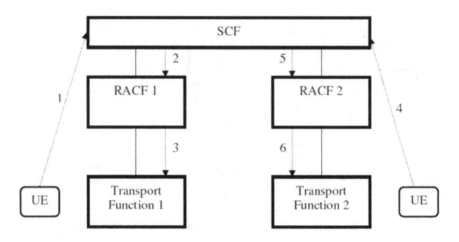

Fig. 7. The scenario for nomadic user

For the case that RACF1 and RACF2 are connected with different SCFs, the scenarios are similar to the above except that in step 2 and 5, the service requests are sent by different SCFs.

Hand-over Procedure for Supporting Mobile Terminals. RACF is required for providing seamless QoS of mobile terminals. Mobile terminals will conform to hand-over procedures when moving between networks. Multimedia services such as Video Phone require seamless QoS to provide regulated bandwidth to users even during the hand-over procedure.

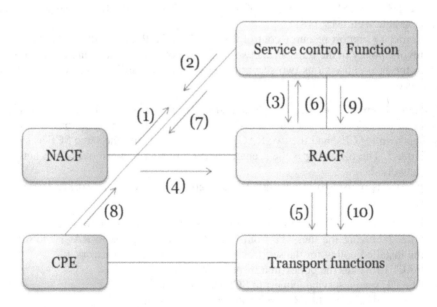

Fig. 8. A possible scenario for providing Seamless QoS

Various types of Access Networks incorporated in NGN may involve possibilities of hand-over between different networks. To provide seamless QoS in this situation, services and policies between access network providers should be defined first. The access network providers need to have QoS parameters that are unified or compatible. In addition, it is required to consider specific cases for RACF during the hand-over procedures, where NACF should deliver QoS parameters corresponding to access networks in response to the request of RACF. Figure 8 illustrates the detailed procedure, including the policy decision and parameter transaction.

(1) A CPE (mobile terminal) moves and detects conditions demanding hand-over. Then it requests hand-over preparation to the SCF.
(2) After SCF receives the hand-over preparation request from the CPE, it starts a decision process on permission of the request to resource allocation.
(3) SCF requests resource allocation to RACF.
(4) RACF collects information including QoS parameters (e.g., DSCP marking) from NACF. Then RACF establishes policies after analyzing the collected information.
(5) RACF applies QoS parameters, corresponding to the policy established for the Access Network, to transport functions.
(6) RACF provides information including QoS parameters necessary for hand-over procedure to SCF to be applied to the CPE.
(7) SCF then applies QoS parameters regarding Access Network to the CPE by sending a response to the hand-over preparation request.
(8) CPE requests hand-over to SCF. SCF then carries out hand-over procedure on receipt of the hand-over request and finally notifies completion of the procedure to CPE.
(9) SCF notifies hand-over status to RACF and requests the release of resources on the Access Network with which previously communicated.
(10) RACF indicates resource release to Transport functions.

The above described procedures are only two possible scenarios for mobility regarding resource management. However this is an open issue and future work is needed to clarify the impact of mobility management to RACF.

5 Conclusion

This paper examined the mobility and QoS control in NGN. These two topics are open issues and there are some challenges in development of the desired models and architectures for them. NGN is needed to be able to deliver generalized mobility and at the same time keep and guarantee the required quality of service for end users. The migration path from legacy toward the next generation mobile networks has discussed and the mobility management architecture and scenarios presented in both. Also the resource management and QoS control architecture and the related activities in standardization bodies have discussed and the RACF proposed by ITU and its mobility considerations studied in more details. It can be seen that there are some open issues which need more studies.

The future direction of NGN is undoubtedly the convergence of fixed and mobile networks and customer equipment. Although there are some problems and concerns in migration toward NGN, most of operators are upgrading their networks to the next generation one. In other words, the NGN is no longer a next generation objective, but is becoming a present generation reality.

References

1. ITU-T Rec. Y.2001: General overview of NGN (2004)
2. Rosenberg, J., et al.: SIP: Session Initiation Protocol. RFC 3261 (2002)
3. Safavi Hemami, M., Pirhadi, M., Iravani Tabrizipoor, A.: Analysis and Optimization of Resource Control Schemes in Next Generation Networks. ITU/IEEE K-INGN08, Geneva (2008)
4. ETSI ES 282 003 v1.1.1: Resource and Admission Control Sub-system (RACS); Functional Architecture (2006)
5. ITU-T Rec. Y.2011: General principles and general reference model for Next Generation Networks (2004)
6. Lee, C.-S., Morita, N.: Next Generation Network Standards in ITU-T (2006)
7. Huber, J.F.: Toward the mobile Internet. Computer 35 (2002)
8. Huber, J.F.: Mobile next-generation networks. IEEE Multimedia (2004)
9. Zahariadis, T.B., et al.: Global roaming in next-generation networks. IEEE Communications Magazine (2002)
10. ATIS: Next Generation Network (NGN) Framework (2006)
11. ITU-T Rec. Q.1706: Mobility management requirements for NGN (2006)
12. ITU-T Rec. Q.1707: Generic Framework of Mobility Management for Next Generation Networks (2008)
13. ETSI ES 282 003 v1.1.1: Resource and Admission Control Sub-system (RACS); Functional Architecture (2006)
14. Snir, Y., et al.: Policy Quality of Service (QoS) Information Model. RFC 3644 (2003)
15. Moore, B., et al.: Policy Core Information Model; Version 1 Specification. RFC 3060 (2001)
16. Moore, B.: Policy Core Information Model (PCIM) Extensions. RFC 3460 (2003)
17. ITU-T Rec. Y.2111: Resource and admission control functions in Next Generation Networks (Release 2), NGN-GSI/DOC – 301 (2007)
18. Song, J., et al.: Overview of ITU-T NGN QoS Control. IEEE Communications Magazine (2007)

Mapping Rule of Workflow-XML Resource Model for Asynchronous Web Service

Myung-ju[1], Jin-Sung Kim[2], Dong-Soo Kim[1], and Yong-Sung Kim[1]

[1] Division of Electronics and Information Engineering, Chonbuk National University,
664-14 1ga Duckjin-Dong Duckjin-Gu Jeonju, Repubic of Korea
{silk,dskim,yskim}@chonbuk.ac.kr
[2] Center for Teaching & Learning, Wonkwang University, Repubic of Korea
kpjiju@wku.ac.kr

Abstract. Workflow has an important role that provide back-end services to response font-end requirements. The workflow technique reduces the time of process, allocates resource powerfully and improves the performance of enterprises. Workflow-XML(workflow-XML) is the language defining XML-based protocol suggested for the mutual interoperability of workflow engine, as an asynchronous web service protocol. We define rule that change Workflow-XML document to UML's class diagram and collaboration diagram. And each entity that compose Workflow-XML resources model in class diagram, interoperability between entity verifies proposal method mapped by collaboration diagram. For this, this paper defines the mapping rule to convert Workflow-XML document to UML class diagram and collaboration diagram, and suggests a technique to model each entity of Workflow-XML resource model to a class diagram and the interaction between entities to a collaboration diagram.

1 Introduction

Recently, many companies struggle to construct the web service in which unique business process formalized in association with other companies as well as in-house is connected to participating partners in order to secure profitability[1]. The web service is the method independent of a platform, through the standardized XML based interface and not affected by a specific language and hardware, as the activities connecting to application on a network[2]. By organically interoperating every inter-related application, a company integrates and manages any necessary information and standardizes the business process that executes the collaboration between and among the applications in accordance with the defined procedure, improving the efficiency and productivity of the business environment[3]. 'Workflow' is the representative technique to standardize the above business process and the standard for the 'workflow' is presented as the reference workflow model by the 'Workflow Management Coalition' so that a part of the process between and among services executing homogeneous or different workflows is delivered to a different workflow service, providing collaborative work[4]. Then, the workflow-related providers have developed and used Workflow-XML, a XML-based protocol language in order for the inter-working between workflow engines.

T.-h. Kim et al. (Eds.): FGCN 2008, CCIS 27, pp. 105–115, 2009.
© Springer-Verlag Berlin Heidelberg 2009

Therefore, this paper suggests a modeling facilitating business partners to comprehend the workflow for their interlink of workflow engines and cooperation by modeling the resource model provided by Workflow-XML through UML(unified modeling language)[5, 6] diagram.

2 Related Studies

The chapter compares and analyzes the previous studies relating to XML schema and Workflow-XML document modeling. First of all, the studies of [5, 6 and 7] are related with modeling XML schema to UML class diagram. [5] suggests a way of modeling XML schema structure to UML class diagram. The study adds, based on the expression of [5], the correlation between classes and establishes the rule to convert XML schema to ULM class diagram. In addition, [6] and [7] describe the modeling procedure of XML schema for the major objects. Especially, they suggest the modeling procedure such as stereo type, number of repeat, inherited attribute of class and others in detail. And, looking into the several studies about XPDL document modeling, there are study [8] expressing the business process in a production system using the workflow concept as UML activity diagram and study [9] designing a distributed collaborative work flow as UML diagram. The study [8] expressed each entity of which a production system applied with the workflow concept consists as an UML class diagram and models the detail process activities as an UML activity diagram. Since the study models the work flow of a specific stream mainly with an activity diagram, the mapping technique is not mentioned in detail.

Therefore, the study defines the mapping rule and mapping table to model the entity for Workflow-XML resource model and the message transfer between entities and suggests, based on the foresaid definitions, a method to execute the object modeling for Workflow-XML resource model and the interaction modeling by using UML class diagram and collaboration diagram. If using the modeling method suggested in the study, an expression method standardized for the Workflow-XML resource model can be provided and the method also can be applied over the entire process of the workflow process modeling.

3 Asynchronous Web Service Protocol

Web service interface can be classified into two types; synchronous web service and asynchronous web service. These two architectures can be distinguished by the request-response process method. While a client makes a request for service in the synchronous service and waits for the response, a client makes a request for service and continues the previous work, instead of waiting for the response.

3.1 ASAP

ASAP(Asynchronous Service Access Protocol), an asynchronous web service protocol of OASIS, defines web service as instance, factory and observer, depending on the roles between entities and operates it accordingly. If the 'Observer' method requires Factory method to create an instance, the 'Factory' method responds to it and requires

'Instance' method to create an instance. Finally, an instance is completely created in the 'Instance' method.

3.2 Workflow-XML

Workflow-XML, an asynchronous web service protocol of OASIS, defines the XML-based protocol suggested by WfMC for the inter-working of workflow engines.

3.2.1 Workflow-XML Resource Model and Method

The workflow system using an asynchronous web service provides asynchronous service based on the workflow system resource model suggested by Workflow-XML standard as major components are interoperating with each resource. Workflow-XML defines 5 types of resources according to the roles of operation as presented in [Fig. 1].

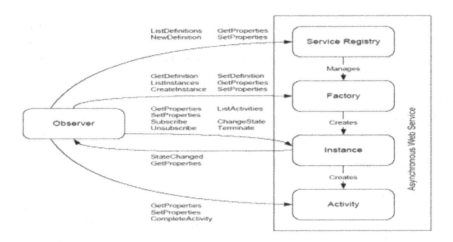

Fig. 1. Workflow-XML resource model

(1) Observer Resource Type Entity

'Observer' is the resource to detect and interpret a service requested to use an event that occurs when business process related service is executed or a service of work flow from the outside.

(2) ServiceRegistry Resource Type Entity

ServiceRegistry resource plays a role of saving the data to define a work flow process, the main body providing service and can load the process definition from the existing system or add it.

(3) Factory Resource Type Entity

Factory resource entity describes how to work with the service content and creates the instance service that actually executes the service.

(4) Instance Resource Type Entity.

Instance resource actually executes a work; for instance, it executes the start, stop, resume and end of a process service.

(5) Activity Resource Type Entity

Activity resource, a resource extended for Workflow-XML in ASAP, executes a designated service.

3.2.2 XML Schema Modeling

XML Schema[14] is XML document structure phenotype that extend and supplements function that is not offered in existent DTD. Examine element's role and characteristic that compose XML Schema in this section, and recognize about XML Schema modeling to apply in Workflow-XML schema modeling.

(1) <Element> Element

<Element> in class diagram to do modeling, express reference relation because express <<element>> Stereotype and Element name on class name part, and use dependence with <<has type>> Stereotype about each elements that Element refers.

(2) <ComplexType> Element

<ComplexType> is element that define type and attribute about Element and sub Element etc. This in UML class diagram to do modeling, express name of <<ComplexType>> Stereotype and ComplexType on class name part and class attribute part expresses low rank Elements that ComplexType includes.

(3) <SimpleType> Element

<SimpleType> is element that declare simplicity style about Element. This in UML class diagram to do modeling, express name of <<SimpleType>> Stereotype and SimpleType on class name part and class attribute part expresses low rank Elements that include simplicity style in SimpleType.

(4) Identification

Identification uses in case division is vague like when there is no name complexType or simpleType or <sequence> tag. Method to do modeling in UML class diagram expresses this as "Element name : *" in case there is no ComplexType's name that is included in specification Element.

4 Data Modeling about Workflow-XML Resource Model

The chapter describes modeling the schema of each entity of which Workflow-XML resource model consists as an UML class diagram and modeling the collaboration procedure between entities to execute web services as an collaboration diagram.

4.1 Workflow-XML Resource Type Entity Modeling

The entity of Workflow-XML resource model is expressed with Workflow-XML schema. The following shows the definition to map the Workflow-XML schema as an UML class diagram.

> **[Definition 1]** To execute a web service, the Workflow-XML schema for each entity of Workflow-XML resource model is mapped as UML class diagram.

4.1.1 Observer Resource Entity

Observer resource entity is expressed as <<observerPropertiesGroup>> in the Work-flow-XML, and the modeling rule is as follows.

> **[Rule 1]** The observerPropertiesGroup element is expressed in the <<Group>> stereotype and the sub element is expressed as a grouping relation(◆).

The following figure shows the results when applying the above [Rule 1] to the ob-server resource element.

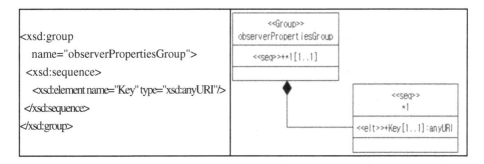

Fig. 2. <observerPropertiesGroup> Example of an element and the modeling results

4.1.2 ServiceRegistry Resource Type Entity

ServiceRegistry entity is expressed as <<serviceRegistryPropertiesGroup>> and the modeling rule is as follows.

> **[Rule 2]** The serviceRegistryPropertiesGroup is expressed in <<Group>> stereotype, the sub element is expressed as a grouping relation(◆) and the external reference element is expressed as a <<elt>> stereotype.

The following figure shows the results when applying [Rule 2] to the service registry element.

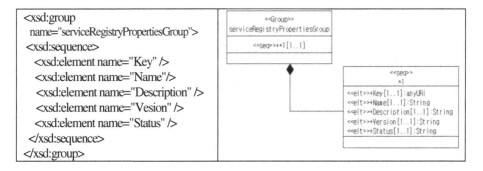

Fig. 3. Example of <serviceRegistryPropertiesGroup> element and the modeling results

4.1.3 Factory Resource Entity

Factory resource entity is expressed as <<factoryPropertiesGroup>> in the Workflow-XML and the modeling rule is as follows.

> **[Rule 3]** The factoryPropertiesGroup is expressed in <<Group>> stereotype, the sub element is expressed as a grouping relation(◆) and the external reference element is expressed as a <<elt>> stereotype.

The following figure shows the results when applying [Rule 3] to the service registry element.

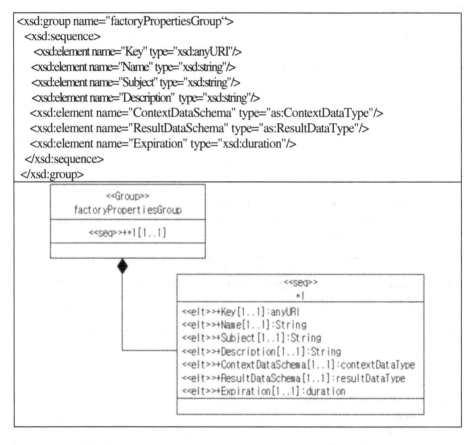

Fig. 4. Example of a <Factory> element and the modeling results

4.1.4 Instance Resource Type Entity

Instance resource entity is expressed as <<InstancePropertiesGroup>> in Workflow-XML and the modeling rule is as follows.

[Rule 4] The instancePropertiesGroup is expressed in <<Group>> stereotype, the sub element is expressed as a grouping relation(◆) and the external reference element is expressed as a <<elt>> stereotype. In addition, the composite data type of Observers, ContextData and ResultData is expressed in <<ComplexType>> stereotype.

The following figure shows the results when applying [Rule 4] to the service registry element.

```
<xsd:group name="InstancePropertiesGroup">
 <xsd:sequence>
  <xsd:element name="key" type = "xsd:anyURI"/>
  <xsd:element name="state" type="stateType"/>
  <xsd:element name="Name" type="xsd:string"/>
  <xsd:element name="Subject" type="xsd:string"/>
  <xsd:element name="Description" type="xsd:string"/>
  <xsd:element name="FactoryKey" type="xsd:anyURI"/>
  <xsd:element name="Observers">
 </xsd:group>
```

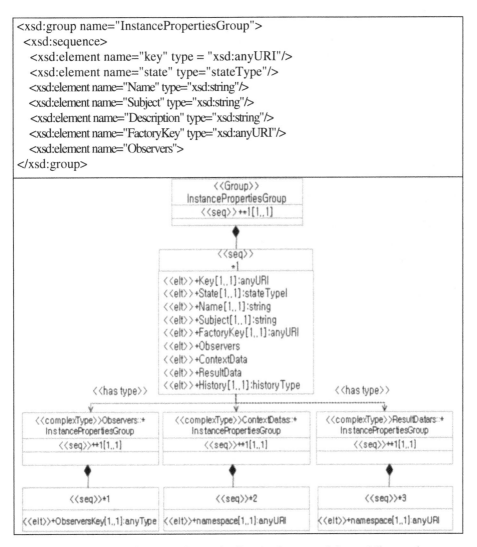

Fig. 5. Example of <InstancePropertiesGroup> element and the modeling results

4.1.5 Activity Resource Type Entity

The activity resource entity is expressed as <<activityPropertiesGroup>> in Workflow-XML and the modeling rule is as follows.

[Rule 5] The activityPropertiesGroup expressed in <<Group>> stereotype, the sub element is expressed as a grouping relation(◆) and the composite data type of external reference elements is expressed in <<ComplexType>> stereotype.

The following figure shows the results when applying [Rule 5] to the service registry element.

```
<xsd:group name="activityPropertiesGroup">
<xsd:sequence>
  <xsd:element name="Key" type="xsd:anyURI"/>
  <xsd:element name="State" type="as:stateType"/>
  <xsd:element name="Name" type="xsd:string"/>
  <xsd:element name="Description" type="xsd:string"/>
  <xsd:element name="ValidStates">
  <xsd:complexType>
   <xsd:sequence>
     <xsd:element name="ValidState" type="as:stateType" minOccurs="0" maxOccurs="unbounded"/>
   </xsd:sequence>
  </xsd:complexType>
  </xsd:element>
  <xsd:element name="InstanceKey" type="xsd:anyURI"/>
  <xsd:element name="RemoteInstance" type="xsd:anyURI"/>
  <xsd:element name="StartedDate" type="xsd:dateTime"/>
  <xsd:element name="DueDate" type="xsd:dateTime"/>
  <xsd:element name="LastModified" type="xsd:dateTime"/>
</xsd:sequence>
</xsd:group>
```

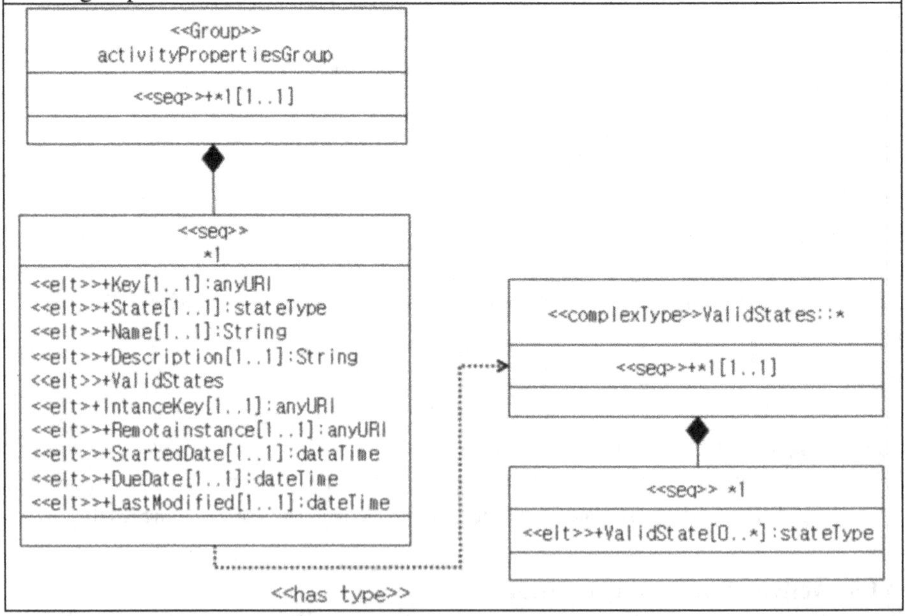

Fig. 6. Example and modeling result of <activityPropertiesGroup>

4.2 Workflow-XML Interaction Resource Entity Modeling

Make rule that map Workflow-XML resources model's interaction resources in UML interaction diagram and do modeling in Workflow-XML resources model's Collaboration Diagram.

> **[Definition 2]** Cooperation and interaction between each Entity of Workflow-XML resources model becomes mapping with UML Collaboration Diagrams.

4.2.1 Observer and ServiceRegistry Entity's Interaction

Because Observer requests information of usable process to ServiceRegistry, newest version etc.. about process name, technology, each process justice respond. Observer interaction between ServiceRegistry Entity rule to do modeling as following.

> **[Rule 6]** Process request and response between Observer Entity and ServiceRegistry express with ListDefinitionsRq/ListDefinitionsRs' method. Also, new process definition request and response express with NewDefinitionRq/NewDefinitionRs method..

Next figure interaction between Observer and ServiceRegistry Entity modeling result that apply [Rule 6].

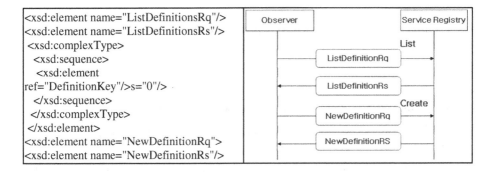

Fig. 7. Interaction example of Observer and ServiceRegistry Entity and modeling result

4.2.2 Observer and Factory Entity's Interaction

Because Observer requests information about acquistition and justice of data to Factory Entity result respond. Observer interaction between Factory Entity rule to do modeling as following.

> **[Rule 7]** Data acquisition request and response between Observer entity and Factory express with GetDefinitionsRq/GetDefinitionsRs' method. Also, definition request and response of data express with SetDefinitionRq/SetDefinitionRs' method .

Next picture interaction between Observer and Factory Entity modeling result that apply[Rule 7].

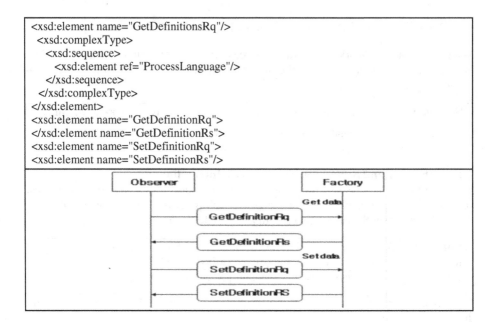

```
<xsd:element name="GetDefinitionsRq"/>
 <xsd:complexType>
   <xsd:sequence>
     <xsd:element ref="ProcessLanguage"/>
   </xsd:sequence>
 </xsd:complexType>
</xsd:element>
<xsd:element name="GetDefinitionRq">
</xsd:element name="GetDefinitionRs">
<xsd:element name="SetDefinitionRq">
<xsd:element name="SetDefinitionRs"/>
```

Fig. 8. Interaction example of Observer and Factory Entity and modeling result

4.2.3 Observer and Instance Entity's Interaction

Observer supplies process service contents to achieve work to instance resources. And instance resources communicate process state that change to observer, and indicate work achievement state.

[Rule 8] Business process request and response to achieve between Observer Entitiy and instance Entity express with ListInstanceRq/ListInstanceRs' method.

Next figure interaction between Observer and Instance Entity modeling result that apply [Rule 8].

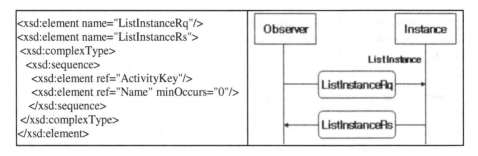

```
<xsd:element name="ListInstanceRq"/>
<xsd:element name="ListInstanceRs">
 <xsd:complexType>
  <xsd:sequence>
   <xsd:element ref="ActivityKey"/>
   <xsd:element ref="Name" minOccurs="0"/>
  </xsd:sequence>
 </xsd:complexType>
</xsd:element>
```

Fig. 9. Interaction example of Observer and Instance Entity and modeling result

5 Conclusion and Further Works

In the age of e-commerce, workflow has an important role that provides back-end services to response font-end requirements. The workflow technique reduces the time of process, allocates resource powerfully and improves the performance of enterprises. Process definition in the workflow contains all of the necessary information related to business process and executed by the workflow management system.

Resource model who offer in Workflow-XML for interoperability of different workflow engine in this paper does modeling in UML diagram. Also propose model who ease analysis for business flowing for interoperability and cooperation. So, we define rule that change Workflow-XML document to UML's Class Diagram and Collaboration Diagram. And each entity that compose Workflow-XML resources model in Class Diagram, interoperability between entities verifies proposal method mapped by Collaboration Diagram. The Contribution of the works is (1) standardization that propose new modeling techniques and apply mapping rule historically with UML's notation. (2) basis technology for corporation interior and external workflow integration. (3) system design and implementation method for Workflow integration.

Future works are Apply actuality situation about business process that is achieved web service and embody by Workflow-XML. Also, result research that can be selected by standard about workflow process justice in inside and outside of the country corporation because do modeling by normalized way achieve .

References

1. Moon, K.-Y.: XML XML information protection abstract. KIPS journal 10(2), 108–116 (2003)
2. Ogbuji, U.: The Past, Present and Future of Web Services (2002),
   http://www.webservices.org/index.phparticle/articleview/663/4/61/
3. The Workflow Reference Model(WFMC-TC-1003) (January 1995),
   http://www.wfmc.org/standardsmodel.htm
4. Routledge, N., Bird, L., Goodchild, A.: UML and XML Schema. In: Australasian Database Conference (ADC 2002), vol. 5, pp. 157–166 (2002)
5. Carlson, D.: Modeling XML Vocabularies with UML: Part I□III (October 2001),
   http://www.xml.com/pub/a/2001/10/10/uml.html
6. XMLmodeling.com UML Models of W3C XML Schema (November 2004),
   http://www.xmlmodeling.com/models/w3c_xsd/v1.0/index.html
7. Bastos, R.M., Duncan Dubugras, A.: Extending UML Activity Diagram for Workflow Modeling in Production Systems. In: Hawaii International Conference on System Sciences (HICSS 2002), vol. 9, pp. 291–301 (2002)
8. Jiang, P., Mair, Q., Newman, J.: Using UML to Design Distributed Coolaborative Workflow: from UML to XPDL. In: Proceedings of the Twelfth IEEE International Workshops on Enabling Technologies: Infrastructure for Collaborative Enterprises (WETICE 2003), pp. 71–77 (2003)
9. Thompson, H.S., Beech, D., Mendelsohn, N., Maloney, M.: XML Schema Part 1: Structures, W3C Recommendation (October 2004),
   http://www.w3.org/TR/xmlschema-1
10. WfMC, Workflow-XML Demo Observer Information Sheet (2003),
    http://www.wfmc.org/standards/wfxml.html

In Search of Unstructured Documents Categorization

Debnath Bhattacharyya[1], Poulami Das[1], Kheyali Mitra[1], Debashis Ganguly[1],
Purnendu Das[1], Samir Kumar Bandyopadhyay[2], and Tai-hoon Kim[3]

[1] Computer Science and Engineering Department, Heritage Institute of Technology,
Kolkata-700107, India
{debnathb,dasp88,DebashisGanguly,kheyalimitra}@gmail.com,
purnendu_das@yahoo.com
[2] Department of Computer Science and Engineering, University of Calcutta,
Kolkata-700009, India
skb1@vsnl.com
[3] Hannam University, Daejeon – 306791, Korea
taihoonn@empal.com

Abstract. Transferring information from one part to another of the world is the main aim of communication. Now a day, the information is available in forms of documents or files created on requirements basis. The more the requirements the large the documents are. That is why; the way of creation which is random in nature as well as storage bends the documents unstructured in nature. The result is that, dealing with these documents becomes a headache. For the ease of process, the frequently required data should maintain certain pattern. But being unfortunate enough, most of the time we have to face problems like erroneous data retrieving or modification anomalies or even a large amount of time may be given for retrieving a single document. To overcome the situation, a solution has raised named unstructured document categorization. This field is a vast one containing all kind of solutions for various type of document categorization. Basically, the documents which are unstructured in nature will be categorized based on some given constraints. And through this paper we would like to highlight the most as well as popular techniques like text and data mining, genetic algorithm, lexical chaining, binarization methods in the field of unstructured document categorization so that we can reach the fulfillment of desired unstructured document categorization.

Keywords: Unstructured Documents, Categorization, Text and Data mining, Genetic Algorithm, Lexical Chaining, Binarization.

1 Introduction

The growth of organizational repositories having large and unstructured document collection is the result of e-commerce and corporate intranets. To understand the need of user and also the state of data, online knowledge transfer, processing, and interpretation of data has led to a new era. To explore this technique properly, the approach to data management, combine and share data sources and data interpretations in a digital world has got the prime priority. But the reality is different. In this world,

T.-h. Kim et al. (Eds.): FGCN 2008, CCIS 27, pp. 116–125, 2009.
© Springer-Verlag Berlin Heidelberg 2009

all documents and data are scattered over the data recovery. The main reason either may be a huge data size or mismanagement of data. And thus it creates problem to retrieve relevant documents from such collections [1]. It is relatively less cumbersome to define categories broadly classifying the information contained in the collection. So, information retrieval and archiving of data as well as efficient storage and transmission of documents to databases have become important issues in research fields. Structured documents have explicit semantics for structural parts.

For many decades, Document summarization became a well-known field for computational linguists among the all which are available for documentation. The existing statistical text learning algorithms can be trained to approximately classify documents. Manual categorization techniques were defined as well as applied to data or document repositories and the actual categorization was done on human judgment. But this was not at all a good technique to accept. So, automation of categorization and filtering of documents was required. This requirement gave birth of various methods and applications. They were used for the purpose of automatic document classification. The Text Mining incorporates methods like information retrieval, computational linguistics and data mining so that it can achieve the goal of an automatic analysis of large and unstructured corpora of digital documents.

In this paper, we have tried to present a detail survey on unstructured document categorization and we hope and believe that this work will definitely provide a perfect overview of what had, have and will be done in this field.

2 Overview

Document categorization is not at all a new field for researcher. It has been started since long pats days. The founder of modern information science, Paul Otlet proceeded to build a structured document collection. The US Department of Defense, along with the National Institute of Standards and Technology (NIST), cosponsored the Text Retrieval Conference (TREC) in the year of 1992. It was built up to look into the information retrieval community by supplying the infrastructure that was needed for evaluation of text retrieval methodologies. In the mid-1980s, the Labor-intensive manual text-mining approaches first surfaced.

Until recently, the only way to capture an unstructured document was to have somebody read it and indexes it. The only way to populate it was to have a live human look at the document and decide where it belongs. That's an expensive way to capture a document. But now there's hope for doing the same far more economically. Auto-classification and extraction technologies arc promising tools for automatically classifying unstructured documents within an index or taxonomy structure. This is the biggest advance in information capture since the invention of document, imaging. But this technology is still relatively new. Gartner Group says auto-classification and extraction am years away from reaching their full potential. On the other hand, governments around the world use it extensively today. And some of the biggest software companies in the world, e.g. Oracle and PeopleSoft, have employed it in their applications.

Many have done, several are eager to be invented. For example, the concept of Neural Network has included neuroscience as a future researching field. A particularly important part of the investigation in recent years has been the exploration of the role of neuro-modulators such as dopamine, acetylcholine, and serotonin on behavior and learning. Biophysical models, such as BCM theory, have been important in understanding mechanisms for synaptic plasticity. Research is ongoing in understanding the computational algorithms used in the brain, with some recent biological evidence for radial basis networks and neural back-propagation as mechanisms for processing data.

3 Approach

3.1 Text and Data Mining Technique

This technique has a great impact in the field of document categorization. Generally this is used in the following approaches.

- GENERATION OF TAXONOMY FOR LARGE DOCUMENT COLLECTION:

Text and data mining are two closely related approaches for information retrieval. Here the main aim is to create automatic taxonomies by using the text and data mining concept and comparing documents on the basis of certain characteristic features they contain. For automatic generation of Taxonomy of   collected documents Lexical Affinity (LA) followed by Linguistic Features (LF) extraction and hierarchical clustering algorithm (HCA) are used. These methods are (LA, LF) generating the output for clustering. Starting from the individual documents HCA algorithm first generates the lower (bottom) cluster. Then it goes higher by grouping the lower level clusters according to necessity. As a result, the automatic taxonomy is generated for the given set of documents [2].

The HTML output from this technique (LF based Taxonomy) is given in the Fig. 1. The output is generated based on names, terms etc. The result is quite satisfactory and stable at about 5000 documents.

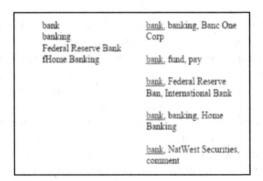

Fig. 1. Node within LF based Taxonomy

- SIMPLE AND FAST TERM SELECTION PROCEDURE FOR TEXT CLUSTERING

Vector–Space Model algorithm is proposed for enhancing the text clustering process by reducing the dimensionality of feature space [3]. This model is generated from the given unstructured documents and used the document as a document to term matrix for calculation procedure.

Thus it gives the limitation to the higher ranked terms of a document. And this is purely concern with saving the time and labor in computation. The result is also quite satisfactory due to cluster with pure efficiency and the number of terms involved in computation is very less which yields computation speed.

3.2 Lexical Chain Technique

Lexical Chain and concept of natural language processing (NLP) are used to generate the concept of document summarization [4]. This summarizer can process the simple" flat" documents as well as complex ones. For generating document summarizer; certain step-by-step approach is followed.

(i) Analyze the structure of documents and classification of the documents and make sets according to predefined categories.
(ii) Using of natural language technique for summarization of documents.
(iii) The summaries (gained from the above steps) are amalgamated with the structure of the actual document to give the exact summary.

Through the structured analysis and concept of lexical chain method, structured as well as unstructured documents can be summarized in a perfect manner. Ultimately the output in XML is given in the Fig.2 and Fig.3.

BCL Corpus

This document describes the creation, maintenance and modification of the BCL Corpus created at BCL Technologies. BCL Technologies develops software solutions necessary for document management and web publishing. It specializes in developing software that analyzes, manipulates and uses information that is stored in different file formats. As part of the customer support BCL Technologies responds to individual queries from customers who are using BCL products and who have questions regarding the products we sell.

The BCL corpus is a written corpus comprised of email messages we receive from our customers. These email messages contain questions, comments and general inquiries regarding our document-conversion products. These email messages were collected between June 2000 and May 2001. We modified the raw email programmatically by deleting the attachments, html and other tags, header files, and senders' information. In addition, we manually deleted salutations, greetings, and any information that was not directly related to customer support. There are around 34,640 lines and 170,000 words in the BCL Corpus. We constantly update our corpus with new email from our customers.

We further pruned down our corpus to create subsets of testing corpora in order to test various modules of the Spoken Language User Interface Toolkit (SLUITK) system. For example, from the BCL corpus, we created a sample test corpus of 1000 mono-clausal inquiry-format sentences to test the end-to-end frame generation module of our system. Similarly, we created a sample test corpus of 50 generic sentences from our corpus to do a preliminary testing of the whole system.

Fig. 2. Given Text

```
<Head>Support BCL Corpus <Head> <ContentWeight>
<1412> <\ContentWeight> <Image Weight>0<\Image Weight> <Link Weight>0<LinkWeight>
```

Fig. 3. After extraction from the above text

3.3 Genetic Algorithm (GA) Technique

This is one of the techniques that are followed in the world of structured documentation. This is specially used in information retrieval (IR) method [5]. It was expected that the combination of GA along with the well-known matching functions would give the satisfactory result than using single matching function. The following figure expresses the general method for information retrieval.

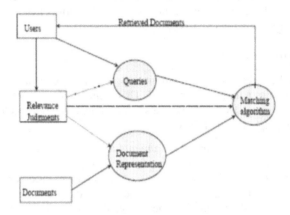

Fig. 4. Information Retrieval System

GA is used to change the descriptions of documents or queries and also the matching functions those are used for IR from any document. In this case, documents and queries are spaced in multi-dimensional vector space for convenience of work. Now, while retrieving the documents those are accepted who are close to the vector-associated with query. The implementation of the algorithm is shown in the Fig.5. The steps are given below.

- GENERATE MATCHING FUNCTION VARIANTS: Randomly chosen values are assigned to each and every matching function.
- MATCHING FUNCTION VARIANTS FITNESS EVALUATION: Overall matching value corresponding to respective documents of a population is computed and then the calculated documents are organized in non-ascending order.
- GENETIC MODIFICATION: It includes four different stages.
  - Selection and reproduction, Crossover, Mutation, Process termination.

Now the total process will be terminated when it finds that after applying genetic modification to individual generation, no such modified out put is found through few consecutive generations.

3.4 Artificial Neural Network Technique

Basically, the neural networks are categorized with respect to their corresponding training algorithms. They are fixed-weights networks, unsupervised networks, and supervised networks. No learning method is required for the fixed-weight networks. That is why a learning mode is supervised or unsupervised in nature [6].

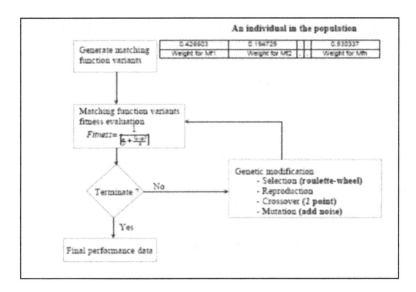

Fig. 5. Genetic Procedure

This is a well-known approach for classification of documents. Automatic document classifications are done using the concept of Self Organizing Maps (SOM) and Learning Vector Quantization (LVQ) algorithm [7].

Self Organizing Maps (SOM) do automatic classifications .SOM is based on Artificial Neural Network concept. Through this concept automatic clustering can be done. Learning Vector Quantization (LVQ) is for maximizing the correctness of classification of data.

The two algorithms SOM and LVQ are used individually for checking the validity. For each case the algorithms are generated then trained and tested .Two simulations are used for both the processes (SOM, LVQ). Each simulation is arranged in different pattern. In one case 70% are training set and 30% are for testing. For the other one 30% are for training, and 70% are used for testing.

The result is tabulated in the following Table 1.

Table 1. The experimental Result

	SOM	(Unsupervised)		LVQ	(Supervised)	
	100%	70%-30%	30%-70%	100%	70%-30%	30%-70%
Learn	72.69	70.84	72.98	74.74	74.43	76.71
Test	NA	67.08	56.72	NA	67.39	64.45

3.5 Binarization

Paleography is the study of ancient handwritten manuscripts. It generally deals with timing and localizing of ancient scripts. Most of the analysis of the manuscripts is based on the character shape. That is why threshoulding with acuteness is required to use in this field. To get rid of the corrupted condition of the documents, multi-stage accurate binarization scheme is applied. The multistage threshold technique is adapted in Paleographical analysis [8]. The steps that are followed are:

- GLOBAL THRESHOLDING: This stage reduces the volume of search space of foreground elements.
- DISCARDING IRRELEVANT OBJECTS: After passing through the 1st stage, the document will be free from small blobs and letters. The line extraction method is there to extract the text lines from the documents.
- LOCAL COMPONENT PROCESSING: Now the foreground pixels are accumulated and sets are generated. The neighbors of a certain data have the effect on it.
- POST PROCESSING: At last the holes that are generated by corrupted parts of some words i.e. the faded parts are processed accordingly.

The total procedure is explained by the given figures (Figure 6, Figure7) of Hebrew text .The 1st one is the input and the 2nd one is the processed text that is the desired output.

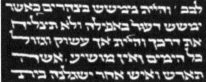

Fig. 6. Input Text   **Fig. 7.** Modified output from given text

4   Application

Document categorization of unstructured documents can be done in any field; where ever it is required. There are many reasons for document categorization, but the main reason behind it to access the desired document in a sophisticated manner so that in future the data or the document itself can be modified and retrieved with out loosing any information.

In the business world document categorizations   are used to achieve the above-mentioned goal so that the data will be securely stored in data repository. This is also used in industrial field for betterment of information storage. Not only that, to retrieve the information from a corrupted document like ancient historical documents can be achieved by the concept of classification of documents.

The text and data mining concept used in taxonomy and automatic text clustering methods are giving quick access to data from repository. As they are giving their desired output (with certain limitations); those concept can be used in large number of document for being categorized in faster process. The commercial summarizers those are available in the market, can be used in case of those data used in banking system, organizations or in industry. Especially the binarization process can easily be implemented for extracting data from corrupted (specially the ancient manuscript) documents.

In future, the concept of automatic taxonomy of documents can be amalgamated with the concept of paleographical search technique of information retrieval process. The features, which have explained, should be modified for fastest categorization process. The technique used for taxonomy generation along with data retrieval process of binarization can lead to the better result than before. Not only this concept, there are several possibilities to find new technique. The data extractions from corrupted documents are quite similar to image processing. So amalgamating the concept of image processing and the data extraction method can emerge a new and more concrete concept of categorization of documents in future.

5 Evaluation

5.1 Text and Data Mining Technique

For generation of taxonomy of documents, the process that have discussed, gives satisfactory and stable result at about 5000 documents. But as we increased the size of the sample, the saturation point changes some how. For LA based input data when it is tested, the stability is gained above 4000 documents. It is required to increase the size of the sample by 50% of data for the higher dimensional Input data.

In case of text clustering process, the result is also quite satisfactory as it does clustering with pure efficiency and the number terms involved in computation is very less which yields computation speed.

5.2 Lexical Chain Mechanism

The commercial summarizer, which follows this technique, is still under process. So there is a vast field to improve the desired out come from this approach.

5.3 Genetic Algorithmic Approach

The information retrieval process using this algorithm gives expected results in certain fields like Simulated and Canfield for document retrieval .Yet other fields are there where this algorithm must be checked and also with new different kinds of matching functions (except those which are used).

5.4 Artificial Neural Network

Automatic document classification based on ANN, gives   result, where it is found that the supervised learning is giving better than the unsupervised one. This is limited to small cluster size. More improvement is required in this field.

5.5 Binarization

Extraction of information from corrupted documents using this method is quite satisfactory. But in future the following must be achieved for using this process in paleographical work;

(i)   Writer's authentication checking mechanism
(ii) Writing style identification
(iii) Dating-timing and localization of manuscript.

6 Conclusion

Many techniques and algorithms for categorization have been devised. According to published literature, some are more accurate than others, and some provide more interpretable classification models than others. The detection of categories should be such that it must not lead to lose any sorts of information related to that field. The more the method will be applied, the more the approach will be analyzed. So we need to choose the field where to apply those concepts. Like genetic algorithm must be tested in many other fields except the mentioned ones. Not only that the matching functions must enhance its flexibility towards the problems. For neural network, the concept of neuroscience must be combined in future to provide a new pace in document categorization.

Medical field gives an environment where we can use document categorization efficiently. The interest in automating the collection, organization and analysis of biological data is creating the platform for this. Data in the form of images in online literature present special challenges to organize those. To understand the contents of a figure and determining the type of each panel, we need categorization. The system identifies panels among figures to further analysis of the sub cellular patterns in such images. This system contains a pertained classifier that uses image features to assign a type to each separate panel. As the types of panels in a figure are often correlated, we can consider the class of a panel to be dependent not only on its own features but also on the types of the other panels in a figure. Data will be secured only when it is well structured. Some kind of security is also needed. So document categorization should be merged with several security processes, which develop themselves for future revolution.

References

1. Bond, C.E., Shipton, Z.K., Jones, R.R., Butler, R.W.H., Gibbs, A.D.: Knowledge transfer in a digital world: Field data acquisition, uncertainty, visualization, and data management. Geosphere 3(6), 568–576 (2007)
2. Müller, A., Dörre, J., Gerstl, P., Seiffert, R.: The TaxGen Framework: Automating the Generation of a Taxonomy for a Large Document Collection. In: 32nd Annual Hawaii International Conference on System Sciences, Maui, HI, USA, January 5-8, vol. Track2, p. 9 (1999)
3. Gonzaga, L., Grivet, M., TerezaVasconcelos, A.: A Simple and Fast Term Selection Procedure for Text Clustering. In: International Conference on Intelligent Systems Design and Applications, October 20-24, pp. 777–781. Rio de Janeiro (2007)
4. Alam, H., Kumar, A., Nakamura, M., Rahman, F., Tarnikova, Y., Wilcox, C.: Structured and Unstructured Document Summarization: Design of a Commercial Summarizer using Lexical Chains. In: Seventh International Conference on Document Analysis and Recognition, August 3-6, pp. 1147–1152. Edinburgh, Scotland (2003)

5. Pathak, P., Gordon, M., Fan, W.: Effective Information Retrieval using Genetic Algorithms based Matching Functions Adaptation. In: 33rd Annual Hawaii International Conference on System Sciences, Hawaii, January 4-7, vol. 1, p. 8 (2000)

6. http://www.gc.ssr.upm.es/inves/neural/ann1/concepts/
    Suunsupm.htm

7. Goren-Bar, D., Kuflik, T., Lev, D.: Supervised Learning for Automatic Classification of Documents using Self-Organizing Maps. In: First DELOS Network of Excellence Workshop on Information Seeking, Searching and Querying in Digital Libraries, Zurich, Switzerland, December 11-12, pp. 1–4 (2000)

8. Yosef, I.B., Kedem, K., Dinstein, I., Beit-Arie, M., Engel, E.: Classification of Hebrew Calligraphic Handwriting Styles: Preliminary Results. In: First International Workshop on Document Image Analysis for Libraries, Palo Alto, CA, USA, January 23-24, pp. 299–305 (2004)

A Medical Charts Management Using RFID System with Enhanced Recognition Property

Sung-hee Jeon, Jung-eun Kim, Dong-hun Kim, and Joon-goo Park[*]

School of Electrical Engineering and Computer Science
Kyungpook National University, Daegu, South Korea
{shjeon72,atongs,jgpark}@knu.ac.kr, dh29kim@ee.knu.ac.kr

Abstract. In this paper, to introduce ubiquitous sensing system for medical service, we propose to apply RFID system for medical chart management service. RFID system can identify multiple tags simultaneously. Also, it has a wide applicable frequency range and a strong security characteristic. These kinds of advantages induce various business systems to adopt RFID system. When adopting RFID medical chart management system, there are two issues which should be considered. First one is how to identify more tags simultaneously and correctly. For this we propose optimized reader allocation methods. Second one is how to reduce read time. For this we suggest new double tag elimination method.

Keywords: RFID, RFID system, Medical service, Double tag elimination, Optimized reader allocation, WSN, USN.

1 Introduction

Many hospitals adopt hand-in-out system for patient management and patient's disease history report. It causes medical report sheets in-out to complicate in a hospital's related department and it is a heavy burden to worker. Sometimes it can give rise to exchange medical report sheets between their patients by mistakes. That can result in a serious medical accident, especially for complete cure or emergency cure.

At present, barcode system is frequently used in medical service for bio-application service. According to reports, the turnover volume for barcode systems was totaled around 3billion DM in Western Europe at the beginning of the 1990s(Virnich and Posten, 1992).

The barcode is a binary code comprising a field of bars and arranged in a parallel configuration. Since this barcode with a binary code is very useful for swift physical distribution control, barcode system has been successfully used for industry part including medical chart management area over the past 20 years.

We can find barcode system is frequently used in large hospitals for medical chart management but it is very inefficient in aspect of labor and time waste because it has to scan per medical chart whenever it is in or out though it is possible hand-recording

---

[*] Corresponding author. Tel.: +82 53 950 7567

T.-h. Kim et al. (Eds.): FGCN 2008, CCIS 27, pp. 126–135, 2009.
© Springer-Verlag Berlin Heidelberg 2009

work reduces. The charts on a cart passed are about two-hundreds per in or out, barcode scanning needs per one pass cart per one chart and workers perform barcode scanning about two-hundreds times per one cart. These works are repeated per medical sheets lending time and per medical sheets return time. It needs a lot of time spent.

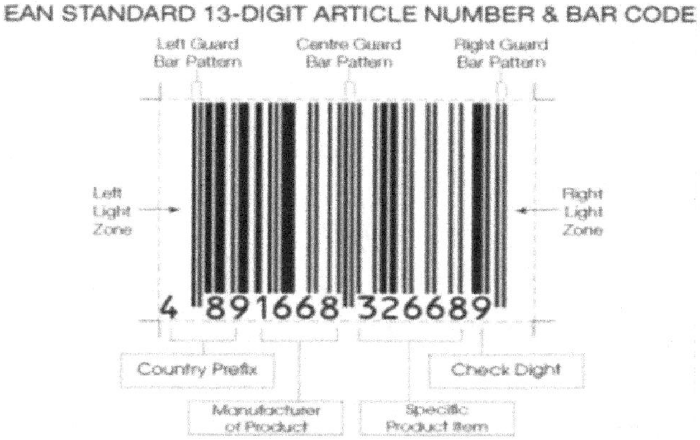

EAN STANDARD 13-DIGIT ARTICLE NUMBER & BAR CODE

Left Guard
Bar Pattern

Centre Guard
Bar Pattern

Right Guard
Bar Pattern

Left
Light
Zone

Right
Light
Zone

4 891668 326689

Country Prefix

Check Dight

Manufacturer
of Product

Specific
Product Item

Fig. 1. Barcode is printed on the back of goods

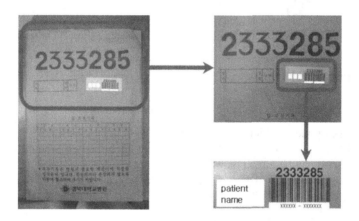

Fig. 2. Barcode on a medical sheet for management

Therefore, RFID system is more good solution for medical chart management because of no scanning per chart. Repeatedly speaking, because of it can read many tags' information simultaneously.

Figure 3 shows barcode system for medical sheets management in hospital. This example is Kyungpook National University hospital case of Korea. After medical sheets take out they are loaded on cart and they are arranged. Then workers process lending work using barcode scanner. When these handling is finish a cart is placed in front of an entrance of storage room(recording room). Next, it is moved for medical examination. Commonly storage room for medical sheet is located on anywhere in hospital.

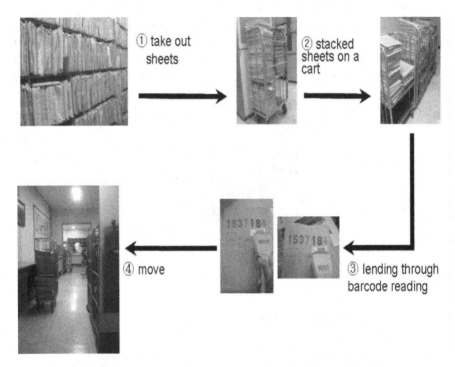

Fig. 3. Barcode reading in-out system for medical sheets in hospital

2 Review of RFID

RFID system is generally made up of two main components.

- Transponder, which is located on the object to be identified.
- Interrogator or reader, which, depending upon the design and the technology used, may be a read or write/read device (in this paper – in accordance with normal colloquial usage – the data capture device is always referred to as the reader, regardless of whether it can only read data or is also capable of writing).

Application range of RFID system is dependent upon several factors.

- Positional accuracy of the transponder
- Minimum distance between several transponders in practical operation
- Speed of the transponder in the interrogation zone of the reader.

For contactless payment applications – e.g. public transport tickets – the positioning speed is very low, since the transponder is guided to the reader by hand. The minimum distance between several transponder in this case corresponds with the distance between two passengers entering a vehicle. For such systems there is an optimal range of 5-10 cm. A longer range would only give rise to problems in this case, since

Table 1. Comparison of Barcode, OCR and RFID

System parameters	Barcode	OCR	RFID
Typical data quantity(bytes)	1-100	1-100	16-64k
Data density	Low	Low	Very high
Machine readability	Good	Good	Good
Readability by people	Limited	Simple	Impossible
Influence of dirt/damp	Very high	Very high	No influence
Influence of (opt). covering	Total failure	Total failure	No influence
Influence of direction and position	Low	Low	No influence
Degradation /wear	Limited	Limited	No influence
Purchase cost / reading electronics	Very low	Medium	Medium
Operating costs(e.g. printer)	Low	Low	None
Unauthorized copying / modification	Slight	Slight	Impossible
Reading speed (including handling of data carrier)	Low -4s	Low -3s	Very fast -0.5s
Maximum distance between data carrier and reader	0-50cm	<1cm Scanner	0-5m(over) microwave

several passengers' tickets might be detected by the reader simultaneously. This would make it impossible to reliably allocate the ticket to the right passenger.

The write/read distance of the RFID system used must therefore be designed for the maximum required range. The distance between the transponders must be such that only one transponder is ever within the interrogation zone of the reader at a time. In this situation, microwave systems in which the field has a directional beam offer clear advantages over the broad, non-directional fields of inductively coupled systems.

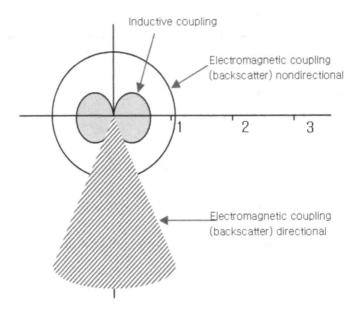

Fig. 4. Comparison of the relative interrogation zones

The speed of transponders, relative to readers, together with the maximum write/read distance, determines the length of time spent in the reader's interrogation zone.

3   Reader Placement for Reading Out Good Sensing Value

Reader needs arrangement for getting correct tag value. According to position, perception performance is different. We propose several reader placement methods for reading out good sensing value.

If measurement area is a rectangle zone, reader antenna should be placed long opposite side on wall.

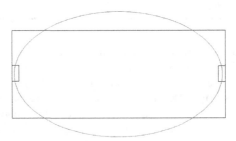

Fig. 5. Reader deployment for a rectangle zone

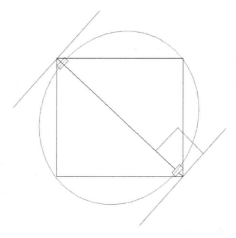

Fig. 6. Reader deployment for a true square zone

If measurement area is a true square zone, reader antenna should be placed diagonal opposite side on wall.

We have other methods of reader deployment for getting correct tag values. But we explained two methods as cases of rectangle zone and true square zone because reader placement scope of our work is medical charts recognition for recording room or in-out medical sheets space in hospital and it needs simple implementation. Other methods can use more complex environment and more varied environment.

The proposed methods are based on backscatter distribution of an antenna direction and the spread shape. Rectangle zone and true square zone, both cases are considered beam loss region of electromagnetic waves. There is no influence about these beam shade effect for medical charts recognition because it just depend on a cart pass route stacked medical sheets. Generally, we can think a path of a cart is middle area (It is not mean correct middle point) of room if anyone do not pass a corner on purpose. And middle area of room is always good position for medical charts recognition.

4   Solution for Double Recognition

We call Middleware Filtering that has a role of prevention to updating double tag ID through filtering of same tag ID for twice or more reading.

Filtering method of double tag ID reading shows Figure 7. A parameter 'A' exists for first 10 data and a parameter 'B' exists for 11-20th data. Both parameters are compared on same tag ID existence then these tag ID's elimination are carried out. Another parameter 'C' exists for 21-30th data and compare parameter 'C' with previous comparison results, then double tag ID's elimination are carried out again. This work is reiterated till all tags are read. Recently RFID system adopted Middleware Filtering method as like above contents. This system has advantage of double read tag elimination but has disadvantage of larger processing time.

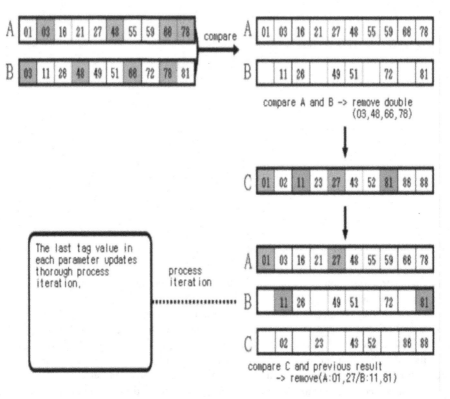

Fig. 7. Double tag value elimination of general method

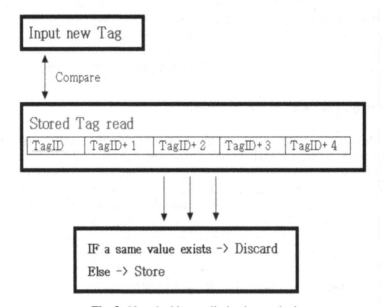

Fig. 8. New double tag elimination method

Therefore, we suggest index method which doesn't use parameters(A, B, C, ...) for comparison of double tags as new double tag elimination method to avoid iteration delay. Figure 8 shows a principle of new double tag elimination method simply.

If a new tag appears at system using the proposed double tag elimination method, its value is directly compared and stored or discarded. There are index forms such as 'TagID, TagID+1, TagID+2, TagID+3 .... TagID+N' for implementation when it is read. We can think function 'find' for this case. That time, if we want to search some value, after we give the value at system then it takes out the value from anywhere in system.(e.q. 'Instring' function in Visual Basic).

5   Experimental Results

We propose several optimized conditions for getting good recognition results in this paper. These conditions are set through several experiments and basic tests. The number of medical sheets and movement speed at actual hospital are considered as parameters for optimized conditions.

Table 2. Performance results - medical sheets amount

Tag Real time	50	100	200	300	400
900 ms	100%	100%	100%	100%	98%
Real time	100%	100%	100%	100%	98%

Table 3. Performance results - movement speed

Speed Tag	0 m/s	1 m/s	2 m/s	3 m/s	5 m/s
50	100 %	100 %	100 %	100 %	100 %
100	100 %	100 %	100 %	100 %	100 %
200	100 %	100 %	100 %	100 %	98 %
300	100 %	100 %	100 %	97 %	94 %
400	100 %	100 %	99 %	97 %	94 %

To have the best recognition rate within shorter time, following conditions should be met:

- Use of circular antenna. Maintain 6m distance between tags and antenna
- Horizontal even leveling between antenna and tags
- Use real time recognition method

As the results, recognition success ratios for several tests are all over 98% for general case of medical chart management. It means that the proposed system has high performance and can be applicable to the medical chart management of hospital.

6 Conclusion

We proposed RFID system for medical charts management with optimized reader allocation and new double tag elimination algorithm for stable recognition success ratio over 98%.

Our RFID system for medical charts management has an advantage of time delay reduction compared to the existing Barcode medical chart management systems. Therefore, by applying the proposed system to medical chart management of hospital, management process time and its exactness can be enhanced to considerable extent.

Currently, more than two-hundred medical record sheets are being used in general hospitals. Therefore, by considering the potential of proposed system's capability, we expect that proposed system can contribute to the best medical service in hospital.

Acknowledgment

This research was financially supported by 'the Ministry of Education, Science, Technology(MEST) and Korea Industrial Technology Foundation(KOTEF) through the Human Resource Training Project for Regional Innovation' and 'RTI-0403-01'.

References

1. Finkenzeller, K.: RFID handbook: Fundamentals and applications in contactless smart cards and identification, WILEY (2002)
2. EPCglobal, EPCTM Radio-Frequency Identity Protocols Class-1 Generation-2 UHF RFID Protocol for Communications at 860MHz~960MHz, Version 1.0.9 (January 2005)
3. RFID journal, http://www.rfidjournal.net/PDF_download/ RFIDJ_CaseStudy_Mar07.pdf
4. RFID journal, http://www.rfidjournal.net/PDF_download/ RFIDJ_BestPractices_Jan07.pdf
5. RFID KOREA "Solutions", http://www.rfidkor.com
6. RFID WORLD, Tag, reader and antenna spec., http://www.rfidworld.co.kr/shop
7. RFID medical devices - Opportunities and challenges, http://wistechnology.com/articles/2384/

8. RFID: Medical Information and Security, `http://www.aimglobal.org/`
9. Digitizing hospitals with the right tools,
   `http://wistechnology.com/articles/1905/`
10. RFID Applications in Hospital Equipment Tracking,
    `http://www.supplyinsight.com/`
    `RFID_in_Hospital_Equipment_Tracking.htm`
11. rPlatform - The RFID Platform,
    `http://www.supplyinsight.com/rplatform.htm`
12. RFID Case Studies knowledgebase,
    `http://www.idtechex.com/knowledgebase/en/nologon.asp`
13. RFID to improve patient safety and hospital savings,
    `http://www.rfidgazette.org/2004/07/rfid_in_the_hos.html`
14. Radio Frequency Identification (RFID)-ISO & ISO/IEC Standards-2006.3.-Craig K. Harmon, President & CEO Q.E.D. Systems (2006)
15. 2.4 GHz RTLS Technology and Applications Overview-2006.3-Tim Harrington, Where-Net Corporation (ISO RTLS/2.4 GHz Editor)
16. RFID Forecasts, Players and Opportunities 2005 to 2015-2006. 2-Dr. Peter Harrop and Raghu Das IDTechEx
17. Information about RFID wristband for hospital application,
    `http://www.rfid-in-china.com/products_669_1.html`
18. RFID in the hospital : reduces patient management errors,
    `http://www.newdesignworld.com/press/story/9158`
19. Library RFID Management System,
    `http://www.rfid-library.com/e_rf07.html`
20. RFID Communication Systems And Methods (WO/2006/122008),
    `http://www.wipo.int/pctdb/en/wo.jsp?wo=2006122008&IA=US20060`
    `17687&DISPLAY=DESC`

A Variable Bandwidth Allocation Scheme Using Effective Multicast Traffic Share in Heterogeneous Networks

Hao Wang, Furong Wang, Xu Xie, Kewei Li, Zhiwu Ke,
Zhe Guo, and Benxiong Huang

Department of Electrical and Information Engineering,
Huazhong University of Science and Techonology,
Wuhan 430074, Hubei, P.R. China
{wh.hust,furongwanghust,xiexuhust,keweilihust}@gmail.com,
{zhiwukehust,zheguohust,benxionghuanghust}@gmail.com

Abstract. Bandwidth allocation and frequent handoffs are serious problems in heterogeneous networks. A Variable Bandwidth Scheme (VBS) using effective multicast traffic share improve the quality of services (QoS) in heterogeneous networks. Compared with the Time-based Channel Predictive Control (TCPC) schemes, the VBS reduces call dropping probability (CDP) and call blocking probability (CBP). And the weight call loss probability (CLP) is the function of CDP and CBP. The variable bandwidth allocation scheme using effective multicast traffic share improves performance in resource control and wireless channel utilization. These are the characteristic of standardization QoS. Simulation results demonstrate the effectiveness of the scheme.

Keywords: Heterogeneous Networks, Bandwidth Allocation, Traffic Share, CLP, Channel Utilization Rate, QoS.

1 Introduction

Heterogeneous Networks provide seamless coverage services with the low propagation delay, low-power terminals and the good QoS. GSM networks with 3G networks are classic examples of heterogeneous networks. Call Dropping Probability (CDP) and Call Blocking Probability (CBP) are important indexes for heterogeneous networks. Furthermore, it should be noted that blocking a handover call is more unsatisfying to the user than blocking a new call; more attention has been paid to the handover issue.

Many schemes to address the Call Admission Control (CAC) strategy and Channel Resources issue of heterogeneous network have been proposed. One of noticeable schemes is the Dynamic Handover Priority (DHP) scheme [1,2]. DHP proposes a Channel-Locking Mechanism and defines two kinds of users, one is the priority users or DHP users, and another is the regular users. The locked channels are reserved for the DHP users to avoid calls' dropping. DHP has low system complexity and low call dropping probability. The disadvantage of DHP is the channel utilization rate is low.

The Time-based Channel Predictive Control (TCPC) [3] is proposed recently to improve the channel utilization rate when handovers happen in system. It reserves the channel for a priority user during a suitable time interval in the cell. The channel can

T.-h. Kim et al. (Eds.): FGCN 2008, CCIS 27, pp. 136–150, 2009.
© Springer-Verlag Berlin Heidelberg 2009

be used by other users in other time interval. The Dynamic Time-based Channel Resources Control (DTCRC) mechanism is based on the TCPC. It divides traffic flows into two classes, the stream flow and the elastic flow. The transmission rates of elastic flows are variable in order to improve the whole channel utilization of the mobile communication system. These schemes improved the channel utilization rate while demanded a higher system complexity and longer processing time.

The Variable Bandwidth Scheme (VBS) is proposed in this paper to balance the channel utilization rate and the system complexity. In the scheme, the bandwidth resource of a cell is divided into two states according to the traffic load. In low traffic load state, the main purpose of the system is to decrease the system complexity and processing time; and in high traffic load state, the main purpose of the scheme is to improve the bandwidth utilization rate, and provide the services for more users.

In addition, heterogeneous networks are a huge system due to its low propagation delay and good QoS. However, the growth of mobile broadband services so that there is a shortage of wireless bandwidth resource. A new scheme which provides better services to use limited resources becomes a general demand. The real-time priorities of ongoing services are adjusted with the change of bandwidth occupancy rate. In accordance with the protocols, an ongoing service sends Measurement Reports (MR) to the base station every 480ms. The information in the MR includes traffic type, call duration and channel occupation.

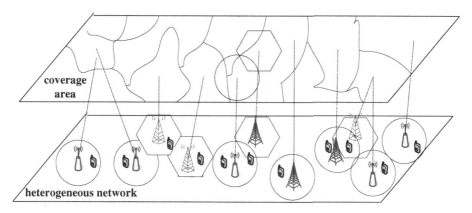

Fig. 1. Heterogeneous networks and their coverage area

Many schemes to address the bandwidth allocation strategy and Channel Resources issue of heterogeneous network have been proposed. One of noticeable schemes is the Max-Min fair bandwidth allocation algorithms, before packet transmission, an input port claims portion of the bandwidth of each output port for its traffic. However, since each input and output has only local bandwidth information, it does not know how much bandwidth other input claimed at a specific output. [4]For the under-utilized case, clearly, the unused bandwidth should be allocated to make full use of the transmission capacity, and it has to be carefully handled to allocate the leftover bandwidth in a fair manner. For the over-utilized case, it is also necessary to fairly scale down the claimed bandwidth of each user to make the scheme feasible. [5]Another bandwidth allocation scheme based on games considers the problem for a consumer multi-provider system, where a consumer may have access to only a subset of all providers. [7] A user demands bandwidth from the base stations it has access to by submitting bids. Once the bidding process is complete, a base station distributes its bandwidth to the users in proportion to their bids. Because all the data needed for this scheme that stays in MR. The data acquisition server takes the supplied MR and looks it up in a large table of E1 addresses to a data format. Great capacity database is built of MRs and the data real-time analysis becomes a challenge and the second step in this system.

Information of Measurement Result:

field name	data type	values range	frame name
Time	date/time	18decimal	Measurement Result
TEI	tinyint	0-127/7bits	Measurement Result
CI_Num	big int	0□42949672 95/4 bytes	Config File
CI_Name	varcha	100bytes	Config File
BTS_Num	bigint	0□42949672 95/4bytes	Config File
BTS_Name	var-char[50]	100bytes	Config File
Latitude	float	±1.175494E-38□±3.402823E+38/4bytes	Config File
Longitude	float	±1.175494E-38□±3.402823E+38/4bytes	Config File
BSC_Num	bigint	0□42949672 95/4 bytes	Config File
BSC_Name	var-char[50]	100bytes	Config File
LAC	bigint	0□42949672 95/4 bytes	Config File
MSC_Name	var-char[50]	100bytes	Config File
Channel_type	tinyint	0-31/5bits	Measurement Result
Time_slot_num	tinyint	0-7/3bits	Measurement Result
Measure-ment_result_num	tinyint	0-255/8bits	Measurement Result
RXLEV_all_up	tinyint	0-63/6bits	Measurement Reasult
RXLEV_subset_up	tinyint	0-63/6bits	Measurement Reasult
RXQUAL_subset_up	tinyint	0-7/3bits	Measurement Reasult
RXQUAL_all_up	tinyint	0-7/3bits	Measurement Reasult

BS_Power	tinyint	0-31/5bits	Measurement Reasult
MS_Power	tinyint	0-31/5bits	Measurement Reasult
DTX	bit	0-1/1bits	Measurement Reasult
RXLEV_FULL_down	tinyint	0-63/6bits	Measurement Reasult
RXLEV_SUB_down	tinyint	0-63/6bits	Measurement Reasult
RXQUAL_FUL L_down	tinyint	0-7/3bits	Measurement Reasult
RXQUAL_SU B_down	tinyint	0-7/3bits	Measurement Reasult
RXLEV_NCEL L_i(1-6)	tinyint	0-63/6bits	Measurement Reasult
BCCH_FREQ_NCELL_i(1-6)	tinyint	0-31/5bits	Measurement Reasult
BSIC_NCC_N CELL_i(1-6)	tinyint	0-7/3bits	Measurement Reasult
BSIC_BCC_N CELL_i(1-6)	tinyint	0-7/3bits	Measurement Reasult
Timing_advance	tinyint	0-63/6bits	Measurement Reasult
Timing_offset	tinyint	0-255/8bits	Measurement Reasult

A data format of Measurement Result Sample:

```
Measurement results
RXLEV-FULL-SERVING:43
RXLEV-SUB-SERVING:44
RXQUAL-FULL-SERVING:1
RXQUAL-SUB-SERVING:0
BA-USED:1
DTX:Used
Measurement results(MEAS-VALID):Valid
Number of neighboring cell measurements:6
```

N CEll	RXLEV-NCELL	BSIC-NCELL	BCCH-FREQ-NCELL
1	42	23	03
2	40	27	00
3	32	22	01
4	32	45	06
5	29	41	02
6	25	27	07

Bandwidth Allocation Schemes for a multi-services heterogeneous network must guarantee the potentially different QoS requirement. The transmission rates of elastic flows are variable in order to improve the whole channel utilization of the mobile communication system [8]. These schemes improved the channel utilization rate while demanded a higher system complexity and longer processing time.

There is little influence on the quality degree of data service when bandwidth changed within a certain range. Therefore, when there is not enough bandwidth in the system, the bandwidth of data service can be reduced and transferred to the handoff calls. The dropping probability is reduced while the quality of service (QoS) is reduced little. But if the bandwidth grade of ongoing calls is decreased too much, there will be significant influence on their QoS. For different service types, the relationships between the QoS and bandwidth used are different. Through the MR real-time analysis, we get the corresponding parameters of current channel occupancy rate. Resource scheduling among the ongoing calls is feasible.

2 Bandwidth Resource Analysis

Based on the MR real-time analysis that the bandwidth of an ongoing call is variable during its lifetime, the bandwidth used by the call is divided into different grades according to their magnitude. The set of the different bandwidth grades is denoted as $G = \{g_1, g_2, ..., g_n\}$. In the notation, the lowest bandwidth, g_1 is the amount of bandwidth which support the minimum information transmit rate required for the call to be admitted; the highest bandwidth, g_n, is the maximum bandwidth a call used. $g_1, g_2, ..., g_n$ is an increasing sequence. The bandwidth of an ongoing call is adjusted in its bandwidth grade set $\{g_1, g_2, ..., g_n\}$ according to the number of calls in the cell.

The bandwidth resources of the system are divided into two sets: the reserved bandwidth, which is reserved for handoff call specially; the non-reserved bandwidth, which can be used by new call and handoff call. When a new connecting request is sent to the network, the classes of the service and its bandwidth set are transmitted to the network as well. The network assigns the bandwidth as much as possible to accept the call. Only when the available non-reserved bandwidth is less than the demand of the minimum bandwidth grade $g1$, the new connecting request will be blocked.

When handoff call arrives, they can use the total idle bandwidth of the network. The network assigns bandwidth as much as possible to the handoff calls. If the available idle bandwidth is less than the demand of the minimum bandwidth, the network will lower the bandwidth grade of the ongoing call to release some bandwidth resources in order to satisfy the lowest bandwidth requirement of the handoff calls. The bandwidth resources will be released when the calls is finished, and then is assigned to the ongoing calls which are served with lower bandwidth grade in order to improve their QoS.

Let C represents the set of on-going calls, Let b_t^i and b_{t+1}^i represents the bandwidth assigned to call $i(i \in c)$ at time t and the next time $t+1$ respectively. Let y_i be the bandwidth lowered of the ongoing call i. That is $y_i = b_t^i - b_{t+1}^i$. Let $y = \sum_{i \in c} y_i$.

Let u_i represents the QoS, it increases with the bandwidth the relate call used. Let B denotes the total bandwidth the handoff calls need. Let p_{hf} represents the handoff dropping probability of the handoff calls. It is assumed that QoS of the heterogeneous network U is the function of QoS and handoff calls dropping probability. It is expressed as:

$$U = \sum_{i \in c} u_i (b_{t+1}^i) - \gamma p_{hf} \tag{1}$$

Where γ is a parameter indicating the influence of the handoff call dropping probabilities on the QoS. Lowering the ongoing call's bandwidth for handoff call can reduce the dropping probability, but the QoS of the ongoing call will decrease. Our main aim is to maximize the system's QoS which belongs to the classical constrained nonlinear optimization problems, and can be formulated as follows:

$$\max U = \sum_{i \in c} u_i (b_{t+1}^i) - \gamma p_{hf} \tag{2}$$

$$b_{t+1}^i = b_t^i - y_i \tag{3}$$

$$\sum_{i \in c} y_i \leq B \tag{4}$$

$$b_{t+1}^i \geq \min b_i, \qquad \text{for all } i \in C \tag{5}$$

Constraint (4) ensures that the sum of the lowered bandwidth of the ongoing calls cannot exceed the amount of total bandwidth that all the handoff calls need. Constraint (5) indicates the bandwidth left for call i must be higher than the lowest bandwidth it needs, and $\min b_i$ is the lowest bandwidth call i requests.

3 Variable Bandwidth Scheme

The strategy of VBS is described in this section. In VBS, two traffic load states of cells are defined. One state is the Channel Low-Occupancy Rate, called CLOR state; the other is Channel High-Occupancy Rate, called CHOR state. The switch of the two states is determined by a channel occupancy rate threshold. Two classes of calls, voice calls and non-real-time calls are considered in VBS.

A. CLOR state
When the traffic load of a cell is in CLOR state, it means that the traffic load of this cell is not high. For a voice call, the DHP method is adopted. When a voice call sets up in a given cell C_i of the heterogeneous network, a bandwidth reservation request is sent to the first two cells to be visited by the user, the cell C_i and the cell C_{i+1}. The system will judge whether there is enough idle bandwidth for this new call, the occupied bandwidth includes the ongoing calls in C_i and the locked bandwidth for the voice calls in cell. If the condition of bandwidth of the two cells is satisfied, the new call will be admitted. And in the sequent cell C_{i+1} that the call may enter, the sufficient bandwidth will be reserved. When the call enters the sequent cell C_{i+1}, it occupies the locked bandwidth reserved before for itself; and a reservation request is immediately sent to the next cell C_{i+2}, when the bandwidth is enough in C_{i+2}, it is locked to reserve for this call.

Such processes happen sequentially until the call terminate. In order to decrease the complexity of the system, there isn't a bandwidth locking waiting queue in each cell.

For a non-real-time call, a gradational method is used, the transmission rate of the non-real-time call in a given cell divides into five grades, and the transmission rate of the higher grade is twice over the lower grade. When a non-real-time call sets up in the cell C_i, the system will first inquire the non-real-time call grade of this cell, and then judge that if there is enough bandwidth for the call with this rate of the grade in this cell. If the bandwidth is enough, the call will be admitted, otherwise, the grade of service of this cell will be decreased. After the decreasing procedure, the bandwidth is judged again. If the bandwidth is still not enough, then the decreasing process will be repeated until the call get the bandwidth needed. If the grade of this cell is the lowest grade and there is still not enough bandwidth for this call, the call will be rejected. Figure 2 shows the flowchart of the Call Admission Control (CAC) strategy for a non-real-time call.

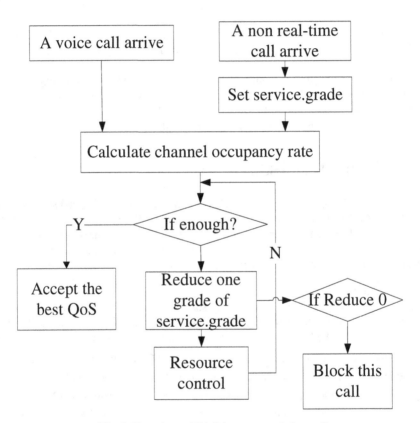

Fig. 2. Flowchart of CAC for a non-real-time call

Because of the simple strategy of the CAC and the bandwidth reservation for channel resources predictive control, the complexity of the CLOR state is low. The system can admit the new call to access more quickly.

B.   CHOR state

In this state, we assume that the user's terminal has the positioning facility to receive its position information. For a voice call, TCPC method is adopted. When a voice call sets up in a given cell C_i of the cell, the system judge that whether there is enough bandwidth in the temporary cell 1 [x-R, x] and the temporary cell 2 [x, x+R], x is position of the new voice call's user, R is the size of a cell, these are showed in Figure 2. If the bandwidth is enough, this call will be admitted to access; otherwise the call will be blocked. When this call is admitted, a bandwidth reservation request is sent to the cell C_{i+1}, the reservation time interval is [T_{iR}, T_{2R}], where T_R is the time of this voice call user reaching the boundary of cell C_i and C_{i+1}, and T_{2R} is the time that the user reaches the boundary of cell C_{i+1} and C_{i+2}. At the time of each voice call's handover, a handover request is sent to the next cell immediately, to reserve the time interval [T_{iR+R}, T_{iR+2R}].

For a non-real-time call, we used the same strategy as that of the CLOR state. The transmission rate of the call is variable according to the traffic in the cell. There won't be a bandwidth reservation for this class of calls.

In CHOR state, the main goal is how to provide services for users as many as possible; in requital for that the cost is the more processing time and the complexity of system.

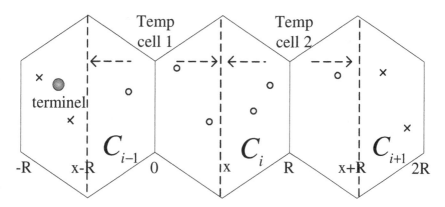

Fig. 3. CHOR state voice call CAC

According to the above, the scheme proposed can be more efficient in CLOR state. For CHOR state, the higher utilization of bandwidth has been obtained.

4   Analysis of the Proposed Scheme

a)   Basic Assumption
Two guidelines of the channel resources predictive control in heterogeneous network were considered in the study, the Call Blocking Probability (CBP) and the Call Dropping Probability (CDP). CBP is the parameter for the new call, and CDP is the parameter for the handover call. The cell of heterogeneous network is single-aspect. Let us assume that the bandwidth resource of the exact cell of the heterogeneous network is a constant, we use B to denote it. And RATE_V denotes the transmission rate of the

voice call, it is a constant. RATE_D denote the transmission rate of the non-real-time call, there are five grades of RATE_D.

b) Evaluation
In the study, the classical traffic assumptions are considered. The new calls are assumed to arrive according to the Poisson process, λ_c and λ_d are respectively the mean arrival rate of the voice new calls and the non-real-time new calls. And the calls durative times are assumed to be according to the exponential process, $1/\mu_c$ and $1/\mu_d$ are respectively the mean serving time of the voice calls and the non-real-time calls. We only need to analyze the new call blocking rate of the cell in CHOR state. A cell of this system is modeled by the Markov chain corresponding to the M/M/N/N queue. In this model, if there are new calls blocked, the grade of RATE_D is certainly down to the first grade according to the rule aforementioned; N is the voice call and the non-real-time call users' number. Let Π_k be the marginal probability to have k users occupying resources. Given the uniform users' distribution position and the uniform arrival of the users in a cell, p_k is the new call blocking probability with the condition of k users in cell C_i, p_k can be derived as follows (only the values of the steady states be considered). Let t denote the initial offset of a new call arrival, and v the actual configuration when a new call arrives.

$$p_k = \frac{1}{\sqrt{R^2 + 1}} \int_{x=0}^{R} \sum_{l,m=0}^{N} P(N \mid v) dx \tag{1}$$

With, v = {t = x, users number in C_{i-1} = l, users number in C_i = k, users number in C_{i+1} = m} as the Figure 2 shows.
   Since PASTA stands, the probability of the new calls blocking P_b is:

$$P_b = \sum_{k=0}^{N} \Pi_k p_k \sqrt{1 - p_k^2} \tag{2}$$

From the equation above, it can be seen that the probability of new calls blocking depends on the steady state probabilities of the Markov chain.

5 Simulation Results

Simulation experiments have been carried out. Suppose that the simulated heterogeneous network to be an orbicular shape area of 3 cells. All handovers are considered to be the same. In the simulation model of the proposed scheme, there are two classes of users, the voice call users and the non-real-time call users. For comparing the performance of the proposed scheme, the TCPC scheme have also been simulated.
   The simulation also gets the CBP and the CDP. Figure 5 and Figure 6 show the CBP and CDP curves of the proposed scheme's performance and that of TCPC and Figure 7 shows the BUR curves of VBS scheme's performance and that of TCPC.

- The new call arrivals are assumed to obey Poisson process with the parameter λ, it is a variable.
- The user call duration is exponentially distributed. The mean duration time of the voice call is 180s, and the mean duration time of the non-real-time call is 300s. The voice call users belong to class 1 users, the proportion of it is 40%, and the non-real-time call users belong to class 2 users, the proportion is 60%.
- The threshold of the state is that the bandwidth which has been occupied is 80% of the bandwidth in the cell.

According to the results, the VBS reduces the CBP with respect to TCPC schemes, and has better performance of CDP than TCPC. The complexity of VBS is close to the DHP scheme, and is lower than the TCPC. So the proposed scheme has both good performances in complexity and guide lines of channel resources predictive control.

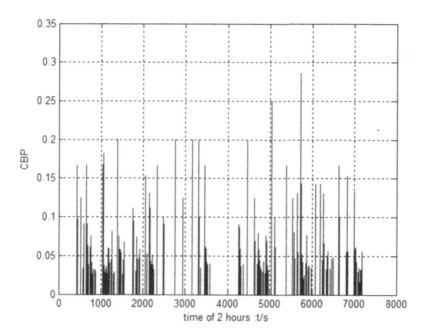

Fig. 4. CBP for VBS in 2 hours

- New call blocking probability is recorded as CBP and handoff call dropping probability is recorded as CDP. As we know, CDP impacts on the QoS greater than CBP. The weight call loss probability(WCLP) is:

$$WCLP = \alpha \cdot CBP + \beta \cdot CDP \tag{7}$$

The Parameters α and β are assigned 1 and 2.
- Standardized QoS is decided by weight call loss probability, channel occupancy rate and average Service Level.

The simulation results show the effectiveness of QoS-adaptive Bandwidth Allocation Scheme.

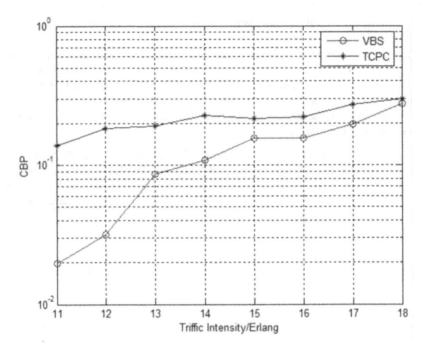

Fig. 5. CBP for VBS and TCPC schemes

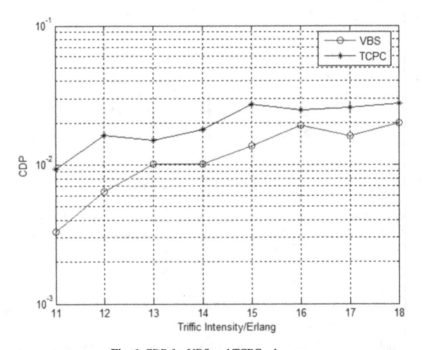

Fig. 6. CDP for VBS and TCPC schemes

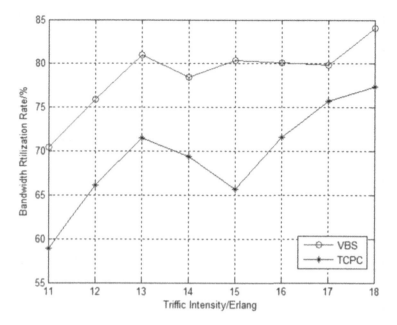

Fig. 7. Bandwidth Utilization Rate for VBS and TCPC schemes

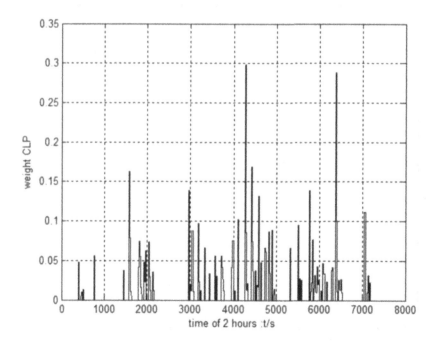

Fig. 8. weight CLP in 2 hours

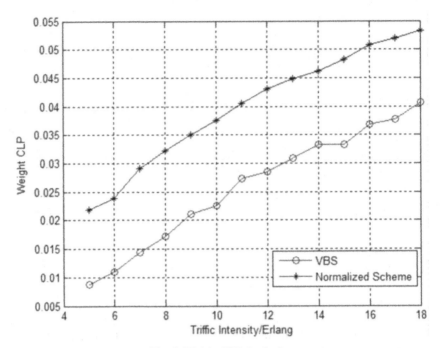

Fig. 9. Weight CLP Analysis

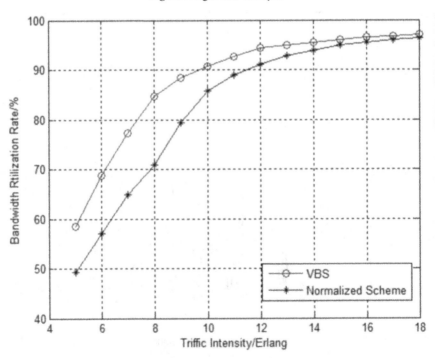

Fig. 10. Bandwidth Utilization Rate Analysis

Table 1. Average QoS Level comparison

Traffic Intensity	4	6	8	10	12	14	16	18
Average QoS Level/BAS	g_5	g_5	g_4	g_3	g_2	g_1	g_1	g_1
Average QoS Level/QBAS	g_5	g_5	g_5	g_5	g_4	g_3	g_2	g_1

6 Conclusions

A new Variable Bandwidth Scheme (VBS) for channel resources predictive control in heterogeneous network was proposed in this paper. VBS defines two traffic load states of cells, the CLOR state and the CHOR state. In CLOR state, the main purpose of the scheme is to decrease the system complexity and processing time; and in CHOR state, the main purpose of the scheme is to improve the bandwidth utilization rate, and provide the services for more users. Compared with TCPC, the simulation results demonstrate the effectiveness of VBS.

Acknowledgement

We would like to express our gratitude to the National Nature Science Foundation of China (NSFC) for financial support of our work under grant No. 60572047, the Program for New Century Excellent Talents in University No.NCET-06-0642, and the Graduate innovation fund of HUST. No. HF04122006181.

References

1. Xhafa, A.E., Tonguz, O.K.: Handover performance of priority schemes in pcs networks. IEEE Transactions on Vehicular Technology 57(1), 565–577 (2008)
2. Chen, H., Kumar, S., Kuo, C.-C.J.: Dynamic call admission control scheme for QoS priority handoff in multimedia heterogeneous systems. In: WCNC 2002, March 2002, vol. 1, pp. 114–118 (2002)
3. Fang, Y., Zhang, Y.: Call admission control schemes and performance analysis in wireless mobile networks. IEEE Transactions on Vehicular Technology 51(6), 371–382 (2002)
4. Kulavaratharasha, M.D., Aghvami, A.H.: Teletraffic performance evaluation of microcellular personal communication network (PCNs) with prioritized hand-off procedures. IEEE Trans. Vehicular Technology 48, 137–152 (1999)
5. Garcia, D., Martinez, J., Pla, V.: Comparative evaluation of admission control policies in cellular multiservice networks. In: Proc. Int. Conf. Wireless Communications, pp. 517–531 (2004)
6. Vassileva, N., Barcelo-Arroyo, F.: A new CAC policy based on traffic characterization in cellular networks. In: Harju, J., Heijenk, G., Langendörfer, P., Siris, V.A. (eds.) WWIC 2008. LNCS, vol. 5031, pp. 1–12. Springer, Heidelberg (2008)
7. Xhafa, A.E., Tonguz, O.K.: Handover performance of priority schemes in cellular networks. IEEE Trans. Vehicular Technology 3(1), 57, 565–577 (2008)

8. Iversen, V.B.: Handbook in Telegraphic Engineering. ITC/ITU-D (2006)
9. Feldmann, A.: Impact of non-Poisson arrival sequences for call admission algorithms with and without delay. In: Proc. IEEE GLOBECOM 1996, pp. 617–621 (1996)
10. Vassileva, N., Barcelo-Arroyo, F.: Performance of a traffic-based handover method in high-mobility scenarios. Accepted for publication in Proc. 4th Int. Workshop PMAC-2WN 2008 (December 2008)
11. Fang, Y., Chlamtac, I., Lin, Y.-B.: Channel occupancy times and handoff rate for mobile computing and PCS networks. IEEE Trans. Computers 47(6), 679–692 (1998)
12. Jedrzycki, C., Leung, V.C.M.: Probability distribution of channel holding time in cellular telephony systems. In: Proc. IEEE VTC, vol. 1, pp. 247–251 (1996)
13. Barcelo, F., Jordan, J.: Channel holding time distribution in public telephony systems (PAMR and PCS). IEEE Trans. Vehicular Technology 49, 1615–1625 (2000)
14. Rajaratnam, M., Takawira, F.: Hand-off traffic modeling in cellular networks. In: Proc. IEEE GLOBECOM 1997, pp. 131–137 (1997)
15. Yavuz, E.A., Leung, V.C.M.: Computationally efficient method to evaluate the performance of guard-channel-based call admission control in cellular networks. IEEE Trans. Vehicular Technology 55(4), 1412–1421 (2006)
16. Zhang, Y., Soong, B.-H., Ma, M.: Approximation approach on performance evaluation for guard channel scheme. IEEE Electronics Letters 39(5), 465–467 (2003)
17. Xhafa, A.E., Tonguz, O.K.: Does mixed lognormal channel holding time affect the handover performance of guard channel scheme. In: Proc. IEEE GLOBECOM, vol. 6, pp. 3452–3456 (2003)
18. Barcelo, F.: Performance analysis of handoff resource allocation strategies through state-dependent rejection scheme. IEEE Trans. Wireless Communications (3), 900–909 (2004)
19. Pan, D., Yang, Y.: Credit based fair scheduling for packet switched networks. In: IEEE INFOCOM 2005, Miami,FL, March 2005, pp. 843–854 (2005)
20. Hosaagrahara, M., Sethu, H.: Max-min fairness in inputqueued switches. In: ACM SIG-COMM Student Poster Session, Philadelphia, PA, USA (August 2005)
21. Sun, J., Modiano, E., Zheng, L.: Wireless channel allocation using' an auction algorithm. IEEE Journal on Selected Areas in Communications 24(5) (2006)
22. Erwu, L., Gang, S., Shan, J.: Bandwidth Allocation for 3-Sector Base Station in 802.16 Single-Hop Self-backhaul Networks. In: Proc. IEEE VTC 2006-Fall (September 2006)
23. Lee, H., Kwon, T., Cho, D.-H., Lim, G., Chang, Y.: Performance Analysis of Scheduling Algorithms for VoIP Services in IEEE 802.16e Systems. In: Proc. IEEE VTC 2006-Spring (May 2006)
24. Yavuz, E.A., Leung, V.C.M.: Computationally efficient method to evaluate the performance of guard-channel based call admission control in cellular networks. IEEE transactions on vehicular technology 55(4) (July 2006)
25. Chou, C., Shin, K.G.: Analysis of combined adaptive bandwidth allocation and admission control in wireless networks. In: Proc. IEEE INFOCOM, June 2002, vol. 2, pp. 676–684 (2002)
26. Wu, S., Wong, K.Y.M., Li, B.: A Dynamic Call Admission Policy with Precision QoS Guarantee Using Stochastic Control for Mobile Wireless Networks. IEEE/ACM Trans. Networking 10(2) (April 2002)

RFID-Enable Real-Time Management
for Multi-experiment Training Center

Q. Y. Dai[1], R. Y. Zhong[1,2], M.L.Wang[1], X.D. Liu[1], and Q. Liu[1]

[1] Faculty of Information Engineering Guangdong University of Technology,
Guangzhou, 510006
[2] Department of Industrial and Manufacturing Systems Engineering,
The University of Hong Kong, Pokfulam Road, Hong Kong
zhongzry@hku.hk

Abstract. This paper proposes a real-time web system based on RFID, B/S+C/S (Browser/Server + Client/Server) module and wireless communication named 433MHz which are used to solve some crucial problems existed in multi-experiment training center such as real-time data collection, task tracking and agile training etc. The system integrated teaching management, equipment management, materials management, personnel management, and other information effectively to achieve real-time collection of various basis data so as to conduct statistics for dynamic statements, real-time queries, tracking and analysis. This management mode could guarantee the unified management, deployment of the experimenters and laboratory equipment, and utilization of laboratories effectively. In addition, a scientific evaluation mechanism for experimental teaching could be established by the real-time information, in order to evaluate the experimental skills, practical abilities and innovation abilities of students. Then the quality guarantee system of experimental teaching was further improved. After application in representative of training center in Guangdong University of Technology.

1 Introduction

Development of network technology accelerates the transferring and interactions of information, especially for enterprises, institutions, companies, and education institutions. Management has brought new vigor and vitality. Microsoft has introduced a new generation of Web technology which could combine with the traditional RFID technology effectively so as to create a new Web application development platform [1]. And this combination is also capable of excellent cross-platform interoperability and the level of clarity, high maintainability and good scalability. As a result, web systems development combined with traditional tech become a popular choice.

Under this definite possibility of combination of B/S and C/S, which is applied in training system, a Web-based system combined with RFID network owns more prominent advantages. B/S is the web system which is mainly focus on the management and

T.-h. Kim et al. (Eds.): FGCN 2008, CCIS 27, pp. 151–168, 2009.

user operatoin. C/S is a communication system which puts weight on information transfering in the lab. The methodology combined with Web and RFID is full of excellent controllability, timeliness, and openness. What is more, it highlights the real-time data intercommunication. According to the same methodology which MES (Manufacturing Execution System) is used; the workshop present management model applies to college engineering training courses, combined with the using of RFID. Programs are designed which include WEB-based management system, C/S-based communication system. Those systems are a tool for information engineering training in colleges and universities in promoting the construction of multi-experiment engineering training.

College engineering training centre is mainly responsible for mechanical and manufacturing engineering training, electrical and electronic engineering training, computer assembly and network training, innovative design and production training, engineering survey training, automotive engineering training, management technology and industrial engineering training and other multiple professional teaching tasks for different professional students. It is a practical teaching base for cultivating and improving the engineering quality and skills of students comprehensively.

With the expansion of the scale of enrollment, the permeability of cross-discipline is strengthened, so that college engineering training centers are provided with more advanced equipment, more and more comprehensive training projects, wider areas, more beneficiaries and stronger model. As a result, there is an urgent need to introduce advanced management mode to improve the management efficiency with maximum extent. Although colleges and universities now have a relatively perfect management and corresponding management system, the manual management and statistics are mainly popular. According to the teaching plans of academic administrations, the centers conduct macroscopic practical and teaching arrangements (workshop as planned), and the microscopic practical arrangements (equipment as planned) are carried out by the guidance teachers after the macroscopic plans are issued to the workshops based on the plans and equipment resources. Because the information of students, the status of equipment, student scores and other information in the practice process are entered mainly by hand, the real-time monitoring capacity of the centers for the teaching plans is really weak. Those training centers are with low level of visualization, and failing to give full play to advantages of the existing resources of schools by far.

In order to trackle this challenges, RFID technology is the best solution for an innovation management. RFID cards of managers, teachers and students are bundled. An embedded multi-functional intelligent data terminal (IDT) has been explored and used to integrated equipment management, teaching management, materials management, personnel management and other information organically (Figure 1). And resources may be shared to the maximum extent by using RFID integration. The service efficiency of the equipment and related resources can be increased.

This paper is mainly aimed to enhance the efficiency of the practical resources of engineering training centers, improve the flexibility about studying of trainees and take the state teaching pilot demonstration base – the engineering training center of Guangdong University of Technology in Guangzhou High Education Mega Center (GHEMC) as an application background. RFID technology is used as identity tags of teachers and students. The IDT with independent intellectual property right is used as an information exchange platform for workshops. IDTs are also used to establish a three-layer architecture combined with B/S infrastructure for the overall planning of the system structure. Then the templates such as the teaching management, equipment management, materials management, monitoring management, performance management, system management are developed. Learning plans for different training engineering projects can be scheduled, appointed and implemented to achieve the off-site real-time monitoring, visualization and paperless management.

Fig. 1. IDT and deployment

The system interacts and integrates with information of the teaching management system of the academic administration, the equipment management system of the equipment office. It also bundles trainees and teachers with the equipment separately, and issues the teaching plans and production process and other experimental guidance information directly to the IDTs related with equipments. Thus teachers and students through IDTs can simultaneously understand the practice plans and process status of all working procedures in the entire process. And real-time practice, teaching outlines, practice guidance and other help documents can also be got from them. Teachers can also submit real-time equipment condition, practice results and feedback of students through IDTs, so as to conduct real-time monitoring and visualization management of the entire practice process. All of this achievements are based on RFID technology which is justified to be excellent scenanrio.

2 RFID Tech

RFID (Radio Frequency Identification) is an advanced automatic identification technology [2-3]. Compared with traditional bar code and magnetic cards and IC cards, RFID is excellent in non-contact identification, fast reading speed, environmental impact, long service life, and easy-to-use. Futher more RFID also contains anti-collision function, which can simultaneously handle more than one card [4]. This system used RFID is to achieve application of automated information collection, which is to ensure that items can be identified. This typical system consists of RFID tags, readers, antenna, and base station and computer (Figure 2). The required information will be encoded into the electronic label, using electromagnetic induction or microwave non-contact two-way communication. And it achieves identification of targets through the exchange of data, which would effectively guarantee data reliability and accuracy. At present, with the maturation of RFID technology in the asset management applications, costs related products continue to decline, and their use will become more and more widely [5-11].

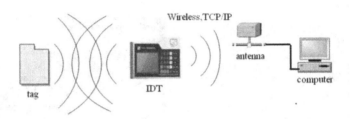

Fig. 2. Principle of RFID

The management of equipment can not be separated from the application of information technology. Equipment management process focuses on how to obtain reliable and valid data and information (especially the equipment operating status information) which is particularly important in the system based on the adoption of RFID technology. The condition information of operation machinery could be monitored and real-time accessed via RFID tech. Further more, information about users on the equipment could also be accessed so as to provide sufficient data to support decision-making when the dynamic curriculum frequently changes.

RFID is very qualified in multi-experiment training center because of its environmental adaptability, the ability of read and write, and its excellent advantages: (1) small, non-contact, reusable; (2) security, anti-cloning; (3) anti-pollution, flexible identification; (4) rewritten; (5) multi-tag identification at the same time. Using the features of RFID, which is the best available methodology improved the present management in the workshop, manufacturing fields have used this technology to tracking production and processes. Notwithstanding RFID has been used in large quantity of fields, multi-experiment training center has not been awaked as some intricate reasons such as magnetic interference, cost, oil pollution, etc.

3   Overview of RFID-Enable Real-Time Multi-experiment Training Center Management System

3.1 Hardware

The hardware of RFID-enable Rea-time Multi-experiment Training Center Management System (RRMTCMS), taking the network as an instance (figure 3), is a platform which contains IDT (Intelligent Data Terminal), BS (Base Station), cable, PCI cards, WS (Work Station) and server. There are three types of network could be used according to the workshop environment and wiring way, including RS485, TCP/IP and 433MHZ wireless communication [9]. And two types of IDT have been developed, one is fixed one and the other is hand-held one, however they have the same function but the hand-held type is much more convenient especially for the warehouse holders and quality checkers. The communication speed could reach 2400bps to 115200bps as the networks and the workshop environments after some basic configurations. The following figure shows a classic network which is set up in RRMTCMS, where are deployed IDTs, WS and servers. After testing with the connection of each component such as computer and cable, cable and BS, PCI-1612 card of four or eight COMs is used for each WS depended on the channel deployed in the workshop.

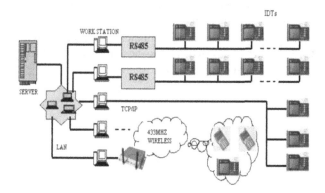

Fig. 3. Hardware and network design

3.1.1 Intelligent Data Terminal (IDT)

From figure 3, the mainly function of IDT is to input/output data and display some basic information which is deployed in the workshops. There are seven main components of IDT, which are showed in figure 4.

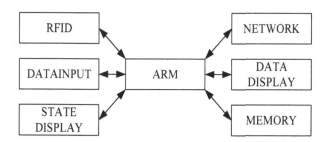

Fig. 4. IDT components

The IDT based on RFID is controlled by the communication procedure up located in WS connected with BS via cable. Data communication protocol is definition followed this rule:

Start (1) address (4) CID (1) STEP (1) INFOLEN (4) XXXX (information contents) CHECK (4) End (1): start: beginning of character string, (1)-represents the length which means 1 Byte; address: the address of IDT with the length of 4 Byte; CID: Current window identity uses one Byte to represent; STEP: the next CID of window when there are some commands took place; INFOLEN: using 4 Byte to record the context length of information communication between IDTs and BS; CHECK: sum of all characters of the string as ASCII then 'and' the sum and FFFF; end: flag of the end .

For example: CID=0, STEP=0 represents an identity code of one window. The string "#1'0105'#$A#$A'0000019A'#2" could be interpreted as: #1: data head, #2: data tail, '0105': IDT address, '#$A#$A': compiled by the object-oriented language, stand for CID=0, STEP=0, '0000': information contents, '019A': check code. IDT sends such string to BS, and then WS receives the string and analyzes them. If the window code is CID=3, STEP=0, the communication procedure converts CID and STEP into '#$D#$A', then reads and judges the information. The principle of IDT how to process production data was shown in figure 5:

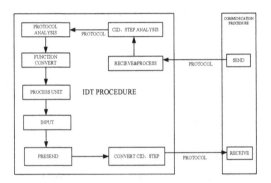

Fig. 5. Principal of IDT

Two types of products of IDT have been produced. As mentioned above, IDT had integrated primary components which RFID is one of the most vital one that could read tags and display information which is auxiliary for the training. Students or trainers usually operate machines, which IDTs are located on or near as convenient as possible. And another reason is the convenience of fetching power sources from machines, as a result, each machine is fixed a IDT for display all the instructions and technologies. After some trails, this deploy methodology is considered to be best one as it is costumed to operators and ambidextrous to the view of technologies while working.

Notwithstanding there are mainly two types of frequency used for RRMTCMS, one was 125KHz as low frequency, and the other was 13.56MHz as high frequency which are used most as the reason of the function range and anti-interference [10-14]. Compared those two kinds of frequency, identification speed of high frequency is less one second than that of low one. Despite the high frequency is the most suitable one for RRMTCMS, as to be a universal and ambidextrous terminal for all manufacturing fields, two frequencies are available after configuration where you could choose one of them as you want. Some technical indicators of IDT are shown in the following texts:

IDT technical indicators:

Power Supply :(DC3.3~7.5) ±10%;   Keyboard: 32;

Screen: 320*240;   Network Interface: TCP/IP, RS422,

433MHz;   BPS Avialable:

Communication Distance :> 500m;   1200/2400/4800/9600/19200;

Working Frequency: 430~434MHz;   Temperature:-10~55°C

Power :> 10mW;   Humidity: 10~90%

3.1.2 Base Station

BS (Base Station), a bridge between WS and IDTs is the other hardware for communication between IDTs and computers, which is the mainly distributing and transferring part in this system which contains five main parts: net control, data process, memory, MCU, send/receive unit. The following figure shows the components of BS and product which has been produced.

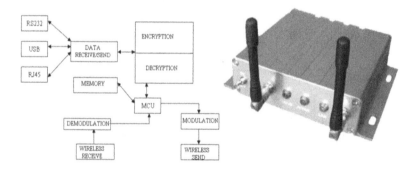

Fig. 6. BS and its Components

Some technical indicators of BS are shown as following:

Power Supply: DC7.5;

Channel available: 8;

Connection: cable, DB-9;

Network: 433MHz;

Communication Distance :> 500m;

Working Frequency: 430~434MHz;

Power :> 10mW;

BPS Available: 1200/2400/4800/9600/19200;

Temperature: -10~55C

Humidity: 10~90%

Terminals do communicate with BS through a wireless networks while each IDT is controlled by WS located in the workshop office centrally, which connects with BS by PCI-1612 card and masked-cable. The BS occupies one frequency with the aim of interference with 50 KHz as bandwidth.

3.2 Software Frameworks

The system mainly serves schools, enterprises, shop staff and equipment managers, students. It also provides some features of serves such as the management of teaching process, information, engineering training for colleges and universities [12-13].

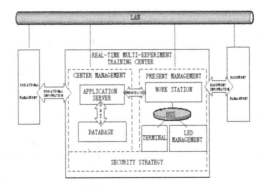

Fig. 7. System framework

This system mainly includes two parts: center management and present management which are shown in figure 7 based on the campus LAN.

3.2.1 Center Management System
Center Management System is a real-time Web management system, mainly realized user-oriented management and learning function such as query and scanning. And center management system provides engineer training processes management via B/S module. Users through center management system are able to monitor and manage the implementation of projects carried out at the scene so as to guide the process of training. But it could also conduct real-time access to learning and operational guidance.

Centre management subsystem includes an application server and database server.B/S network structure is used to form the presentation layer, business layer and data storage layer of thin clients based on WEB browser. Different types of practice resources are uniformly scheduled and managed so as to assist school leaders, academic

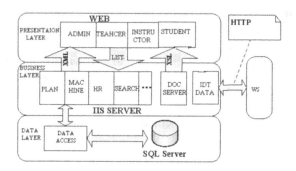

Fig. 8. Centre management system structure

administrators, teachers and students to conduct the overall management and learning of day-to-day teaching tasks. The frame construction of the centre management system is shown in Figure 8.

The main tasks of the centre management subsystem provides users with a convenient , friendly visualization platform and focuses on management of teaching, equipment, assets , personnel, and has teaching management, authority management, system monitoring, statistical inquiry, system management, assets management, materials management, teaching inquiry, user information modification and other functional modules.

3.2.2 Present Management System

Present management system uses C/S structure which is divided into a workshop and operation of Terminal System. The terminal system is a distribution of hardware that main major is to display and collect training data with 433MHz wireless communication protocol [9].

The site management system is achieved by C/S structure and divided into two levels: workshop workstation and operating terminal system. The workshop workstation can communicate with the workshop data inquiry terminals through site workshop bus or TCP/IP or 433M wireless or others. The structure of the site management system is shown in Figure 9:

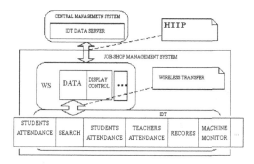

Fig. 9. Structure of the site management system

3.2.3 Workstation

Workstation as a server for the terminals provides data services to upload and transfer information to every student who is going to have this training.

Terminal operation system is involved in training students in the entire process, whose main function is to identify student via RFID cards, track attendance, search information, and view operation guidance [14]. At the same time teachers are provided for the services of attendance querying, information querying, performance evaluation, equipment management and some other functions. The following figures show some system running windows.

The workshop workstation is placed in each workshop and is responsible for the information collection and management of the corresponding intelligent management terminals in each workshop .It provides workshop information data to the management service program and is a bridge of communication between the workshop site and the management. First of all, the operation authorities of all users are input and defined. The data collected for various needs and the production processes applicable to the characteristics of each station are defined. In accordance with the requests of various needs, all display information and course information as well as practical tasks is issued IDTs. At the same time workshop panels are controlled, information display panels is customized; the data collected by the IDTs are submitted to the interface of the center management subsystem. The workshop managers can adjust appropriately the trainees and plans.

IDTs are installed and bundled on the practice site with specific equipment, that means the IDT mentioned correspondingly communicate or connected with the specific equipment. They collect the dynamic operating information of the corresponding equipment or working stations directly or indirectly, such as operating status of the equipment, operating time, the maintenance time and results of the learners who practice on the equipment. They also provide the site practice process with attendance, data inquiry, operating guidance. At the same time, they provide an exchange platform for attendance, inquiry, results evaluation and equipment information management. All data collected by the IDTs are timely sent to the workshop workstations. Functions of

Fig. 10. System running windows

IDT are as follows: (1) acquisition of practice program, (2) acquisition and display of equipment information, (3) inquiry of practice processes, (4) report of equipment status, (5) evaluation of teacher results.

The communication management module is separately connected to more than eight IDTs .In the circumstance of wireless connectivity; one or more wireless base stations are set up in order to prevent data signals from excessive collisions. System windows are shown in figure 10.

4 Optimization

4.1 Modular Optimization

As data interaction relatively frequent between the functional modules and real-time Web system, all the functional modules above are required to be optimized to meet the needs of users and management requirements.

In order to increase transmission efficiency of the data, some simple data are processed and calculated by the client in the system by means of XML technology, so an independent service program forming into a virtual four-layer B/S organizational structure is designed (figure 11). The necessity for expansion of the three-layer B/S is also explained by the development environment of visual studio 2005. The independence service program increased can reduce data transmission of client and server and improve the utilization rate of resources and implementation efficiency.

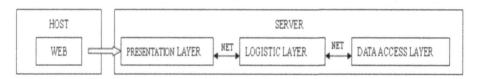

Fig. 11. Frame organization method

In addition, the adjustment scheme of the system also includes the entity data, data types, local and global variables and so on. First of all, the data cache mechanism is used for the page data. And .NET owns strong data processing ability. When a user sends the page request, the system first checks whether there is the object inside the cache, and then returns to the client.Afer the check, the system will inquire the database and then return the inquired results via the web. Data exchanges between all pages and database or the information of pages obtained could be viewed by session. Once again, excessive data going back and forth between the database and Web pages are well designed, the client resources are used to verify the input data, and the press of database is reduced. The data types are appropriately adjusted, and the new requirements can be met as long as the values of the parameters are modified when the program is modified to establish a re-load mechanism. The global variables and local variables are appropriately arranged because the global variables play a role in the survival period of the whole program, it is necessary to verify them because of their impact. On the data of the whole program; the local variables should act locally in the survival period, so have no impact on other data. The resources are timely released, that is, the resources occupied must be released after completion, and if too many objects have not been released, the working space is increased and the system resources are reduced. The resources of the objects are released by the function named close (). At last the in the lower layer, terminals which collect and upload data by wireless are operated in the database as far as possible, so as to prevent the duplication of data flow to the database through Web system.

In this system, the application layer on a separate independent is on the server. As long as the client-side interfaces and services could deal with some simple calculations so as to release the client, what is more important is to reduce the data processing pressure of server-side.

There are some advantages by applying the above methodology:

a) sharing of the server data processing pressure, the simple logic operations and calculation are completed on the client so as to reduce server press;

b) reducing the flow and stream exchanges of data between client and server, saving bandwidth constraints during data flow requirements;

c) acilitating the realization of modular interface, which could also enhance the independence of the function modules to achieve a good design goal under bandwidth limitations ;

d) reducing refresh frequency to facilitate the realization of "WYSIWYG" design philosophy;

e) preventing a variety of database connections by a unified database connection interface standardization;

f) reducing unnecessary data transmission, and improving resource utilization and process efficiency, as the aim of increasing system stability;

g) reducing maintenance time and cost;

As the interaction of data and Web system requirements for real-time requirements, it is necessary to optimize the function modules, so as to achieve excellent performances. Module optimizations are mainly illustrated in the following texts: (1) using data package and interface design features to achieve data coherence ; (2) using sub-level methodology to design the function of sub-module, between each levels with AOE Network modules required for the completion; (3) whole system is divided by functional modules into several levels of abstraction, so each object is distinct; (4) forecasting data integrity and consistency; (5) In order to maintain data flow consistency, the entire system data is monitored by the management of whole approach to prevent, produce and read "dirty data".

4.2 System Adjustment

System adjustment programs include data physical adjustments, data type adjustment, local and global variables adjustment, etc. Firstly, page of data uses data caching mechanism, which is .Net's own strong data processing. When one user requests a page, the system first checks the cache, if there is existed, and then returns to the client, if not then queries the database. Last query results are returned to the customer through the web page. All pages and data exchanges between databases are available through session. Secondly, to avoid too much data intercommunication between database and Web page, appropriate server control is introduced to reduce the database pressure. Thirdly, the modification process as long as the amendments to the value of the parameter is to meet the new requirements. Then establishment of heavy-duty mechanism is rebuilt. Fourthly, global variables and local variables are made appropriate arrangements. As global variables for the survival of the whole process work period, it is necessary to be verified, because it affects the whole process of data. Local variables should accomplish the partial role in the survival period so as not to have an impact on other data. Fifthly, it is primary to release resources timely. When the code is not released after the completion of sharing of resources, too much created objects would occupy resources, in the results of increasing of threads and the reduction of system resources. Thus the overall system performance will be depredated. Close () method is used to complete the release. Finally, low-level data, especially collected by wireless terminal is completed to prevent the adoption of Web system to write back to the database once again to repeat the operation data streams.

4.3 Code Optimization

4.3.1 Optimization Methodologies

Test results show that the code quality directly affects the whole performance and maintenance of a system. Code reusing and reconstruction not only could improve the quality of code, but also could improve the maintainability of the procedure. So it is necessary to optimize the code. In this system, optimizations follow the texts:

(1) Code testing: to complete this one, confirmation process functions in all cases should be followed output function and design object method. After that, this code would have a high reliability;

(2) Code reusing: some methods are used for code design. As long as program could call functions, this system uses common.cs and CSS documents, such as public static void LogEMOperation () {~}, to complete the logging operation;

(3) Database connection: the definition of a unified database of links is proposed to operate string public class ConnStr (public static string ConnString = onfigurationManager.ConnectionStrings ["ConnStringName"]. ConnectionString;);

(4) exception monitoring: database operation that may arise in the operation of a number of anomalies, so we used the following code to monitor abnormal: try (~) catch (Exception) (~);

(5) e-forms package: all the documents in electronic form are abstracted into a category. Then object operation is achieved to complete the form processing, which could be inherited, such as derivatives to achieve the same treatment.

4.3.2 Improvement

This system has been implicated in the Engineering Training Center in Guang Dong University of Technology since Sep.2007. After one year testing and improving, great benefits have been achieved via accelerate information transmission and real-time tasks assignment using 433MHz wireless communication and RFID which mainly used for the identification of users and attendances. Some indicators were informed in the following tables.

At present, Guangdong University has developed into a set of turner, fitter, CNC, casting, and assembling etc. It also owns more than 10 workshops, which have the training capacity of 500 persons/day in the large-scale comprehensive training center. The information intercommunication between teachers and students, teaching management and the teaching departments, engineering training center and management department is greatly increasing for exchanging and sharing sources. Engineering Training Center through this RRMTCMS enables to deal with a variety of data processing and analyze the increasing workload and complexity.The traditional extensive manual management methods can not meet the teaching issues to establish a highly efficient and flexible management information system. As a result, RRMTCMS obtains the achievement of dynamic and self-configuration teaching, freely information exchanging, practice plans and issues real-time reporting, online scheduling, timely practice and teaching evaluation. Moreover, equipment, materials and other functions are also maintained in this system so as to achieve agile response to every emergency.

At present, the engineering training practice management system has the following characteristics:

1) Management System and more students to practice based on the curriculum management style, stay in the upper deck, not taking into account the specific plant and equipment management.

2) Management system with B / S mode or C / S mode to achieve;

3) Management System integration is not high, can only be carried out with the teaching-related practices, achievements, simple fragmented management courses.

As the system based on B/S+C/S, there is not only campus networks but also Internet could logon this system which meant the resources sharing is more higher than before as operated by hand only in the past. Some good results have been achieved from the tables.

Table 1. System indicators

ITEMS	DATA
Furthest Range	500m
Number of Terminals	60sets
Picture Download Time	<5s
BER	<0.001
Resend Rate	<0.01
Packet Loss Rate	<0.0001
Keyboard Average Response Time	<1s

Table 2. Improvement

Items	Comparisons	
	Before	**Now**
Information Respond	Slow (cross Depart.)	Real-time
Task correction	90%	99%
Paper saving	100%	0%(Paperless)
Teacher's work	100%	50%
Resources sharing	Low	High
Data input	100%	10%
Visualization	20%	>95%

This paper introduces a real-time experimental training system integrated the use of C/S+B/S as system structure, which is proofed to be a good method which is able to meet the requirements of real-time teaching and tracking. With the traditional combination of C/S and B/S, this system has achieved such following obvious advantages after practice in Guangdong University of Technology Traning Center:

1) Real-time processing
Using of the above data processing system, WEB page could entered and modified data in real-time spread of system C/S structure with RFID terminals. So this system can reach a high real-time requirement to meet the training process of the timeliness of information transferring issues;

2) Good system stability
Because of the advantages of C/S+B/S, the system uses this architecture best met the functional and performance requirements. After the relevant data processed in the two modes, this system achieves a consistency of data by testing in high-intensity.

3) Optimization under limited resources
Based on B/S greatly affected by network bandwidth, we use such combination of B/S and C/S to reduce the bandwidth limitations of the data traffic. In accordance with the requirements of actual system, we optimize data packet and made use of relevant WEB server programming techniques to alleviate the pressure.

4) Various forms of data views
The system has various forms of data presentation. One is shown on RFID terminal screen with the experiment content, equipment information etc. The other is LED displaying with workshop teaching tasks, student information. Third, workstation with teaching information monitoring is viewed in the computer. The last one is the adoption of RFID terminal displayed in monitor via cable.

5 Key Technologies

Some key technologies which are illustrated in the following passages included all the functions of real-time multi-experiment training center.

(1) Bulk data processing techniques
BS (Base station) based on 433MHz wireless communication is a bridge between data collecting and displaying terminals. And WS (Work Station) uses multi-serial card to connect to the corresponding BS. Terminals are set up through channel number and address to identify its distinction. The same line has same channel frequency, so as to distinguish different lines. The addresses are different from a distinction between different terminals. BSs communicate by differ frequencies with the terminals. Communication program which is mainly to control communication mechanisms used multi-thread synchronization techniques and DLL to solve bulk data upload and download issues which are frequently occurred.

(2) BLOB (Binary Large Object) data-processing technology
BLOB data is a binary large object data, such as pictures, documents, and multimedia data. In the C/S structure, the graphics is saved in a binary file, so the using should be in the form of packet transmission. However in B/S structure, it is general to use relative path to access its file name, but in this system it uses byte [] binData method to get those files, and myFile2.PostedFile.InputStream.Read to process. The using of binary data stream technology and realization of BLOB data in the database access is a realization of two structural data compatibility mode.

(3) C/S+B/S real-time data processing technology
The system uses C/S+B/S combination of design method. In both modes, it must adopt a certain degree of effective transfer mechanism in order to achieve real-time data transmission. Accordingly, the system mainly carries out following data transmissions. In C/S model, using real-time data communication program for all bus terminals is a good way to achieve enquiries. When the terminals are in operation and communication controlled for access data from the database, the obtained data is sent to the terminal. Communication program uses 1/N seconds repeatedly polling interval (N for the terminal number). In the other hand, B/S model uses JavaScript to detect database. When database updated, data accessing is sent to Web page.

(4) Data consistency Tec
As the system database preserves text data, binary data streams, multimedia data, XML data, and other data, which must be processed under C/S and B/S module. It is important to maintain the consistency. We adopt the following techniques to achieve the goal:

●Services Technology: Service is used to access and modify the procedures of various kinds of   data units, which are panels during the data-processing. It should be either completed or not, known as "atomic" Therefore it is also to prevent "read repeat", "write repeat", and "read dirty data".

●Concurrency control techniques: it is a realization of affairs orderly. In order to achieve this implementation, each data item sets up a mutually exclusive lock, which is mutually exclusive and marked as resource.

6 Conclusion

RFID technology is used timely and accurately to access real-time information, which could track and retrospect the staff, materials, equipment status, and the implementation of teaching plans, detect the bottlenecks in practice and realize the real-time scheduling in practice. The workshop processes practice information which is timely feeded back to the top management system, which not only provides scientific decision-making for the school with support, but more importantly provides the share resources of more than 10 colleges and universities in GHEMC. This system plays very much great significance on realizing the fine management of the experimental center, enhances the workshop tracking capability, improves the utilization rate of laboratory equipment, reduces training costs, promotes the comprehensive applications of scientific research results in the experimental teaching field, and builds the engineering training center into a state scientific research, teaching and experimental demonstration. Base with a combination of scientific research and teaching experiment the relevant research results could also be applied and promoted in other colleges and universities. Other engineering training aspects are promoted with very broad application prospects.

Real-time multi-experimental training center management system is a good tool to aide teachers and students to get dynamic information and operation guidance via RFID terminals. And this system is easy logon as long as you could use the IE address bar enter the URL to get the crucial information in advance. The other is through the RFID card registry. Both of which could monitor the entire system data, management, setting parameters etc. Students could view the information operations, usage of varied and flexible manner of data information collection and integration of examinations and self-established studying.

However there are some limitations and improvements for this system. First, interface intercommunicated with other systems should be set up in order to accelerate information delivering speed. Then, dynamic training plan scheduling is one of the most vital problems which should be solved urgently as all of the works should be input by hands. Some of the machinery distribution can be automated by system itself, but most of tasks achieved by hands.

Overall, this system proposed in this paper provides a great implementation of integration of RFID, wireless communication, Web tech and C/S module. Great progress is achieved according to the practice. This paper would like to bring some brainstorms to this research fields.

Acknowledgements. The authors thank to the nation R&D which gave partial finance support and the chance to accomplish the research. Thanks to all members of project team, Faculty of Information Engineering of University of Guangdong University of Technology, Department of Industry & Manufacturing System Engineering the University of Hong Kong, especially the constructive guidance from great many experts and engineers. Finally thank you very much to Guangdong University of Technology.

References

[1] Runyang, Z., Qingyun, D., Ke, Z., Meilin, W., Jin, W., Zexi, L.: Instruction and Realization of Real-time Web System Based on RFID. Modern Computer 9, 7–9 (2008)

[2] Poon, K.T.C., Choy, K.L., Lau, H.C.W.: A real-time manufacturing risk management system: An integrated RFID approach. Portland International Center for Management of engineering and Technology, 2872–2879 (2007)

[3] Rizzi, A., Montanari, R., Volpi, A., Tizzi, M.: Reengineering and simulation of an RFID manufacturing system. Int. J. Dynamics in Logistics, 211–219 (2008)

[4] Budak, E., Catay, B., Tekin, i., et al.: Design of an RFID-based Manufacturing Monitoring and Analysis System. In: RFID Eurasia, 2007 1st Annual, pp. 1–6 (2007)

[5] Huang, G.Q., Zhang, Y.F., Jiang, P.Y.: RFID-Based Wireless Manufacturing for Walking-Worker Assembly Islands with Fixed-Position Layouts. Int. J. Prod. Res. 23/4, 469–477 (2007)

[6] Zhong, R.-y., Dai, Q.-y., Zhou, K., Dai, X.-b.: Design and Implementation of DMES Based on RFID. In: International Conference on Anti-counterfeiting, Security, and Identification 2008, pp. 475–477. IEEE, Los Alamitos (2008)

[7] Liu, W.-n., Huang, W.-l., Sun, D.-h., Zhao, M., et al.: Design and implementation of discrete manufacturing industry MES based on RFID technology. CIMS 13, 1886–1890 (2007)

[8] Hua, J., Liang, T., Lei, Z.: Study and Design Real-time Manufacturing Execution System Base on RFID. In: Second International Symposium on Intelligent Information Technology Application, pp. 591–594 (2008)

[9] Dai, Q., Liu, Y., Jiang, Z., Liu, Z., Zhou, K., Wang, J.: MES Wireless Communication Networking Technology Based on 433MHZ.2008ASID, pp. 110–114.

[10] Keskilammi, M., Sydänheimo, L., Kivikoski, M.: Radio Frequency Technology for Automated Manufacturing and Logistics Control. Part 1: Passive RFID Systems and the Effects of Antenna Parameters on Operational Distance. Int. J. Adv. Manuf. Technol. 21, 769–774 (2003)

[11] Penttilä, K., Keskilammi, M., Sydänheimo, L., et al.: Radio frequency technology for automated manufacturing and logistic control. Part 2: RFID antenna utilization in industrial applications. Int. J. Adv. Manufacturing Tec. 31(1-2), 116–124 (2006)

[12] Run-yang, Z., Qing-yun, D., Ke, Z., Mei-lin, W., Ze-xi, L.: Study on key data processing technology in the real-time multi-experimental teaching management system. Modern Manufacturing Engineering 12, 122–125 (2008)

[13] Run-yang, Z., Qing-yun, D., Mei-lin, W.: Design of Engineering Training System Based on Improved Three B/S Layer. Journal of Jiang Xi Normal University 32(5), 530–533 (2008)

[14] Kim, C., Nam, S.-Y., Park, D.-J., Park, I.J., Hyun, T.-Y.: Product control system using RFID tag information and data mining. In: Stajano, F., Kim, H.-J., Chae, J.-S., Kim, S.-D. (eds.) ICUCT 2006. LNCS, vol. 4412, pp. 100–109. Springer, Heidelberg (2007)

[15] Poon, K.T.C., Choy, K.L., Lau, H.C.W.: A real-time manufacturing risk management system: An integrated RFID approach. In: Portland International Center for Management of engineering and Technology, pp. 2872–2879 (2007)

[16] Run-yang, Z., Qing-yun, D., ke, Z.: Realization of Program Based on Plug-Universal Database-Aided Design. In: International Conference on Information Management, Innovation Management and Industrial Engineering, vol. 11, pp. 377–380. IEEE Computer Society, Los Alamitos (2008)

Secured Resource Selection in Grid Computing: Trust and Reputation Sentient Scheme

V. Vijayakumar[1] and R.S.D. Wahida Banu[2]

[1] PhD Research Scholar, Faculty of Information and Communication Engineering
Anna University, Chennai, Tamilnadu, India
vijayakumarphd@yahoo.com
[2] PhD Research Supervisor, Faculty of Information and Communication Engineering,
Anna University, Chennai, Tamilnadu, India
rsdwb@yahoo.com

Abstract. The primary concern in proffering an infrastructure for general purpose computational grids formation is security. A majority of the grid implementations tend to address the safety concerns by authenticating the users, hosts and their interactions in an appropriate manner. Sophisticated and secured resource management systems are mandatory for the efficient and beneficial utilization of grid computing services. The wide range of selection and the high degree of strangeness have been identified as the problem factors in the secured selection of grid. Efficient resource allocation and utilization can not be achieved with the lack of a higher degree of confidence relationship. Owing to the large scale applications in e-commerce and on-line communities, reputation mechanisms have been widely acknowledged as one of the significant techniques supporting distributed application and system safety lately. We have proposed a novel approach in this paper that is aimed at providing trust and reputation aware security for resource selection in grid computing. In this approach, the self-protection capability and reputation weightage of an entity is utilized to obtain the Trust Factor (TF) value of that particular entity. In addition, jobs are probably allocated to entities that posses higher TF values. The proposed approach has been found to satisfactorily manage the increase in number of user jobs and grid entities. Extensive experimental evaluation of the performance shows that ascertaining grid entities intended towards the secured execution of the job with the aid of the proposed approach is competent and acceptable.

Keywords: Grid Computing, Computational Grids, Security, Resource Management, Trust, Self-Protection Capability, Reputation.

1 Introduction

The escalating amounts of resources present in the Internet and the recent advancements in wide-area network performance have aided in the emergence of grid computing as a feasible archetype to satisfy the continuous growth of computation power demand that cannot be fulfilled utilizing the inner resources of a single organization [33]. The objective to share processing resources among many organizations so as to

T.-h. Kim et al. (Eds.): FGCN 2008, CCIS 27, pp. 169–183, 2009.
© Springer-Verlag Berlin Heidelberg 2009

resolve large scale problems has led to the introduction of computational grids [1, 2]. A collection of resources (computational devices, networks, online instruments, storage archives, etc.) that can be utilized as a collection is termed as a Grid. Grids are becoming widespread platforms for high-performance and resource-intensive applications owing to the fact that they possess vast potential of capabilities that can aid large distributed applications [34]. A concept or methodology where in the intent is on combining a set of distributed resources that can be applied at diverse computer system levels like computation, data, software, agents, users and the like.

Besides proffering pervasive, dependable, consistent, and cost-effective access to the various services provided by the distributed resources grids can support problem solving environments that might be created using such resources [35]. High performance distributed resources analogous to high performance systems, networks, databases and the like are made use of by the Grid applications. These have enabled via grid middleware for instance Globus [12], Gridbus [15]. The grid resources are dynamic in nature. The grid computing resources fall into various levels ranging from a small number of large clusters (for example the TeraGrid [6]) to millions of PC-class machines (for example SETI@Home [7]). Dynamic allocation and release of resources is necessitated by a powerful Grid system. Allocation of resources to ensure that the desired computing power is yielded besides enhancing the security at the same instant are vital things to be accomplished to create assured trust in grid computing [36].

Uncertainly, a considerable challenge for Grid computing is the development of a comprehensive set of mechanisms and policies for protecting the grid. Currently, Grid security research and development concentrates on developing enhanced solutions to cater the subsequent requirements: Authentication, Secure Communication, Effective Security Policies, Authorization, and Access Control. A range of security functionality like the authentication, authorization, credential conversion, auditing, and delegation need to supported by the applications and services of the Grid environment so as to ensure secure operation. It is mandatory for the Grid applications to interact with the other applications and services which posses a wide variety of security mechanisms and requirements [37].

The two elementary necessities in Grid applications are resource and security guarantee [8, 9]. The concrete and precise problems underlying the grid concept are coordinated resource sharing and problem resolving in dynamic, multi-institutional virtual organizations [10]. Infected grid resources can possibly ruin the applications running on the same grid platform via the malicious codes implanted by intruders. The apprehensive sharing is not principally file exchange but rather direct access to computers, software, data and other resources that are necessary for various collaborative problem-solving and resource-brokering strategies emerging in industry, science and engineering [11]. Various phenomenons like (a) geographical distribution of resources, (b) resource heterogeneity, (c) autonomously administered Grid domains having their own resource policies and practices, and (d) Grid domains using different access and cost models create huge challenges for resource management in grid systems.

Currently security is incorporated in the grid toolkits (e.g. the Globus toolkit [12]) utilized at the provider sites (parties that offer resources for use in the grid). Secure channels, authentication [13], unsupervised login, delegation, and resource usage [11] are all managed by the toolkit. However the security of the grid user is not taken into account by these mechanisms (the person or entity desires to utilize resources). The user if forced to trust the provider without confirming the justification of the trust [16]. Users submit jobs to distant resources and normally have no explicit control over the resources themselves. Thus mutually users and resources can be looked upon as independent agents, having control of their own behavior. This independence provides rise to intrinsic insecurity due to the fact that an individual cannot predict the response of another to varying situations. The grid service providers must proffer guaranteed definite security, privacy protection, and dependable accessibility of all Grid-enabling platforms [9].

Majority of the grid computing environments highlight their security concerns in authenticating users and hosts and in the communications between them in an appropriate manner. To automatically and clearly ensure the fulfillment, the effective and efficient exploitation of Grid computing facilities requires advanced and secured resource management systems. This fulfillment is for both the functional requirements and the non-functional ones. The wide range of selection and the high degree of strangeness paves way for problems in secured grid resource selection. Beneficial resource allocation and utilization can not be achieved devoid of the assurance of a higher degree of trust relationship. Lately, reputation mechanisms have developed into one of the most significant techniques supporting the distributed application and system safety for its better scalability and robustness owing to the huge applications in e-commerce and on-line communities.

Here we have presented an improved version of our earlier works [31], [32] with more security factors for self-protection capability and attributes for reputation weightage calculation. The primary intent of this research is to develop a solution that could avail trust and reputation aware security for resource selection in grid sites for scheduling large number of independent and indivisible jobs. The scheduling of the incoming jobs is carried out by the proposed approach on basis of the trust factor value. The feed back from user community on past behavior of the resource is used in determining its self-protection capability and reputation weightage which in turn are used in estimation of the resource's trust factor (TF) value. The ability of a site to detect intrusions, viruses, unauthorized access and secured file storage and job completing abilities is termed as self protection capability of that site. Reputation mechanisms pave a way for creating trust through social control with the aid of community based feedback about past experiences of entities. Our approach is intended to inflict security in grids through security- assured resource allocation.

The remaining sections are organized as follows; Section 2 presents a brief review of related work. Section 3 confers an overview of Trust and Reputation. The proposed approach for secured resource selection for scheduling incoming jobs is discussed detailed in Section 4. Experimental results are given in Section 5 and conclusions are summarized up in Section 6.

2 Related Work

Our work is inspired by a number of previous works related to trust management and reputation based security enhancement for sustaining performance of grid computing. These related works are reviewed below.

Farag Azzedin and Muthucumaru Maheswaran [14] proposed a formal definition of both trust and reputation and discussed a model for incorporating trust into Grid systems. Rajkumar Buyya and Srikumar Venugopal [15] proposed an overview of an open source Grid toolkit, called Gridbus, whose architecture is fundamentally driven by the requirements of Grid economy. Gridbus technologies provide services for both computational and data grids that power the emerging eScience and eBusiness applications.

Ernesto Damiani et al. [24] proposed a self-regulating system for P2P network using robust reputation mechanism. In their system reputation sharing is realized through distributed polling algorithm. Chuang Liu et al. [26] proposed a general-purpose resource selection framework by defining a resource selection service for locating Grid resources that match application requirements and evaluated them based on specified performance model and mapping strategies, and returned a suitable collection of resources, if any are available.

Yao Wang and Julita Vassileva [22] proposed a bayesian network-based trust model and a method for building reputation based on recommendations in peer-to-peer networks. Sepandar D. Kamvar et al. [25] proposed a reputation management system, called EigenTrust, which can effectively reduce the number of downloads of inauthentic files in a P2P system. The reputation value of each peer is determined by the number of successful downloads and the "opinions" of other peers.

Shanshan Song and Kai Hwang [18] proposed a new fuzzy-logic trust model for securing Grid computing across multiple resources sites. They have developed a new Grid security scheme, called SARAH supported by encrypted channels among private networks. Justin R.D. Dyson et al. [17] described a trust framework model for Grid computing, which enables users to execute their jobs on reliable and efficient resources, thereby satisfying clients' quality-of-service (QoS) requirements.

Farag Azzedin and Muthucumaru Maheswaran [23] proposed a trust brokering system that operates in a peer-to-peer manner. They have developed a security-aware model between resource providers and the consumers that separates the concepts of accuracy and honesty. Shanshan Song et al. [27] proposed a new fuzzy-logic trust model for securing Grid resources. They have developed a SeGO scheduler for trusted Grid resource allocation.

Li Xiong and Ling Liu [28] proposed a reputation-based trust supporting framework, which includes a coherent adaptive trust model for quantifying and comparing the trustworthiness of peers based on a transaction-based feedback system and a decentralized implementation of such a model over a structured P2P network.

Ian Foster [12] reviewed briefly the current status of Globus, focusing in particular on those aspects of the GT4 release that should be of interest to those wishing to work with the software. Chunqi Tian et al. [29] proposed ARTrust—an Attack Resistant Trust management model, a novel recommendation based trust model for P2P networks.

Baolin Ma et al. [30] proposed a trust model, which is used to compute and compare the trustworthiness of entities in the same autonomous and different domains. This model provides different methods to deal with the problems of users and related resources belonging to the same or different domains. Nadia Ranaldo and Eugenio Zimeo [3] proposed a framework for brokering of Grid resources, virtualized through web Services, which can be dynamically configured with respect to multiple syntactic and semantic description languages and related matching strategies.

Zhiguo Shi et al. [10] proposed a novel anonymous coordination authentication scenario which can provide efficient and reliable anonymous identity authentication and remote platform attestation for Grid computing systems. Lohr et al. [16] proposed an approach to enhance the Grid security using a combination of trusted computing and virtualization technologies.

3 Trust and Reputation

This section furnishes a short foreword regarding trust and reputation in the context of Grid Computing.

3.1 Trust

Trust is the foundation of both human society and cyberspace security. All of us are aware of the significance of trusting some one. The nature of trust is decentralization since the parameters of trust are often personal. A feeling of confidence that a particular party would work in an anticipated fashion regardless of monitoring or controlling the party can be termed as Trust. Generally trust is positive and envisages a good outcome in indecisive circumstances. Trust is not a black and white substance. Frequently grey area exists in conveying the trustworthiness of a computer site [18]. Similar to human relationship, trust is expressed by a linguistics term rather numerically. Trust differs with respect to time and environment. The concept of trust is a multipart subject related to a firm belief in attributes for instance reliability, honesty and competence of the trusted entity. The definition of trust proposed by Farag Azzedin and Muthucumaru Maheswaran [14] is as follows: Trust is the firm belief in the competence of an entity to act as expected such that this Firm belief is not a fixed value associated with the entity but rather it is subject to the entity's behavior and applies only within a specific context at a given time. The firm belief is a dynamic value and spans over a set of values ranging from very trustworthy to very untrustworthy. The trust factor has built on the basis of past experiences and has given for a specific context. The trust factor is specified within a given time since the trust level between two entities is not necessarily the same from today to a year ago.

3.2 Reputation

In recent times, with larger applications in e-commerce and on-line communities, reputation mechanisms have become one of the most important techniques underpinning the distributed application and system safety for its better scalability and flexibility. Since one can trust another on basis of good reputation, the latter acts as a means of building trust. A measure of trustworthiness in the sense of reliability is called Reputation. Reputation systems [19] provide a technique for building trust through social control without trusting third parties. Using community based feedback about past experiences of entities; reputation mechanisms provide a technique for building trust through social control. This helps in making suggestion and judgment on quality and consistency of the transactions [20]. The definition of reputation proposed by Farag Azzedin and Muthucumaru Maheswaran [14] is as follows: The reputation of an entity is an expectation of its behavior based on other entities' observations or information about the entity's past behavior at a given time.

4 Secured Resource Selection for Scheduling Jobs

This section explains our proposed approach for resource selection designed for safe scheduling of independent and individual jobs to grid sites. The scale of resources and the strangeness of entities cause difficulties in the process of resource selection. Since a high-efficient society cannot go with a high-trustworthy social relationship, efficient resource sharing cannot be attained in Grid without certain trust relationship core. Entities can depend on others for information pertaining to a particular entity while making trust based decisions. This can be achieved by the reputation mechanism. By considering the above conditions, we have proposed an approach by combining both trust and reputation. The proposed approach aims for secure scheduling of incoming jobs based on the Trust Factor value to available resource sites. The Trust Factor (TF) value of each resource site is calculated through its self-protection capability and reputation weightage obtained from user community on its past behavior. Two necessary assumptions are made below: (a) all resource sites have prior agreements to participate in the Grid operations; and (b) the Grid sites truthfully report their self-protection capability to Grid organization manager (GOM). Selfish Grids [21] are not considered in our approach.

4.1 Self-protection Capability

The grid organization manager maintains the self-protection capability of all entities in a grid organization. Every so often each entity reports its self-protection capability trustfully and honestly to the GOM. The self-protection capability of an entity is calculated by aggregating the values of the below mentioned security factors. The value of these factors differs in the range between 0 and 1.

- *IDS Capabilities:* - The ability of an entity to protect the system against host and network based intrusions.
- *Anti-virus Capabilities:* - The ability of an entity to defend against viruses and malicious codes.
- *Firewall Capabilities:* - The ability to protect the entity from other network accesses.
- *Authentication Mechanism:* - The ability of the mechanism to verify an identity claimed by or for a system security.
- *Secured File Storage Capabilities:* - The ability of an entity for securely storing the files needed for the execution of job.
- *Interoperability:* - The ability of an entity to restrict the interfacing between concurrent jobs.
- *Secured Job Execution:* - The ability of an entity for the secure execution of the job.
- *Authorization:* - The mechanism used by an entity to determine what level of access a particular authenticated user should have to secure resources controlled by the entity.

Based on their contribution to security, a weightage is given to all the security factors and as a final point aggregated to compute the self-protection capability. The weightage assigned to the security factors are listed in Table1.

Table 1. Weightage of Security Factors

Security Factors	Weightage (W)
IDS Capabilities	0.825
Anti-virus Capabilities	0.85
Firewall Capabilities	0.9
Authentication Mechanism	0.8
Secured File Storage Capabilities	0.7
Interoperability	0.6
Secured Job Execution	0.75
Authorization	0.87

The self-protection capability is calculated using the following formula

$$SPC = \sum_{i=1}^{n} W(i) * A(i)$$

Where n is the total number of factors, W is the weightage and $A(i)$ value of the factor.

4.2 Reputation Computation

Since reputation is a multi-faceted concept [22], it has many aspects for instance truthfulness, honesty and so on. Reputation weightage is calculated via the feedback on quite a lot of security characteristics provided by the user community about their previous experiences. After the usage, users will provide feedback on the attributes to the Reputation manager (RM) based on their experience. The feedback is a value in the range between 0 and 1. An entity's feedback from all the users has aggregated. The reputation weightage is calculated with the algorithm in section 4.2.1. The RM in grid organization maintains the reputation weightage of all entities. The security attributes considered for the reputation are as follows.

- *Consistency:* - The ability of an entity to perform its required functions under stated conditions for a specified period of time
- *Confidentiality:*- The ability to keep information from being disclosed to unauthorized users
- *Truthfulness:* - The ability of the entity to ensure that the data is protected from unauthorized modifications
- *Security:* - The ability of the system to provide protection to job execution and file storage.
- *Privacy:* - The ability to keep some information solely to oneself
- *Non-repudiation:* - The inability of something that performed a particular action to later deny that they were indeed responsible for the event

- *Authentication:* - Defined as the process of verifying an identity claimed by or for a system entity. An authentication process consists of two steps: Identification and Verification
- *Authorization:* - Refers to the process of granting privileges to processes and, ultimately, users. This differs from authentication in that authentication is the process used to identify a user. Once identified (reliably), the privileges, rights, property, and permissible actions of the user are determined by authorization.
- *Reliability:* - Defined as the probability that all the programs involved in the grid system execute successfully.
- *Robustness:* - Defined as the capability of a system in coping well with the attacks to that system.

4.2.1 Algorithm for Reputation Weightage Calculation

The aggregated feedback of all the security attributes of an entity is represented as a Reputation Vector (R_V) as follows.

$$R_v = [SA_1, SA_2, \ldots\ldots, SA_n]$$

Where n is the total number of security attributes.

The aggregated feedback of all the entities in the Grid domain is represented as a Reputation Matrix (R_M) as follows. Each row in R_M represents the reputation vector R_V of an entity.

$$R_M = \begin{bmatrix} SA_{11} & SA_{12} & SA_{13}\ldots\ldots SA_{1j} \\ SA_{21} & SA_{22} & SA_{23}\ldots\ldots SA_{2j} \\ SA_{i1} & SA_{i2} & SA_{i3}\ldots\ldots SA_{ij} \end{bmatrix}$$

Where i represent the number of entities and j represent the number of attributes.

The reputation weightage of each entity is evaluated by its relativity with other entities in the Grid domain by forming a relativity matrix. The relativity matrix is formed as follows.

$$\mathrm{Re}\,l_{Mat} = \begin{bmatrix} \varphi(E_1, E_1) & \varphi(E_1, E_2) & \varphi(E_1, E_3) \cdots\cdots \varphi(E_1, E_n) \\ \varphi(E_2, E_1) & \varphi(E_2, E_2) & \varphi(E_2, E_3) \cdots\cdots \varphi(E_2, E_n) \\ \varphi(E_3, E_1) & \varphi(E_3, E_2) & \varphi(E_3, E_3) \cdots\cdots \varphi(E_3, E_n) \\ \vdots & \vdots & \vdots & \vdots \\ \varphi(E_n, E_1) & \varphi(E_n, E_2) & \varphi(E_n, E_3) \cdots\cdots \varphi(E_n, E_n) \end{bmatrix}$$

Where n is the number of entities and $\varphi(E_a, E_b)$ represents the relativity between the entities E_a and E_b and calculated as follows

$$\varphi(E_a, E_b) = \begin{cases} 1, E_a > E_b \\ 0, E_a < E_b \\ 0.5, E_a = E_b \end{cases}$$

Finally the reputation weightage is calculated using the following equation.

$$RW(E_a) = \sum_{b=1}^{n} \varphi(E_a, E_b)$$

4.3 Trust Factor Calculation and Resource Selection

The trust factor (TF) of each entity is calculated by utilizing the self-protection capability (SPC) and Reputation Weigthage (R_W) calculated as discussed in above sections using the following equation.

$TF(E_a) = SPC(E_a) + RW(E_a)$

The resource is selected for the execution of incoming jobs using the following algorithm.

      for each entity in Grid domain
            Obtain SPC from GOM
            Obtain RW from RM
            Calculate TF
    end
    $[STF, Ind] = DescSort(TF)$
    for all i jobs
            Allocate Entity [Ind[i]] to job J_i
    end

5 Experimental Results

In this section, we first describe the experimental setup and present the analysis of our experimental results. The proposed algorithm is implemented in Java. The experimental setup consists of ten grid entities and a Grid Organization Manager (GOM). At first, the users submit their jobs to GOM. The GOM will calculate the trust factor value of all the entities based on their Self protection capability and Reputation weightage. An entity with high trust factor value is selected for the execution of current job. The GOM will inform the user with the selected entity for their job execution. After the completion of job, the user is asked to provide feedback about the entity on some security attributes. The selected entity has provided high security for the job execution. The self protection capability of all the entities is updated by the GOM in a periodical manner. The reputation weightage is frequently updated for all the entities based on the feedback value from user communities.

The security factors utilized for determining the self-protection capability of the ten grid entities are enlisted along with their respective values in Table2. The security attributes that eventually aid in the estimation of reputation weightage with their respective values are as well listed subsequently in Table 3.

Table 2. Values of Security Factors for Ten Entities

Entity	IDSC	AVC	FC	AM	SFSC	I	SJE	A
E1	0.245	0.535	0.555	0.605	0.605	0.65	0.56	0.68
E2	0.21	0.5	0.7	0.57	0.61	0.44	0.39	0.92
E3	0.6	0.37	0.89	0.51	0.67	0.73	0.79	0.1
E4	0.15	0.21	0.45	0.57	0.39	0.23	0.38	0.456
E5	0.145	0.7725	0.7775	0.675	0.7075	0.675	0.7	0.7
E6	0.5	0.6	0.65	0.4	0.5	0.35	0.3	0.3
E7	0.51	0.42	0.5	0.56	0.7	0.4	0.61	0.21
E8	0.4	0.5	0.59	0.68	0.74	0.79	0.62	0.57
E9	0.6	0.37	0.89	0.51	0.67	0.73	0.79	0.605
E10	0.21	0.5	0.7	0.57	0.61	0.44	0.39	0.42

Table 3. Values of Security Attributes for Ten Entities

Entity	Consi stency	Confid entiality	Truth ful ness	Security	Privacy	Non Repu dia tion	Authen tication	Authori zation	Relia bility	Robust -ness
E1	0.245	0.285	0.305	0.355	0.355	0.4	0.31	0	0.605	0.245
E2	0.65	0.66	0.97	0.5	0.4	0.1	0.35	0.21	0.57	0.21
E3	0.6	0.7	0.8	0.58	0.25	0	0.21	0.6	0.51	0.6
E4	0.71	0.77	0.85	0.67	0.52	0.23	0.58	0.15	0.57	0.15
E5	0.46125	0.46375	0.47375	0.44625	0.43125	0.3875	0.44	0.1975	0.675	0.145
E6	0.54	0.725	0.75	0.6	0.465	0.4	0.5	0.5	0.4	0.5
E7	0.75	0.8	0.9	0.55	0.28	0.15	0.32	0.51	0.56	0.51
E8	0.82	0.75	0.5	0.63	0.21	0	0.3	0.4	0.68	0.4
E9	0.485	0.555	0.595	0.405	0.335	0.16	0.37	0.45	0.405	0.45
E10	0.41	0.5	0.7	0.57	0.31	0.2	0.39	0.21	0.57	0.21

A relativity matrix that is obtained on basis of the proposed approach with the values of various security attributes present in the foreshown table is given below. Further, this relativity matrix is employed in the estimation of reputation weightage.

$$
\text{Rel}_{\text{Mat}} =
\begin{bmatrix}
0.5 & 0.3 & 0.4 & 0.3 & 0.2 & 0.15 & 0.3 & 0.3 & 0.3 & 0.4 \\
0.7 & 0.5 & 0.6 & 0.35 & 0.6 & 0.3 & 0.4 & 0.4 & 0.6 & 0.55 \\
0.6 & 0.4 & 0.5 & 0.2 & 0.6 & 0.5 & 0.3 & 0.45 & 0.7 & 0.6 \\
0.7 & 0.65 & 0.8 & 0.5 & 0.7 & 0.7 & 0.5 & 0.6 & 0.8 & 0.75 \\
0.8 & 0.4 & 0.4 & 0.3 & 0.5 & 0.1 & 0.4 & 0.3 & 0.5 & 0.5 \\
0.85 & 0.7 & 0.5 & 0.3 & 0.9 & 0.5 & 0.4 & 0.6 & 0.9 & 0.9 \\
0.7 & 0.6 & 0.7 & 0.5 & 0.6 & 0.6 & 0.5 & 0.7 & 0.7 & 0.5 \\
0.7 & 0.6 & 0.55 & 0.4 & 0.7 & 0.4 & 0.3 & 0.5 & 0.4 & 0.6 \\
0.7 & 0.4 & 0.3 & 0.2 & 0.5 & 0.1 & 0.3 & 0.6 & 0.5 & 0.5 \\
0.6 & 0.45 & 0.4 & 0.25 & 0.5 & 0.1 & 0.5 & 0.4 & 0.5 & 0.5
\end{bmatrix}
$$

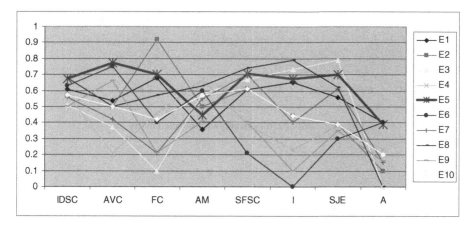

Fig. 1. Security Factors Graph with selected entity E5

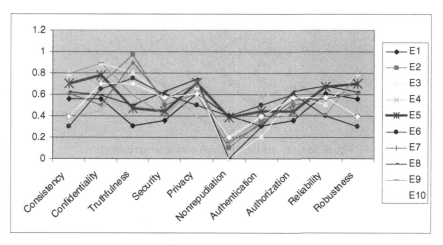

Fig. 2. Security Attributes Graph with selected entity E5

Figure 1-4 are the charts of data obtained from the various experimental setups. From these charts, it is very apparent to make a decision on selecting a secured entity for the current job. But the proposed approach has played witty solution to arrive the most secured entity among the available entities during a particular period of time under varying values of security attributes. The line marked dark is the selected entity.

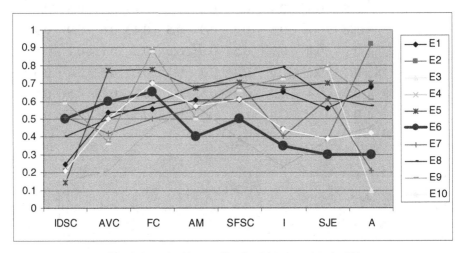

Fig. 3. Security Factors Graph with selected entity E6

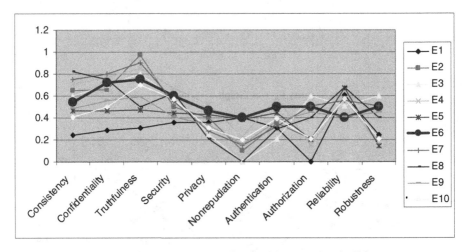

Fig. 4. Security Attributes Graph with selected entity E6

6 Conclusion

Computational Grids are emerging as a realistic technique that can be utilized to implement latest science and develop applications afresh. Highly sophisticated and secured resource management systems are vital requirements for the successful and efficient utilization of Grid computing facilities. The assurance of high trustworthiness is an inevitable factor in resource sharing and accessing. Reputation mechanisms pave a path for creating trust through social control with the aid of community based feedback regarding the past experiences. In this paper, we have proposed a secured approach for the users to decide on the appropriate resource for the execution of their job. Security for the resource selection procedure is offered by the proposed approach by combining trust and reputation. The proposed approach aggregates a number of security related attributes for both self-protection capability and reputation into numerical values that can aid in the determination of the Trust factor of grid entity. Our method has been proved to be efficient in choosing a secured entity from a pool of available ones. Our approach also manages the increase in the number of jobs as well as the number of grids in a satisfactory manner.

References

1. Berman, F., Fox, G., Hey, T.: Grid Computing: Making the Global Infrastructure a Reality. Wiley, Chichester (2003)
2. Cosnard, M., Merzky, A.: Meta- and Grid-Computing. In: Monien, B., Feldmann, R.L. (eds.) Euro-Par 2002. LNCS, vol. 2400, pp. 861–862. Springer, Heidelberg (2002)
3. Ranaldo, N., Zimeo, E.: A Framework for QoS-based Resource Brokering in Grid Computing. In: 5th IEEE ECOWS, the 2nd Workshop on Emerging Web Services Technology, Halle, Germany (2007)
4. Foster, I., Kesselman, C., Tuecke, S.: The anatomy of the Grid: Enabling scalable virtual organizations. Int. J. Supercomputing 15(3), 200–222 (2001)
5. Foster, I., Kesselman, C.: Computational Grids. In: Foster, I., Kesselman, C. (eds.) The Grid: Blueprint for a New Computing Infrastructure, pp. 2–48. Morgan Kaufmann, San Francisco (1999)
6. National Science Foundation TeraGrid, http://www.teragrid.org
7. SETI@Home: The Search for Extraterrestrial Intelligence, http://setiathome.ssl.berkeley.edu/
8. Berman, F., Wolski, R., Casanova, H., Cirne, W., Dail, H., Faerman, M., Figueira, S., Hayes, J., Obertelli, G., Schopf, J., Shao, G., Smallen, S., Spring, N., Su, A., Zagorodnov, D.: Adaptive Computing on the Grid Using AppLeS. IEEE Trans. on Parallel and Distributed Systems 14 (April 2003)
9. Welch, V., Siebenlist, F., Foster, I., Bresnahan, J., Czajkowski, K., Gawor, J., Kesselman, C., Meder, S., Pearlman, L., Tuecke, S.: Security for Grid Services. In: Proceedings of the HPDC-12 (2003)
10. Shi, Z., He, Y., Huai, X., Zhang, H.: Identity Anonymity for Grid Computing Coordination based on Trusted Computing. In: Proceedings of the Sixth International Conference on Grid and Cooperative Computing, pp. 403–410 (2007)
11. Foster, I., Kesselman, C., Tsudik, G., Tuecke, S.: A Security Architecture for Computational Grids. In: ACM Conference on Computers and Security, pp. 83–91 (1998)
12. Foster, I.: Globus toolkit version 4: Software for service-oriented systems. In: Jin, H., Reed, D., Jiang, W. (eds.) NPC 2005. LNCS, vol. 3779, pp. 2–13. Springer, Heidelberg (2005)
13. Basney, J., Nejdl, W., Olmedilla, D., Welch, V., Winslett, M.: Negotiating trust on the grid. In: 2nd Workshop on Semantics in P2P and Grid Computing, New York (May 2004)

14. Azzedin, F., Maheswaran, M.: Towards Trust-Aware Resource Management in Grid Computing Systems. In: 2nd IEEE/ACM International Symposium on Cluster Computing and the Grid (CCGRID 2002), p. 452 (2002)

15. Buyya, R., Venugopal, S.: The Gridbus Toolkit for Service Oriented Grid and Utility Computing: An Overview and Status Report. In: Proceedings of the First IEEE International Workshop on Grid Economics and Business Models, GECON (2004)

16. Lohr, H., Ramasamy, H.V., Sadeghi, A.-R., Schulz, S., Schunter, M., Stuble, C.: Enhancing Grid Security Using Trusted Virtualization. LNCS, pp. 372–384. Springer, Heidelberg (2007)

17. Dyson, J.R.D., Griffiths, N., Lim Choi Jeung, H.N., Jarvis, S.A., Nudd, G.R.: Trusting Agents for Grid Computing. In: Proceedings of the IEEE International Conference on Systems, Man and Cybernetics (SMC 2004), pp. 3187–3192. IEEE Press, Los Alamitos (2004)

18. Song, S., Hwang, K.: Dynamic Grid Security with Trust Integration and Optimized Resource Allocation. Internet and Grid Computing Laboratory, University of Southern California, Los Angeles, CA. 90089 USA

19. Malaga, R.A.: Web-based reputation management systems: Problems and suggested solutions. Electronic Commerce Research 1(4) (2001)

20. Resnick, P., Zeckhauser, R., Friedman, E., Kuwabara, K.: Reputation Systems. Communications of the ACM 43(12), 45–48 (2000)

21. Kwok, Y.-K., Song, S., Hwang, K.: Selfish Grid Computing: Game-Theoretic Modeling and NAS Performance Results. In: Proceedings of CCGrid 2005, Cardiff, UK (May 2005)

22. Wang, Y., Vassileva, J.: Trust and Reputation Model in Peer-to-Peer Networks. In: Proceedings of the 3rd IEEE International Conference on Peer-to-Peer Computing, Linköping, pp. 150–158. IEEE Computer Society, Los Alamitos (2003)

23. Azzedin, F., Maheswaran, M.: A Trust Brokering System and Its Application to Resource Management in Public- Resource Grids. In: Proceedings of IPDPS 2004 (2004)

24. Damiani, E., De Capitani di Vimercati, S., Paraboschi, S., Samarati, P., Violante, F.: A Reputation-Based Approach for Choosing Reliable Resources in Peer-to-Peer Networks. In: Proceedings of ACM CCS 2002 (2002)

25. Kamvar, S.D., Schlosser, M.T., Garcia-Molina, H.: The Eigentrust Algorithm for Reputation Management in P2P Networks. In: Proceedings of ACM WWW 2003 (2003)

26. Liu, C., Yang, L., Foster, I., Angulo, D.: Design and Evaluation of a Resource Selection Framework for Grid Applications. In: Proceedings of HPDC-11 (2002)

27. Song, S., Hwang, K., Macwan, M.: Fuzzy Trust Integration for Security Enforcement in Grid Computing. In: Jin, H., Gao, G.R., Xu, Z., Chen, H. (eds.) NPC 2004. LNCS, vol. 3222, pp. 9–21. Springer, Heidelberg (2004)

28. Xiong, L., Liu, L.: PeerTrust: Supporting Reputation-based Trust to P2P E-Communities. IEEE Trans. Knowledge and Data Engineering, 843–857 (July 2004)

29. Tian, C., Zou, S., Wang, W., Cheng, S.: An Efficient Attack-Resistant Trust Model for P2P Networks. IJCSNS 6(11), 251–258 (2006)

30. Ma, B., Sun, J., Yu, C.: Reputation-based Trust Model in Grid Security System. Journal of Communication and Computer 3(8) (Serial No.21) (2006)

31. Vijayakumar, V., Wahidha Banu, R.S.D.: Trust and Reputation Aware Security for Resource Selection in Grid Computing. In: International Conference on Security Technology (SECTECH 2008), December 13-15, pp. 121–124 (2008)

32. Vijayakumar, V., Wahida Banu, R.S.D.: Security for Resource Selection in Grid Computing Based On Trust and Reputation Responsiveness. IJCSNS International Journal of Computer Science and Network Security 8(11) (November 2008)

33. Foster, I., Kesselman, C., Nick, J., Tuecke, S.: The Physiology of the Grid: An Open Grid Services Architecture for Distributed Systems Integration. Technical Report, Open Grid Service Infrastructure WG, Global Grid Forum (2002)
34. Pautasso, C., Alonso, G.: Parallel Computing Patterns for Grid Workflows. In: The HPDC 2006 Workshop on Workflows in Support of Large-Scale Science, France (2006)
35. Maheswaran, M., Krauter, K.: A parameter-based approach to resource discovery in Grid computing systems. In: Computer Science, University of Manitoba, pp. 181–190 (2000)
36. Song, S., Hwang, K., Rajbanshi, R.: Security-Assured Resource. Allocation for Trusted Grid Computing. Submitted to International Parallel and Distributed Processing Symposium (2003)
37. Arenas, A.: State of the art survey on trust and security in grid computing systems, CCLRC Technical Report, RAL-TR-2006-008 (March 2006), 1SSN 1358-6254

Author Index